Maude Barlow (signature)

The Fight of My Life

Confessions of an Unrepentant Canadian

Maude Barlow

A Phyllis Bruce Book
HarperCollins*PublishersLtd*

http://www.harpercollins.com/canada

HarperCollins books may be purchased for educational,
business, or sales promotional use. For information please write:
Special Markets Department, HarperCollins Canada,
55 Avenue Road, Suite 2900, Toronto, Ontario M5R 3L2.

First edition

Canadian Cataloguing in Publication Data

Barlow, Maude
The fight of my life: confessions of an unrepentant Canadian

"A Phyllis Bruce book."
Includes index.
ISBN 0-00-255761-4

1. Barlow, Maude.   2. Women political activists – Canada – Biography.
3. Women social reformers – Canada – Biography.
I. Title.

HQ1455.B37A3   1998   303.48'4'092   C98-931368-9

98 99 00 01 02 03 04 WEB 10 9 8 7 6 5 4 3 2 1

Printed and bound in Canada

To Andrew

CONTENTS

INTRODUCTION

When my editor and friend, Phyllis Bruce, first suggested I write my autobiography, I balked. For one thing, I thought, an autobiography is what one writes at the end of life. Much as some might wish otherwise, I am feeling fit and feisty and full of life. For another, I write books about policy. An autobiography would be too personal, I worried, somehow self-indulgent. There are so many pressing issues that should claim priority, I reasoned. Anyway, autobiographies are too subjective to be honest. The judgement of one's life and work must be left to others.

The more I thought about it, however, the more I realized a biography would allow me to write about the issues that concern me in a more personal and accessible way. It is perhaps better to describe this book as a "mid-life" exploration of what I truly believe in. So often, I struggle with the big issues: globalization, market liberalism, class and gender politics. But behind these issues are the lives of real people, people I care passionately about.

So here is my story as best I can remember and describe it. It is the story of a naïve young girl whose enthusiasms for traditional life were swept away in the tide of 1970s feminism. It is the story of a political activist who found that the best change comes from outside the system. It is the story of an unconventional life path that has taken me from the Prime Minister's Office and high-level meetings with the OECD in Paris to the slums and prisons of Mexico's infamous *maquiladoras* and to Iraq with an international women's peace mission on the eve of the Gulf War.

1

Mostly, however, this is a story about a love affair. It is the story of a Canadian who took her beloved country for granted and lived in a state of innocence until she saw it "being sucked away as it were by a consuming, swallowing wind" to quote a Welsh poet. My political journey is a journey of discovery of my country — its history, its roots, its soul — and it is a love story.

Finding out who I was as a human being, a citizen, a woman, meant discovering who I was as a Canadian, and so, in the end, this is not so much my story, but the story of the many wonderful Canadians with whom I have worked, cried, laughed, sometimes won, but more often lost, in the last decade. These so-called "ordinary people" are the stars. I try to do them justice.

1

YOUTH

"We think back through our mothers, if we are women."

Virginia Woolf

For more years than I should admit to, I thought the fireworks displays to mark May 24th, Queen Victoria's birthday, were for me and I would thank people very much for the honour. I was born at Toronto General Hospital on May 24, 1947, and was named Maude Victoria — Maude for my father's mother, Victoria for the British sovereign. The irony of this is not lost on my parents today, as I now spend much of my time fighting the very authority, hereditary entitledness, and class divisions that defined the Victorian era.

My father, Bill McGrath, was a newly minted graduate of the University of Toronto with a master's degree in Social Work. The son of William "Big Bill" McGrath — a quiet, hard-working Irish railway man whose family had emigrated to Canada during the potato famine in the 1840s — and Maude Tucker, a gentle, soft-spoken woman with English roots, he had grown up in a big family with much love and little money in the small lobster-fishing village of Pointe-du-Chêne, New Brunswick.

My father was modest, industrious, and a young man in a hurry. He walked miles every day to take piano lessons and worked after school to pay for them; his love of music started early and has nourished him his

3

whole life. He graduated from high school with honours at sixteen, put himself through normal school to obtain a licence to teach, taught public school, and graduated from Mount Allison University as a member of the Canadian Officers Training Corps — all by the age of twenty-two.

During the Second World War, he served as a captain with the New Brunswick division of the Canadian Regiment, Carleton and York, for four years and in 1944, was shot in the head just outside of Rome during one of the fierce battles for the liberation of Italy. Although he lived through the savage heart of this epic war, he seldom spoke of those years to friends or family, and never glorified them. He didn't even claim his numerous medals at the war's end. Several years ago, my sons, seeking to understand this part of their heritage and to honour this dearly loved grandfather, retrieved them from the Department of National Defence, where they and thousands of other medals are still kept. Officials told us that there has been a recent rash of grandchildren searching for these precious family heirlooms while their grandfathers are still alive.

The atrocities my father witnessed in Europe forged in him a deep abhorrence of fascism and totalitarianism. He came to believe that when the powerless in society are considered expendable, democracy cannot survive. He returned to Canada with a commitment to make his life's work the search for justice for those without a voice in our society. He became one of the architects of a postwar social and judicial system based on the tenet that every citizen has fundamental rights, and neither social class nor ethnic background should determine their life's course.

My mother, Flora, was born in Scotland, the only daughter of Jack and Flora Wilkie, proprietors of a small wholesale food business on the docks of Glasgow. A red-haired local beauty, Flora (née Macdonald), was reputedly a descendant of the lass by that name who smuggled Bonnie Prince Charlie out of Scotland disguised as a woman after his defeat at Culloden. Deserted by his business partner, who stole their profits and fled to Australia, my grandfather booked passage to Australia to go after him. At the last minute, my grandmother convinced him to choose Canada instead, and my five-year-old mother set sail for a new life.

Flora grew up in Moncton, New Brunswick, where her father became a salesman and then the Atlantic regional manager for Westinghouse. She lived a stone's throw from Pointe-du Chêne, where she and my father played on the beach as children. But he was older by several years, and she fell in love with and married Stuart Connacher, a young RCAF fighter pilot from Dalhousie, New Brunswick. Tragically, he became one of the war's early casualties, shot down over the English Channel returning from a mission to Germany. At first he was listed as missing in action; it would be a year before Flora would get confirmation of his death. Throughout my childhood, I thought about Stuart a lot, how his life was cut short at the age of twenty-one, and about how hard it must have been for my mother. They had been married only six weeks when he left for the war, having predicted his own death. I probably romanticized him, but their story made the war very real to me years later. Left alone with her infant daughter (my sister Patricia) my mother returned to her parents' home for the duration of the war.

At war's end, my mother met Bill McGrath again when one day he came up her front walk by accident. My determined grandmother had always had her eye on him and decided that, fate having delivered him to the house, this handsome young soldier would be coming in for a visit. "Do I have the right address?" asked my father. "You certainly do, Billy McGrath," my grandmother answered firmly. "You come right in." Flora and Bill were married three months later (my sister, who first saw him from the kitchen as she peeked around my mother's skirt, insisted "Daddy married Mommy and me") with no fanfare, reception, fancy clothes, flowers, or even photographs. They had both been deeply affected by the war experience and thought it wrong to celebrate their happiness too openly when so many others hadn't survived to find or keep their own. Fifty years later, their daughters would give them that wedding, complete with friends and family, a piper, champagne, flowers, and cake. My father even let my mother put a ring on his finger. He promptly lost it.

When they were first married, my dad, plagued by nightmares from the war, got up one night, took all his war paraphernalia, including guns, down to the wharf in Pointe-du-Chêne, and threw it in the water. He and my mother stayed up all night talking about how to make sense of what they had already experienced in their young lives, including terrible losses, and how they could put it behind them only by helping to build a different kind of world.

Shortly after my father obtained his M.A. in Toronto and I was born, we moved to Digby, Nova Scotia, where my dad worked as the regional supervisor of public welfare for the province. My younger sister, Christine, was born there, and my parents were overjoyed to be back in the Maritimes which they consider (as do I) the place we come from. All my childhood summers were spent by the sea at the Pointe, surrounded by extended family. The community was not built up; no fast-food outlets, no cute little tourist shops. Only old cottages and wooden homes with sweeping verandas, dirt pathways, masses of wild roses everywhere, and days without end or care.

My three elderly maiden great-aunts —Margaret, Mabel, and Eileen — lived in a grand old house that was filled with clocks and old rocking chairs, and smelled of ginger cookies and Tweed perfume. I loved visiting them and listening for hours to family stories, which they narrated in great detail, pausing only to laugh until they couldn't breathe. How Great-Aunt Helen made a pass at the priest when he came to visit her on her ninetieth birthday. How Great-Uncle Mike terrified the stuffy old mayor's grandchildren, who fled in tears when he hammered a nail into his leg at a church supper. (He didn't mention that it was a wooden leg to replace the one he'd lost when he fell in front of an oncoming train late one night, after a wild Irish wake for an old sailing-mate.) They revealed the terrible family secret, the ancestor who had a headstone, but no coffin, in the local cemetery. He was a slaver who had been killed and devoured by cannibals on one of his forays into Africa. ("Good for them," my great-aunts said, snorting, and proving I come by my passion for justice honestly.)

Then there was the story of how Great-Great-Aunt Peggy, who lived in a remote fishing village up the coast, "died" when she was twenty-one. This happened in the days before embalming, my great-aunts explained in hushed tones, and Peggy — a beauty and much sought-after — was laid out in the parlour while, with the aid of a great deal of Irish whisky, the local lads said goodbye to her. Suddenly, a sharp gust of wind slammed a door shut, and Peggy sat up in her coffin, scaring people so badly they dived out of doors and windows. Great-Great-Aunt Peggy married one of the boys who attended her funeral and they had eight children and twelve grandchildren.

I loved to drive into the nearest town, Shediac, with these aunts and my Uncle Willy, who was a famously terrible driver. At every turn, he had to stop the car and let all the "young people" — that is, anyone under seventy-five — get out so he could round the corner. When Maude, my father's mother, died, she was laid out in the parlour of the very house in which she was born. I was ten and sat quietly beside her as everyone from the Pointe filed by, in tears, to say goodbye, and then went into the sitting room, where they laughed and told stories about her life well into the night. I learned so much from those people. I watched them grow old with dignity and learned about the rhythm of life and death. I learned about the importance of family and friends and roots, how to tell stories and how to laugh, and that money and its acquisition are false gods.

My love of nature came from roaming the hills, farms, and uninhabited coastlines of rural New Brunswick in these early years of my life. The only event that ever came to threaten our happiness was a severe illness.

At the age of three, I was diagnosed with childhood rheumatic fever and had to spend a year in bed, motionless and on medication. My parents were told I might die, and everything in our world now revolved around this fact. I have since been told that it is unlikely that I suffered from rheumatic fever (or, as I called it, "romantic fever"); there is no sign of a heart murmur now. Likely I had acute toxic carditis, a result of poor drainage of the toxins from an earlier operation to remove my tonsils.

But a near-death experience for a young child is very powerful. My parents bought me a beautiful bed that had a Chinese sailing ship carved into an elaborate headboard "to die in." They didn't say that in front of me, of course, but I overheard them telling this terrible secret to a neighbour. I have vivid memories of watching other children play outside my window, of hearing my mother weep outside my room, of feeling that life was passing by without me. Digby was a small, close-knit community and everyone knew everyone else's business. I would hear visitors downstairs asking after my health in hushed tones, and hear the adults admonishing their children to be quiet "because little Maudie is very ill." I was very angry at having to stay immobile, and more than once I sorely tested my mother's patience by tearing or cutting up toys or dolls she bought me to help me pass the time. I even took apart a radio my dad bought me (a big expense for them) and threw the pieces out the window.

I think now that this period in my childhood shaped me in several important ways, aside from the incredibly close bond I forged with my wonderful mother, who nursed me through it. It gave me a fierce passion for life and for living it my way. It also gave me the courage to take chances. I am not easily frightened or intimidated by authority figures. I seldom take the safe path and I am not a follower. Maybe it was my illness that instilled in me an almost visceral empathy for people in pain, and an intuitive ability to feel if another person is hurt or sad or frightened.

When I was five years old, my father accepted a job in Ottawa with the Canadian Welfare Council. We lived for a few years in a small rowhouse in Manor Park, and then my parents bought a turn-of-the-century, three-storey red-brick family home on First Avenue in the Glebe — that tree-lined, church-on-every-corner Ottawa enclave of civil servants, doctors, and lawyers. It was there we settled and where they lived for thirty-seven years. We didn't have a lot of money. My mother never worked outside the home, and a social worker's salary was not grand. Money was never much of a motivating influence in our lives.

Postwar Ottawa was staid, quiet, and very white. This was a time when traditional values of home, church, and hard work still prevailed and when there was little social divisiveness. Most women stayed home and only "got out" to tea parties with one another, to cocktail parties with their husbands, and to church or to home-and-school meetings. Milk was still delivered in horse-drawn wagons, and buses took men in identical grey suits to identical government offices. The city rolled up its sidewalks promptly at eight o'clock. The streets were safe to walk, and the big event was the Ottawa Ex every August at Lansdowne Park. The Arts Centre hadn't been built; several movie theatres doubled as venues for live performances. I remember my father leading us resolutely through a crowd of protesters and hecklers to see the Soviet Union's Red Army Chorus — the closest thing I had ever seen to political controversy — at the stately old Odeon Theatre when I was about ten.

In many ways, I grew up in a typical middle-class family in the 1950s.

My mother, my sisters, and I belonged to St. James's, our local United Church, where I attended Sunday school and became president of our local Canadian Girls in Training troop. I can still recite our motto by heart: "As a Canadian Girl in Training under the leadership of Jesus, it is my duty to cherish health, seek truth, know God and serve others, and thus, with His help, become the girl God would have me be." I remember, now with mortification, our being taken, in our navy-blue middy blouses, to a home for unwed mothers, where we looked at girls not much older than ourselves as if they were specimens in a zoo. The lesson, of course, was not lost on us. This is what happened when "good" girls went "bad." But there is much that I cherish from CGIT. I learned about female bonding and had some fine women role models.

I know I was fortunate to come from such a loving home. There were books, lots of books. Like all girls my age, I grew up reading Nancy Drew mysteries. But I also loved Kingsley's Roman and Greek myths; Saint-Exupéry's *Little Prince*; biographies of famous women, be they royalty, movie stars, writers, or ancient warriors; and any kind of poetry, especially the Romantics — Shelley and Wordsworth. (I would have to wait until I was older to discover Yeats, who would become my favourite.) And music. Father insisted on piano lessons, and for years "after school" meant piano practice. But surprisingly, he declined to attend church.

My father, whose family had conducted a Protestant–Catholic tug-of-war over his religious upbringing, avoided church. He would say that staying home to listen to the Sunday concert on CBC Radio was better for the soul and the mind. Eventually I came to agree with him. Organized religion simply left me with more questions than answers. But church was an integral part of my youth, not only because it was so significant in my social life, but also because it was influencing my nascent political consciousness. Our minister, Donald Joyce, worked and preached in the long and proud Canadian tradition of the social gospel. Christmas Eve sermons were opportunities to rail against the bomb or to advocate for the poor. When I left home, I also left the church in search of more direct ways to effect social change.

Although I eventually came to share my father's feelings about insti-tutionalized religion, I still believe that its highest calling is to challenge the dominant power structures of society. But I am proud of my church tradition that produced such visionary leaders as Senator Lois Wilson, Bruce McLeod, and now, Bill Phipps, who says the market economy that dominates today's world puts a price on everything but a value on nothing. I know the church has helped shape both my spiritual and my political character.

A conventional education for a girl in the 1950s and 1960s was also a traditional education. In Ottawa, I attended Mutchmore and Glashan public schools and Glebe Collegiate, where I studied as much as necessary to get good but not brilliant marks, sang in the choir, acted in school and church plays, skied, skated, played tennis, and lived a loved and sheltered life. We took sewing and cooking and had to wear hideous baggy blue gym suits with bloomers to hide our changing bodies. We made fun of the "old maid" teachers who couldn't "get a man" and had to work for a living. My grade seven home economics teacher, Miss Lavender — she had lavender hair (from "blueing" it), wore lavender dresses and stockings, and smelled of lavender perfume — kept me in after school one day for singing in class. "Maude Victoria. Why were you singing in class?" she asked. "Because it's spring, Miss Lavender," I said. "I couldn't help it." Instead of punishing me, she told me I could go home and, as I looked back, I saw her put her head down on her desk and weep. It was not until many years later that I understood that women of her generation had to make a choice: they could work as teachers or civil servants, or they could be wives. Not both. These teachers we made fun of were, in fact, pioneers.

As I got older, my musical loves became the Beatles, the Stones, and that precocious rebel, Bob Dylan. I had to take Latin and dissect pregnant cats, both of which I hated. In my first year of high school, I blew up my Bunsen burner, and the whole system had to be replaced. The male teachers addressed all the girls as "Miss So-and-So," not by their first names. I had then, and still have, a hard time learning in the absence of contextualization and had a bad habit of asking "Why?" particularly in math and science classes. My grade nine physics teacher, Cecil Holmes, had a strong lisp, and we had cruel fun with his name. One day, after a long and very boring lecture on electrical currents (all I remember is AC/DC), I asked poor Mr. Holmes "Why?" He spun around and, his lisp stronger than usual, said,

"Becauth, Mith McGrath, God made it tho." The class dissolved in helpless laughter.

The Cold War intruded into this innocent existence on a regular basis. At the sound of a siren, our drill would begin; we would crouch under our desks and in stairwells, it being assumed by authorities that such measures would protect us from nuclear attack. Most of our mothers insisted we stay home during the Bay of Pigs standoff as war was expected on a moment by moment basis. I was in Grade 11 in 1963 when President Kennedy was assassinated. The announcement came over the loudspeaker, and we walked around all day in a silence broken only by tears and whispers. What could it all mean? No one at my school was able to explain it.

In these years, I formed friendships that would last my lifetime. A little girl named Helen Porter, a minister's daughter whose vivid imagination changed my life, came to visit me one day after school in grade five and fell off the back porch into the geranium bed while my mother was serving us lemonade and cookies. I knew immediately this was my best friend for life, and many Saturdays would find Helen (now a noted and gifted Toronto story-teller and writer), Sheila Purdy (an Ottawa environmental lawyer and very close friend to whose son, John, I am godmother), and myself walking or biking the railway tracks outside the city, playing "Nancy Drew" at the deserted Carleton College at the end of our street (now the Ottawa Board of Education), or smoking our first (my last) cigarettes in locked washrooms of Kresge's on Sparks Street.

Helen and I "published" a monthly satire on Diefenbaker and Pearson, the political leaders of the time, called the *Rabbitville Gazette*; Harry Hare was the "Kiberal" and Bunn Bunnifer led the "Bunnservatives." We used it to spread neighbourhood news about other kids and give our ten-year-old views of politics to the world. We also advertised "free hare-cuts" and local movies, starring "Barelin Bunroe," and delivered our little newspaper around the Glebe. A childhood without Helen would have been totally different and Ottawa would have been infinitely more boring. She was the antidote to the unrelenting conformity of 1950s Ottawa and opened my mind to the world of creation, enchantment, and mystery.

My sisters were very important to me, although I suppose we all took one another for granted. Pat was eight years older than Christie; one had left high school long before the other even entered. So I was closer to them than they were to each other and I had to play the classic middle-child role of peacemaker. I probably learned to use the situation to ingratiate myself with my mother in particular and I can still call on that early-learned charm to get myself out of difficult situations. On our summer trips to the Maritimes, we would share the back seat of the car, one moment fighting, the next trading the most intimate confidences. We looked out for one another at school and passed along, one to the next, the treasured secrets of young womanhood.

Paddy and all her friends were, in their words, "boy crazy" in high school, and the object of my sister's affection was always changing. Every April Fool's Day, Christie and I would wake her up early (a teenager, she slept in later than we did) to say that Mike or Frank or Russ was on the line, and then kill ourselves laughing as she ran, breathless, to the phone. Every year, we were threatened with imminent death.

During these years, I experimented with live theatre, at church and at school, and at one point had dreams of an acting career. I played the young queen in *Becket or The Honour of God* by Jean Anouilh at the Ottawa Little Theatre when I was seventeen, and the lead role in Shaw's *Passion, Poison and Petrifaction* at a local café the same year. At York University (where I spent only a year), I had the lead female role in Molière's *Don Juan*, and beat out fellow student Trish Nelligan, better known now as the distinguished actor Kate Nelligan, for the lead role in a modern version of *The Trojan Women*. The *Globe and Mail's* theatre critic, Herbert Whittaker, told my parents that I should study professional theatre and had a real future in it were I to make that choice. I often think this early training helped me with public speaking and with stage fright.

My mother's parents came to live with us when I was still quite young, and my mother devoted herself to them for almost twenty years, until their deaths. Although they greatly enriched our lives in many ways (looking after us several times so that my mother and father could take trips, once to Europe) and loved us very much, we sometimes resented them;

everything had to operate on a time schedule that was good for "Grandma and Grandpa." We were always being told to keep our voices down, not to upset or worry them. Meals had to be at an exact time, and there was important ritual to follow. Once, when we were on holiday, my parents were visiting friends down the beach at dinner time (five o'clock!) and my grandparents were getting anxious. "Why don't we eat without them?" I asked. "Because Bill McGrath is a man who likes to cut his own roast beef," thundered my grandfather, in his sternest Scottish brogue.

Now I realize that I learned from those years and from my mother's selfless behaviour with her parents that growing old and ill is a part of life that must not be shut away out of view. I know now that it is important to be able to say truthfully that you have been a good daughter (or son) when the time comes for your own parents to go. There is no second chance. I will always remember my gruff old grandfather saying softly as he climbed the stairs to his room after my grandmother's funeral, "It was a wonderful day. She would have loved it."

Though I was unaware of it, the world around me was changing rapidly. Postwar Canada was booming. The gross national product doubled between 1950 and 1960; the baby bonus and old-age pension gave families purchasing power; the birth rate and immigration numbers both soared. The Liberals under the courtly and cautious Louis St. Laurent were succeeded by John Diefenbaker's Conservatives in 1957, who were in turn replaced by the Pearson Liberals in 1963. Social upheaval was in the air.

The Civil Rights movement in the United States, the war on poverty, the women's movement, aboriginal claims, consumers' rights — all these and more were shaking up the conservative world of my youth. During Pearson's two minority governments (pushed hard by the newly formed New Democratic Party), Canada got a new flag, bilingualism in the civil service, a labour code, liberalization of the divorce laws, the Royal Commission on the Status of Women, and the Company of Young Canadians. Our universal social programs, including the Canada Assistance Plan, the Canada Pension Plan, and universal health care, were created in these heady years. For the first time, in 1965, federal social expenditures exceeded the nation's defence bill.

During these years, my father was becoming a distinguished advocate and expert in the field of criminal justice, working with young offenders, in aboriginal justice, and for prison reform. He founded what would become the Canadian Association for the Prevention of Crime, a non-government watchdog "half of whose function was to help government, the other half to fight it." He established a biennial conference that brought together for the first time representatives from the criminal justice, mental health, probation, community, and police fields to work with senior politicians of the federal, provincial, and territorial governments. International visitors were drawn to this event, and my mother, who was always at his side, acted as guide, friend, and interpreter to hundreds of distinguished guests from around the world.

In the 1950s, the death penalty was still in force. My father was one of the leaders of the movement to abolish capital and corporal punishment, and, in 1956, just four years before Parliament revoked the death penalty in all but the murders of police officers, he wrote an influential book called *Should Canada Abolish the Gallows and the Lash?* This was a raw and emotional debate, but he believed deeply that Canada could not consider itself a truly civilized nation until state-sanctioned death retribution was abolished. A powerful childhood memory is my dad debating the hangman on television. He wore his dark hair in a brush cut (and would continue to do so long after it was out of fashion) and sported thick, heavy-rimmed "Clark Kent" glasses. "Mr. Ellis" (his pseudonym) was wearing a hood and quite terrified me. He obviously intimidated my fiercely anti-smoking father as well. Bill McGrath smoked one cigarette after another throughout the interview. It was the only time I ever saw him smoke.

When my father entered this field, there was little literature and research on crime prevention in Canada; most of what was available came from American sources. He and several others pioneered the academic study of this field now taught in more than thirty universities and community colleges. He wrote many articles and several books, including *Youth and the Law, Crime and You, The Police Function in Canada,* and the standard university textbook in the field for many years, *Crime and Its Treatment in Canada.* His study *Indians and the Law* was a landmark in identifying and addressing the scandalous large-scale incarceration of Canada's aboriginal peoples.

For over thirty years, my father fought unwaveringly for social justice. He sat on most of the committees, task forces, and enquiries in his field over the years, including the Ouimet Committee on the future of the criminal justice system in Canada, and he was an adviser to the Royal Commission on the Status of Women. He received several major awards, including one from the John Howard Society, for his outstanding contribution to his profession.

In a speech to the United Nations in 1975, he called for the injection of ethics into the debate about global crime, and a recognition that when one race, social class, or nation dominates another by conquest or social order, "criminal law falls most heavily on the dispossessed." He argued that people who live in a country where the law discriminates against certain groups on the basis of race, religion, or social status are justified in refusing to obey that law, and he called for the development of a citizens' code of ethics for government, the courts, and the media. My father was helping to forge a form of global citizens' politics in which I would find my political home many years later.

Ending this speech, he sounded the alarm on environmental crime, years before most of society had even started debating the issue. His words now seem prescient of an economic order to come that would be dominated by the "efficiencies" of the marketplace to the detriment of human values and the Earth: "I am afraid that as we become more professional, more sophisticated, more efficient, we may lose sight of the fact that the drive that leads mankind to seek justice is based on dedication to principle and not to efficiency."

I know now that my father's values have had a profound influence on my own life and work. And this influence started early, even as I was living what truly could be called a carefree childhood. The notions of rights, equality, and entitlement, now again under attack in the neo-con 1990s, were instilled in us with our morning oatmeal. The only time my father would become truly angry was when one of us was unkind or made some negative remark about someone less fortunate than us. Once when Helen and I visited the family of a girl we went to school with and talked to other friends about how dirty her house and parents were, I was grounded for a month.

Racist remarks or jokes were strictly forbidden in our home. I taught all the other kids to sing "Eeny meeny miny mo, catch a rabbit by the toe," which was how my father insisted the childhood rhyme was to be sung. I was very tender-hearted anyway, and I would weep at stories of someone being turned away from a home or a job on account of prejudice. The Christmas story that most moved me was "The Little Match Girl." (I note that this classic has disappeared in the Christmases of the 1990s — that sort of introspection about social class and the real meaning of Christ's birth having given way to group consumerism and random individual acts of charity, as befits our first-past-the-post market system.)

I was traumatized when I first read accounts of the Holocaust and felt horrible fear and panic when I read books or saw films about it. To this day, I empathize so acutely with victims of torture and political repression that I become almost ill when confronted by images of their suffering. Once, at a movie theatre in Ottawa, during the scene in *Marathon Man* when Dustin Hoffman's character is being tortured by an ex-Nazi dentist, played by Laurence Olivier, I jumped up and yelled at the whole audience to walk out of the theatre with me. "This movie is sick," I shouted. I felt it was one thing to portray torture as it really exists but to use it as sensationalism in a commercial thriller cheapens it and further anaesthetizes a society already too jaded about the real suffering of real people. Needless to say, most people in the audience told me to sit down and shut up. Someone threw popcorn. The sole person to walk out with me was a young Jewish woman whose parents had died in a concentration camp and who was so upset by that scene that she called her babysitter to make sure her children were fine.

Despite the kinds of daughters they raised, my parents held more traditional views about the roles of women. It was their belief that men and women have, by and large, different roles to perform in life. But what women did, while it might be different, was not considered less important. My mother, the full-time homemaker, "got dressed" for work every day — skirt and sweater, stockings and nice shoes, hair done, make-up carefully applied. She used to joke that if everyone looked after their families as she did, dad's work would be redundant.

16

I now understand that my mother's devotion to her family gave me enormous stability and confidence, and I owe her a huge debt of gratitude for her love and guidance. I also know it required an enormous personal sacrifice on the part of my mother and many of the women of her generation, a sacrifice that our generation would come to question intensely.

On the issue of dating, my parents were very clear. No sex, period. No alcohol. Early curfews, always. I was allowed to go to my first dance at St. James's Church when I was fourteen and had to be home by nine o'clock. I wasn't allowed to go out alone with a boy until I was fifteen. On one of my first dates, I came down with make-up on my face and my hair done up in a "French twist." My dad told my date I would be back in a minute, and I was sent to wash my face and let down my hair. If my dad said to be home at 10:00, he'd be standing at the front porch at 9:55, and it wasn't worth it to cross him. He had no hesitation in grounding me, and more than one date was chased off the front porch by big, strong Bill McGrath. "Maudie's father" had a reputation as someone not to cross.

My parents have mellowed over the years and followed with pride the changes in their three girls. My older sister, Pat, the most traditional, is now a single mother, community organizer, and chief fund-raiser for a large hospital. Christine, a strong feminist now farming her own land with her partner, Carole Anne Burris, is a member of the National Parole Board, and has worked with poor women, women in conflict with the law, women's health issues, and LEAF (the Legal Education and Action Fund). These incredible women have insisted that their parents walk their journey with them and, as a result, we have grown as a family and as individuals.

Perhaps the most remarkable change has been in my mother, who blossomed as a watercolour artist after we left home and her parents died. She studied and developed an original technique, combining Japanese sumi-e brush painting and watercolour on rice paper. Her paintings hang, among other places of distinction, in P.E.I.'s Confederation Gallery and in the governor general's residence in Ottawa. And, of course, with pride in the homes of all her friends and family.

At the beginning of the sexual revolution, I went off to Toronto to study general arts at York University. But the revolution initially passed me by. Raised as I was, I married, at nineteen, the first boy I fell in love with — a handsome, literary scholar from Regina named Garnet Barlow — and had two babies within two years. (That ended my acting career!) Between babies, we went to Europe and lived in a little town in northern Italy for six months, where I looked after my baby, while Garnet taught English to wealthy landowners. Summers were passed at the Barlow family cottage in Saskatchewan's beautiful Qu'Appelle Valley. I learned to love the prairies, which I found very like the ocean. We wandered over meadows, valleys, and wheat fields, and Garnet taught me how to ride a horse and shoot a gun (tin cans only).

Like many women of my generation, I dropped university and picked it up, one year at York, one at the University of Toronto, finally graduating, one course at a time, with a major in English and history from Carleton University in Ottawa, where Garnet found a job teaching English.

Nothing in my life had prepared me for how much I would love these two little boys, Charly and Billy. They were, for me, so heart-stoppingly beautiful that I can still remember watching them come off a plane after a visit to their grandparents out West, dressed alike in their hand-knit Scottish sweaters and tams, their identical blond bowl-cut hair shining under the bright lights. "Why isn't everyone in the entire airport stopped dead in their tracks to appreciate these perfect kids?

We were so young, my boys and I, that we all but raised each other. On my first time driving the car after getting my licence, I got distracted by their fighting in the back seat and went through a stop sign, hitting another car. Thankfully, no one was hurt, but our car was badly dented. Shaken, I was about to get on the Queensway to go home when three-year-old Charly ordered me to the nearest garage. "Lucky you did that, ma'am," insisted the mechanic. "The car would never have made it home."

My role in the early years of my children's lives was predetermined. I was with them morning, noon, and night. My husband was going to school and holding down two jobs at the same time. So he was out a great deal, and my babies and I spent hour after hour together, reading, cuddling, walking, telling stories. I knew quite early that they were going to be a little wild: every hill had to be climbed, every bridge had to be jumped off, every swollen river dived into head first. One day, when Billy was three and Charly four, they hitch-hiked miles along a busy expressway from their nursery school because they had, they explained, "tried school" and decided they would rather be home with me.

But we were crazy about each other, and very open in our expression of that love. One night, when we were going out and I was all dressed up, I bent over Billy's crib to kiss him goodnight. He spit his soother out of his mouth, and his eyes filled up with tears. "Oh, Mom," said he, who loved red fire trucks and police cars, "you are so beautiful. You look like, you look just like . . . a police car." (This view of the world lasted several years. One day, my mother was teaching the boys how to draw impressions and sat them down in front of a big bowl of fruit. Charly drew a fine likeness of the fruit. Billy drew a big red fire truck. "You said to draw what we felt, Grandma, and I always feel like a red fire truck!")

It is not to deny this bond or to undo the intense beauty of those years to acknowledge that I was having great feelings of conflict. It was in these years at home with my children that the full brunt of the modern women's movement hit North America, and swept me along in its tide. I started reading everything I could get my hands on — Virginia Woolf, Simone de Beauvoir, Germaine Greer, Gloria Steinem, Betty Friedan. They were laying out a whole new analysis of the oppression of women in our society and exposing the systemic flaws in what they were calling "the Patriarchy." Women were as capable as men, they claimed, and perhaps more in touch with their humanity. There is no biological reason that women should have to accept an inferior role to men, from the bedroom to the boardroom, they argued, and the time had come for change.

Andrea Dworkin's *Woman Hating* — an anthology of religious and state oppression of women through the ages — had an enormous impact on my life. In it, Dworkin explained how she became a feminist. She was working with the civil rights movement in the Deep South in the 1960s. A black activist colleague had disappeared, and they were dragging a local swamp for his body. They found lots of bodies all right, the searchers said, but not him; just a bunch of women, black and white — probably hookers, nothing to get worried about or report. These men who so readily dismissed what they had found were

not local rednecks; they were her compatriots in the civil rights struggle. Dworkin never looked back. She became a raging prophet in the
fight against the abuse of women for many years and gave voice to a
generation that would make it our cause.

So here I was, Susy Homemaker by day and night; a feminist incu-
bating in a cocoon, reading late at night or when the children were sleeping. And I was beginning to ask some hard questions. I started to notice
how disrespectfully women were portrayed on television and in film.
Our newspapers had no women on the editorial board and yet felt confident to pass judgement on "bra-burners" — a tag on the early women's
movement that came from one small protest in New York City but that
was used as an epithet against all women who questioned the status quo.

My lawyer was a man. My MP was a man. My dentist was a man. My
gynaecologist, who was eventually convicted for assaulting women, was
a man. My first paediatrician was a man, until I made the conscious decision to choose a woman doctor, Anna Sharpe. The experts on everything
— from fashion and cooking (supposedly areas of female interest) to law,
sports, economics, and politics — were men. When I joked about
"maybe having a career one day" to a throat specialist treating Charly for
an infection, he replied with a sneer that my place was with my husband
and sons, and I should "get over it."

One day, Billy asked me why a scantily clad woman in a movie ad in
the *Ottawa Citizen* was chained up. (She was being tortured by Nazis as
I recall, and was bound in ropes and chains, her breasts exposed.) I
performed my first political act. I called the *Ottawa Citizen* and
complained. The next day, she was still there, being tortured, but they
had whited out the chains and covered her breasts. A minor victory, but
it was enough to whet my appetite.

It was now the early 1970s, and I was helping to set up the first women's
centre and women's career-counselling centre in Ottawa, and sitting with
women in "consciousness-raising" sessions. I was on a fast learning
curve: women and education, women and health, women and spiritual-
ity. I learned the numbers — what women earned, how many sat in our
legislatures and university faculties, how many were battered and raped,
how our view of the world had been ignored or silenced.

I became a real drag at parties. I wanted to talk about violence against women and pay equity and the drowning of baby girls in China. I could never let a sexist or racist joke go. I noticed how all the men at a party treated all the women, and I was often unhappy with what I saw. Jane O'Reilly described similar experiences in her 1980 book, *The Girl I Left Behind*: "'The movement is really over, accomplished, for middle-class women, isn't it?' asserts a well-meaning, white, male corporate lawyer. And I, now resigned to the fact that I will always, for the rest of my life, be the person who shouts at dinner parties, shout 'No! Without a man and his income, a woman is not yet even in the middle class.' He smiles, and his elegant, graceful, talented wife avoids my eyes."

Suddenly, I couldn't fit in with any of the "couple" friends we had acquired; I was a walking question in search of some pretty big answers, and I wasn't finding any of them in the familiar places of my past or present.

This, of course, was bound to have an effect on my marriage. Garnet had also grown up in a very traditional home. On my first visit to his huge extended family in Regina, the women of his family took me aside in the kitchen after dinner and explained that any ambitions I had for myself should now be relinquished for him and his career. We found ourselves too locked into roles to be able to change, and I had no patience, something I now regret. It was just a matter of time before we parted, agreeing to share the parenting of our boys. It was a very painful phase of my life. Dissolving a marriage is always awful, and, in our case it turned out to be nearly impossible. Whether or not you still live together, you get into the habit of caring about what happens to the other person on a daily basis. I continued to care about Garnet long after we parted. We are still good friends.

While the women's movement would redefine my life over the next decade and I would set off to forge a career out of a burning need to challenge the status quo, I can still say that raising my children is the single most important thing I ever did. I do not believe it is a contradiction to be a feminist and a loving woman to those close to you and to whom you are responsible. My boys were a lot of work and worry. They were physically wild, forever breaking a limb, driving a car too fast, jumping out of planes, or diving deep into the ocean. One summer, years later, when Charly was working as a bartender in a hotel, he broke his arm, and had the doctor set a shotglass into the cast so he could keep his job. The head waiter found it funny, and let him work. But then he broke the other arm the next day falling off a motorcycle, and he was fired. So Charly and a bunch of friends went to Europe, where he removed the casts himself with pliers so he could swim in the Mediterranean. I thankfully learned this last detail after the fact.

I lived in terror that I would lose them and cannot today think of anything more devastating. My boys were generous and warm, intensely loyal to their friends and family, and good athletes and students. Our bond never stopped growing.

In 1977, when I was thirty, I met and eventually married Andrew Davis, a funny, generous, and extraordinarily kind man with whom I have lived for twenty years. He actually proposed to me when I was in hospital after major surgery, lying immobile, receiving a blood transfusion. I wasn't feeling well, and proceeded to throw up on him. He insisted on cleaning me, and the bed, himself, and, when he was in the bathroom washing up, the nurses told me if I didn't marry him, they might let me die. We were married three days later.

Originally from Montreal, Andrew is a lawyer who works with victims of childhood sexual abuse and also volunteers for animal rights' groups. His Jewish background opened up a whole new culture and tradition that I have come to love. Because we met after my feminism had formed, we worked out a relationship based on a different set of rules. Andrew has been a wonderful "other" father to my boys and they are very close to him.

As I look back now, I ask myself how I could have emerged from this traditional childhood to become a political nonconformist. I believe the answer is that in some very important ways, my family did not conform to many of the dominant values of the day. They weren't small-minded or racist; they didn't gossip and didn't judge their neighbours; and they raised their daughters to take stands on issues of conscience. Yes, they were conventional. They were very hurt by my marriage break-up and the changes my sisters went through as well. And they were puzzled at first over my and Christie's strong embrace of feminism. But they wanted to understand and they grew and adapted admirably.

From my father, I learned my political conscience. It's true, he worked more within the system than without, as I do. But those were different days, when government was still forming policy and programs to deal with the emerging issues of social justice, and it made sense for him to help them build this infrastructure. Today, governments are retreating as fast as they can from these areas of responsibility and there is more of a need for confrontation from civil society to protect rights already won, which are now being rolled back.

From my mother, I gained the confidence to become myself. Most women of my generation didn't even want to *appear* to be different, and so set themselves against other women as well. My very traditional mother gave me not just her permission, but her blessing, to go into the world and shake it up. I could not have accomplished any of my life's work without the legacy of my mother's emotional strength. It was she who made me understand that I come from somewhere, and that what I stand for will live on through my children. One night recently, leaving my house after dinner, she said, "I won't die, you know. Just as Grandma lives on in me, I am inside you. When you look at the world, you will always see it partly through the eyes I gave you."

2

AN UNTRODDEN PATH

"If a thing must be done, it can be."

Eleanor Roosevelt

It is hard for today's young women to understand just how much has changed for women in a very short historical period. The pre-1917 Canada Elections Act said, "No woman, child, idiot or lunatic shall vote." Women at the turn of the century were considered the property of their husbands, and very few ventured outside their traditional roles in the home, although history has taught us just how rugged and resourceful Canadian pioneer women really were.

A doctor writing about the nature of women in *Collier's* magazine in 1946 said that women's emotional growth had not caught up with their intellectual and economic development, and, as a result, they were closer to a childlike state of elemental nature than men. "Women's total nature — conscious and subconscious — is comparable with that of preadolescent children and of men inclined to criminal propensities. Women have, in common with children and potential criminals, the characteristics of emotional instability, fragility of inhibition between instinctive desires and their fulfillment, and a limited ability to endure disappointment." Of course, women, as do "all low offenders," crave mistreatment: "This almost instinctual fascination with danger and horror would seem to be

24

a vestigial remembrance of the thrill and danger of the ancient hunts in which women were captured and subdued."

When I grew up in the 1950s and 1960s, the legal reality for women was changing. Women had the vote and the right to hold office and were entering the workforce. But a woman still couldn't open a bank account without her husband's signature, or testify against him for beating her, or become ordained as a church minister. Most women had no legal access to information about birth control, and women teachers and government workers had to quit their jobs when they married to make way for a "real" worker. Most senior women living on their own were poor.

The traditional work of women was undervalued by just about everyone, women included. When my sister Christie was a little girl, someone asked her what she wanted to be when she grew up. "Nothing, like my mom," was her answer. At a Children's Aid dinner in Kapuskasing in the early 1980s where I was giving a speech, I sat beside a woman who was being honoured later in the evening. She was all dressed up and sported a lovely corsage. I asked her what she did, and she said, "Nothing." "They give you awards for doing nothing in Kapuskasing?" I joked. "I must come back more often." It turns out she had been a foster parent for more than two hundred children over the years and had set a record in Ontario for her foster work. But, in her own mind, she had done nothing. Her husband apparently shared her low opinion of herself; he was at home watching the hockey game instead of being with her on her big night.

(In my speech that night, I praised the work of women like her and said that women wouldn't advance as a group until we recognized the importance of our nurturing and traditional roles. She called me on the phone several months later to tell me a story. She had been very moved by what I said that night and thought a lot about it. Her eighteen-year-old son was trying to get into a program in social work at his local community college and had been asked by the intake officer what his mother did. "Nothing" was the answer. After some prodding by the female official, he allowed that she had raised him, his four brothers and sisters, and all these foster children. The officer told him to go home and think of a different answer to her question, and then they would see about his entering the course. The son came home perplexed and asked his mother what he had said wrong. "Sit down!" she ordered. "And let me tell you.")

Right into the 1980s, it was assumed by many men in government and business that women worked for "pin money" or until a man came along. There was great resentment against women who competed with men in traditional male-dominated fields, and horrific tales of group and individual harassment aimed at women who tried. Mostly, women entered the "helping" professions — nursing, teaching, social work, child care, secretarial — and brought home paycheques for a fraction of what their male colleagues were paid. Ottawa city hall actually had a separate pay scale for men and women doing the same jobs, and that practice wasn't eliminated until 1960.

In 1966, I worked as a teller in a bank for eight months, just after my first year at university and before I got married. I learned the job so fast that they moved me to training. There, every six weeks, I would train two groups of people: women, who were destined to be tellers and clerks, and men, who were automatically put into the bank's management program, part of which was this basic teller training. The men were earning almost three times my salary, and no matter how well or badly they did (unless it was so badly that they were let go altogether), after six weeks as tellers they were off and moving up the ladder. This was so commonplace a practice at the time that, even though I knew there was something wrong, I couldn't figure out what.

The 1967 Royal Commission on the Status of Women, established by Lester Pearson and chaired by Florence Bird (whom I once correctly called a "national treasure" in the *Globe and Mail*), changed the world for Canadian women. Within a decade, almost two-thirds of the commission's 167 sweeping recommendations on everything from employment and education to family law were implemented, including the creation of the Canadian Advisory Council on the Status of Women and the passage of the Canadian Human Rights Act.

The Canada Labour Code was amended to remove discriminatory statutes, and the federal government funded the creation of women's career-counselling and rape crisis centres, women's research programs and professional associations, and transition houses for battered women. Canada became one of the few countries in the world where the government helped fund a women's revolution.

The American process, on the other hand, was litigation-driven. While the American government didn't fund the American women's movement, it did pass a law obliging any company with a federal government contract to develop an affirmative-action program and it established the legal framework within which women and others could themselves directly challenge discrimination through the courts. The federally established Equal Employment Opportunities Commission was mandated to enforce quota-backed affirmative-action programs on campuses and in the workplace, and became enormously powerful and controversial. Affirmative action and pay equity swept the United States, challenging the entrenched privilege of white, upper-middle-class men in universities, clubs, and the workplace.

Although Canadian politicians were not talking about enforced quotas, the Canadian media, ever filled with American stories as if they were our own, carried tales of "reverse discrimination," lawsuits, and race and gender wars in the workplace. Canadian businesses, government departments, and universities started to get nervous about the possible importation of legislated affirmative action, and many decided to set up their own "equal opportunity" programs to avoid the imposition of something more radical down the line. It was an opportune time to be a young feminist, filled with energy, commitment, and ideas. The path was untrodden; it was ours to clear and walk.

For a while, I searched for a way to become involved. Besides working as a volunteer with the local women's centres, I taught women's studies at our local community college and communications courses for women at the local YWCA. I started speaking out on sexism in advertising and media, and answered requests to be a spokesperson for local groups and in the press. My knowledge in all of this was self-taught; there were still no women's studies courses at universities.

But these new approaches lacked direction. So in 1975, five women — Joyce Denyer, Helen LaFountaine (now dead), and Carol Reich in Toronto, and Penny Shore and myself in Ottawa — set up a consulting firm to help advance the status of women in a systematic way and in every facet of Canadian society. It was the first of its kind in Canada. Modelled after a similar company in New York, for the next five years Women Associates Consulting Incorporated would provide advice, research, and training to organizations all across Canada on how to promote women in-house. There was no blueprint or precedent for what we were doing, and no professional training to teach us the ropes.

I have to confess that we developed our programs as we went along. We studied where we could find anything in our field at all — I attended numerous human-rights courses as well as a University of Chicago intensive training course on implementing affirmative action in the workplace — and read everything we could get our hands on.

But we were one big step ahead of everyone else and we were an idea whose time had come. The contracts came pouring in. We developed Canadian-style affirmative-action and pay-equity programs, and the assertiveness-training programs, career counselling, and management-training courses for women employees in Canada that we designed were among the first. Our forte became our courses for senior management, where we walked executives and decision makers (usually male) through their own stereotypes and forced them to confront their involvement in the gender biases that existed within their organizations.

Major contracts included studies for the Alberta Human Rights Commission, the National Indian Brotherhood (predecessor of the Assembly of First Nations), and Atomic Energy of Canada. We developed extensive training packages for Canada Mortgage and Housing Corporation, Ontario Hydro, the Ministry of Labour, the National Film Board, and the CBC, where we put every manager and more than 1,500 women through equal-opportunity training. I remember one die-hard senior producer telling me, "I can always figure which women have gone through your program on job interviews. They talk back!"

The sessions with senior management were often tense and always revealing. I had a favourite technique: I would divide the managers into three groups and tell the first to list on a flip chart all the attributes that make up the ideal woman, the second to list those of the ideal man, and the third those of the ideal manager. Then I would put these flip charts on the wall and compare them. *Always*, the ideal man and the ideal manager would be interchangeable parts of a perfect being — strong, decisive, not afraid to risk, responsible for those around him, compassionate when necessary but never "soft," and so on. The ideal woman, by contrast, was something totally different: concerned with others, soft and gentle, quiet and supportive. And, of course, beautiful.

I would then have them role-play an imaginary job interview. "You are to hire someone for the management-training program — a long-term employee with a future." I would then send in two candidates, both female. One would be the stereotype of the perfect manager based on their description. Inevitably, she would intimidate and threaten them, all but blowing her chances of getting hired. The second candidate would be the ideal woman they had described. It wouldn't take long for them to realize that, while this was someone they might ask out on a date, she was not likely to be offered the job. It was a quick lesson in the "damned if you do and damned if you don't" position professional women found themselves in all the time in those days.

The assertiveness-training and career-counselling workshops for women were pure magic. We were a generation in the midst of revolution and we knew it. So many talented women had been raised to deny their gifts and bury their ambitions. They had been taught that to be liked was more important than to be respected, and their need for approval, particularly from male superiors, was often incapacitating. Our courses offered women a safe place to release emotion, including anger; ways to value themselves and to admit their ambitions; and the ability to forgive themselves for imperfection. We taught that an assertive woman is allowed to act in her own self-interest (an amazing discovery for many women), to ask for what she needs, to set limits on other people's aggression, and to express (Horrors!) negative feelings.

We put literally thousands of women through role-playing in which they had to analyse their body language, practise saying "No," learn to turn off the internal self-criticisms, and express their rights in the workplace and in the home. Women would sit down for the first time in their lives and plan their futures. They would analyse their workplace for bias and, with a "click" of recognition, realize that the reason they took home half the pay of the man sitting next to them at work was not their fault but the system's — what came to be known as "systemic discrimination."

One moment we would be roaring with laughter at an individual story instantly recognizable for its universal resonance. Another moment we would be helping a woman look into the abyss of breast cancer, a child's death, or a divorce; tears didn't seem out of place when learning to deal with sexual harassment or how to ask for a promotion. We ended many a workshop by going around the room and asking each woman to finish the sentence "I like myself because . . . ." More often than not, a box of Kleenex would have to accompany the process, as woman after woman broke years of taboo by publicly declaring her self-worth. Those were some of the happiest working days of my life.

Several contracts in particular are etched in my memory. Penny and I were the first women ever hired to teach at the Canadian Police College, a national training school for police managers around the country. We designed and taught, for almost three years, two types of courses on a weekly basis. One set of courses dealt with women as victims — of rape, wife assault, and other sex-related crimes. The disturbing statistics on these crimes were just surfacing, and the common practice at the time was to treat them as "private" or "domestic" incidents. Police resented being called in on these cases, which they considered to be nuisances that took them away from their "real" work; when they did respond, it was their practice to calm everyone down so things could get back to "normal." They almost never laid charges in the case of domestic assault, date rape, or incest.

It was our job to sensitize these men to the realities of rape and assault for women (at many a police station, women victims of rape were "interviewed" in a room with walls covered with centrefolds from such magazines as *Hustler* or calendars of nude women) and to impart to them the emerging societal and government consensus that these were real crimes and should be treated as such.

The other type of course dealt with the rights of women in policing — a newly emerging phenomenon most male officers hated and energetically resisted. Women were just entering the municipal and provincial police forces, following a pattern of quota-based integration of American police forces, and to say the issue was controversial is a major understatement. Many — even most, I have to say — of the men I taught were opposed to women in policing at all. As one explained to me, "My job is tied up with my masculinity." He went on to say that he was there to protect the helpless — old people, women, and children — but if he was told that women are his equals and can do his job, he would have to reassess himself as a man.

Every month, we had a whole new group to break in, and every month, they would have some surprise or other for the "lady instructors." One group had papered the whole room with *Playboy* and *Penthouse* centrefolds on our first morning together. I said "Now, boys. You shouldn't have spent all your allowance in one place and at one time. Now there won't be anything left over for bubblegum." Another had their watches synchronized so that every ten minutes they would all stand in unison, bring out an apple for Teacher, and ask to go "pee-pee."

Although I used humour wherever I could, I found this constant testing exasperating to deal with on a regular basis, and sometimes dreaded going to the college. I often felt that I wasn't up to the task and worried that, if I handled a problem badly, life for the women these men dealt with back home might be made more difficult. But I told myself that if I couldn't take the heat, I was being a bad role model for women who wanted to enter the profession, and I became even more determined to carry on.

In the end, most of us learned to respect one another. I like to think some of them learned something from me; I can certainly say that I learned a great deal from them. These were tough men doing a tough job and, although I often disagreed with them, I learned to see the world through their eyes. Behind the hard façade, many were compassionate and caring men, and I learned not to make assumptions based on my first impressions. They taught me to toughen up, not expect perfection, and to keep a sense of humour.

The most important lesson they taught me was professionalism. I was not there to be liked or to approve or disapprove of their attitudes. I was there to teach and to help them change their behaviour. I learned this the hard way. My lesson came in the form of a particularly obnoxious senior officer with the Ottawa force. I was teaching a class on women in the forces, and he had taunted me all morning with racist and sexist comments and sneered and huffed through my entire presentation.

I kept my cool until he called all policewomen "cunts" and then I lost it. I told him to fuck himself, threw a piece of chalk at him (a direct hit, right on the forehead), and stormed out of the room. I counted to a hundred, calmed myself down, vowed that never again in my professional life would I act like that, went back into the room, apologized to the group, and the rest of the morning passed without incident, but the air was thick with tension. Since that day, I have never again lost my temper like that in a professional setting, and I have been grateful many times when up against far harder antagonists than those at the Canadian Police College. (The officer in question was fired from the Ottawa force some time later for brutal behaviour. I will admit to a wee gloat when I heard that.)

In any case, all the stress and any bad memories melted away the fine June morning I attended the ceremony of the first group of women to graduate from the Royal Canadian Mounted Police Training Academy in Regina. While walking the inspection line, I was introduced to the female RCMP officers by the commanding officer as "one of the women who had made this possible for them." One young woman, after being told to stand "at ease," yelled out, "Right on, ma'am!" I grinned like an idiot for the rest of the day.

In 1977, on behalf of Women Associates, I also became involved in the fight to open the armed services to women, and helped design the pilot assessment at the military training base in St. Jean, Quebec, of the trials to bring women into near-combat roles. I had the pleasure of working with some wonderful women: Shirley Robinson, the fiery red-headed military nurse, one of the first women to rise to the rank of lieutenant-colonel (now retired) who has led the public case on this issue; Dr. Susanne Simpson, now a private consultant, who designed the military's research for the project; and Lise Belanger, a lawyer who won a landmark case before the Canadian Human Rights Commission when she challenged the military's refusal to grant her maternity leave.

In 1984, I leaked to the *Globe and Mail* the contents of a Defence Department study which indicated that, even though women had done well on the trials, the military was going to argue against their participation in combat or near-combat roles because males in the military would have serious problems adapting. The study said that, because there were so few women in the armed forces, their small numbers would work against them — an illogical argument for not hiring more women, if ever I heard one.

We formed the Association for Women's Equity in the Canadian Forces and launched a national campaign to force the government to address this issue. Following a Human Rights Tribunal in the late 1980s, all occupations (except submarines) in the Canadian armed forces were fully opened to qualified women.

Shirley Robinson must be given enormous credit for her tireless lobby and the public fight she put up for the women coming after her. She was honoured for this work when she was recently given the prestigious "Person's Award" by the governor general. I had the great pleasure of nominating Shirley for this honour, and all the women from our group were on hand at Rideau Hall to share her special moment.

The idea of women in the military, ironically, was a bone of contention within the women's movement, particularly among feminists in the peace movement. Many felt that women were innately more peaceful than men, and a place in the military was not something for them to aspire to. A heroine of mine, Professor Emerita in Nuclear Physics at the University of Toronto, and a leader in the peace movement, Ursula Franklin, called me to voice her concern. I explained that, for me, this was a matter of simple justice and choice. Whether our military was contributing to world peace or world discourse was another issue, a political matter, I argued, one that all women in Canada should address. In fact, I was at the time on the board of the Canadian Centre for Arms Control and Disarmament, which published a small book I wrote on women and disarmament. The book decried the lack of women in this field in Canada and on the international scene. I did not then, and still do not, see these perspectives as incompatible.

In 1978, I began a project with the Kingston Prison for Women that would prove to be one of the most challenging of my life. Inspired by both my father's work in prison reform, and my sister Christie's career (she was now executive director of the Elizabeth Fry Societies of Canada), I was particularly anxious to work with the women inmates at what they called "P4W," an institution built in 1934 that, until recently, housed all federal female offenders in Canada in infamously poor conditions.

I was first brought in to give several life-skills and anger-management workshops to "lifers." The first time I saw the prison, I physically recoiled, and dread flooded my body. Just down the road from the men's prison, with its heavily armed guards clearly visible from a huge tower, P4W is an imposing building, relentlessly grey, with a rigid and repressive atmosphere. The first thing I had to do was pass through a gruff and rigorous inspection; there were no pleasantries from the guards or any apparent recognition that I was a free agent and not there to be incarcerated. I thought, "If I feel this intimidated, I can imagine how a prisoner must feel." Inside, the prison was a collection of the most disadvantaged and dispossessed people I had ever met, being handled by overworked, understaffed, and very defensive guards.

It was (and remains) my conviction that most women prisoners have been victims of poverty, brutality, and sexual violence, and that they had to learn to reject self-hatred, come to terms with the systemic discrimination that had helped put them there, and learn ways to cope with the daily challenges of life inside and out of prison. I was particularly convinced that they had to form a kind of "sisterhood" and stop brutalizing themselves and one other.

This issue came to a head in the first hour of my first workshop. I had been given a list naming the twenty participants; in the room there were nineteen women. I asked, "Where is the missing person?" "She's a baby killer, miss," said an inmate, "and she's not welcome here. If she comes in here, she'll get hurt." With prodding, they gave me her story. Fay was a young aboriginal woman from a remote northern Saskatchewan community who had sniffed glue and fallen asleep while babysitting a friend's child. Her boyfriend, who had been visiting with her, had started a fire in the basement and left. By the time she woke up, smoke filled the house; she panicked and fled. The two-month-old baby died in the fire. By the rough justice of prison life, she was more hated than anyone, and the women would take the opportunity to punish her if she stepped out of line.

I said, "The week we are about to spend together will help us all understand the larger social origins of Fay's story. She's not your enemy, and your anger against her is misdirected. We won't start the workshop until she is invited to participate." I sat down, my heart pounding. They talked, smoked, shouted at one another, talked some more, and finally one went off to find Fay and bring her, trembling, to the group. I would like to think this early success was a measure of their desire to take my workshop; but the truth is probably more mundane. Life in prison is dull. My session was the only diversion around and they didn't want to blow their chances of attending.

These encounters stand out in my mind as some of the most intense personal interactions of my life. They also made me realize what a privileged upbringing I had had and how different life would have been if I had had any one of theirs. One of the first tasks for each woman was to see her life and crime against the larger social reality of women, so the first days were a crash course in Feminism 101. Although their personal histories were private and to be shared only if they chose, most voluntarily disclosed their own stories and we collectively worked to place them in a larger social context. The feminist adage "the personal is political" came alive for me as never before in that musty old room with its barred windows when some of the most despised and brutalized women in our society revealed the secrets of their lives while armed guards patrolled the hall just outside the door.

One woman had murdered an extremely brutal husband (these were the days before battered women could claim self-defence for this crime) and she told her story to the hushed group for the first time. The abuse she took was so brutal that, when she described sinking that knife into his sleeping back, we all breathed a sigh of relief. Another inmate, with whom she had been having an ongoing, violent feud, wept and held her as she finished her story.

It wasn't all serious. These women were too tough and had seen too much not to have some fun, mostly at my expense. At noon each day, anyone who needed medication went to the nursing station to receive it. One day, returning from her daily trek for her treatment, an inmate named Sandi opened her blouse and showed her breasts to the whole group, who admired them with "oohs" and "aahs." I, trying to be cool, asked, "And just what's so special about your breasts today?" The women howled in unison at my discomfort when she revealed that she used to be a man, and was in the midst of a sex-change operation. The group was monitoring the daily progress of her hormone treatment. Now I understood why Sandi had laughed so hard whenever I talked about how sex-role stereotyping had affected them when they were little girls.

(Years later, when I was hosting a thirteen-part television special on women for CJOH in Ottawa, I asked Maggie, another lifer at P4W whom I had worked with, to be a guest on my show to talk about what life in prison is like for women. The assistant floor director, to make conversation with her as he was putting on her microphone, asked her what she was in prison for. "I killed two men," she answered pleasantly. When he looked distinctly uncomfortable, Maggie quickly added, "Don't worry, dear. I marry them first.")

One woman mesmerized me from the first. Marlene "Shaggy" Moore was a fragile woman with huge eyes ringed by deep circles who sat apart from the group, curled up like a cat on one of the big windowsills that surrounded the room. She would not speak or respond to questions, and the group seemed to give her a wide berth, although they also displayed a certain gentleness with her, as if she were breakable. Over the next decade, I would come to see why as this intelligent, sensitive, and vulnerable woman touched a whole community of people inside and outside P4W. Her life story was chronicled in a brilliant 1989 piece of journalism written by Anne Kershaw and Mary Lasovich and published by the *Kingston Whig-Standard*.

Marlene Moore grew up in a large, poor, rural Ontario family, where corporal punishment was common, and her father beat her for bed-wetting. She had little formal education and she told me she was the victim of sibling incest. By the age of thirteen, she was committed to the maximum-security unit of the ill-famed Grandview training school, where three-quarters of the girls mutilated their bodies. Here Marlene began a lifelong pattern of self-mutilation: she slashed herself with razors, glass, and knives more than a thousand times. By the time I met her, her arms, legs, and stomach were butchered, criss-crossed with new slashes on old scars. She once tried to cut her uterus out, so much did she hate her female self.

Once out of reformatory, she was viciously raped by a stranger who was convicted of the crime but subsequently acquitted because it was discovered that Marlene had been high on speed that night. Enraged, she set out on a rampage, breaking and entering and generally taunting police until she was sent to the Vanier Centre for Women — the provincial facility for female offenders. Here, she fell into a spiral of rage and violence which ended when she and another prisoner took a female guard hostage and Marlene, refusing all offers of psychiatric assessment, demanded to be sent up for "hard time." The court granted her wish and she was sent to P4W. She would never leave this place for any sustained time again, and her self-destructive behaviour at the prison set her up in direct confrontation with the prison authorities.

In fact, eighty per cent of her adult life was spent in prisons, often in isolation. The government twice invoked extraordinary legal measures to block her release from prison, and she was the first woman in Canada to be designated a dangerous offender. When I met her, she was already considered incorrigible.

On the last day of the three-day workshop she attended, Marlene climbed down off the windowsill, and walked over to the flip chart. She wrote: "About leavin the past and every Thing behind. Its my life and Im the one that can change it becuz Im the one liven it. If god should strike me dead rite now, I no I gotta do it my way or no way at all." I was over-joyed. I hadn't thought I was reaching her. Just as she seemed ready to talk about what she had written, the (male) prison chaplain walked unan-nounced into the room, a habit he had developed during my courses. (He was deeply suspicious of what I was doing there.) He picked up a marker pen and proceeded to correct every one of Marlene's spelling mistakes in front of the whole group. Then he dropped the marker, and, with a smile, left the room. Marlene left in a rage, and I was so angry I could hardly carry on. She allowed me to visit her later that day, and we formed a friendship over our mutual feelings about that "man of God." I kept coming back to the prison long after my workshops ended in order to visit with her, and her courage in the face of her terrible demons never failed to amaze me. I have kept some of our correspondence and cannot even now read it without tears.

"I went to the outside shrink," she wrote in 1981, "and I ran. I didn't no were I was running to or from, All I new is I wanted to get cot. All I did was sit on the water front. Thought abit and when I went to run I told the screw to pick me up around the corner. After I got off the water front I was scared, So I walked out to the street and they picked me up. I was so happy I got cot.

"They charged me outside kort. for a 45 minute walk. But Im not sure I care what they do to me, cuz when I was out, I was to affraid of people of everything. not becuz the cops were after me, just my thoughts. I ended up slashin, 40 stitches, I brought the razor blades to the shrink cuz I new I was gonna get cot & go to seg when I got back. I don't no if I'll ever get out of here. And yet, I wanna make it. Does that make sense? I'm walkin a thin line."

Marlene had a sense of humour that drove the officials at P4W crazy, especially when she was in segregation. "I refuse to let our so called warden get to me. I drawed a couloured Granata TV on my wall, rite. And on the screen I put Betty Davis starrin in Hush Hush Sweet Charlotte. And when he comes up, rite, I goes be quiet, I'm watching a movey rite. That way I don't give him a chance to get me goin. He gets confused and when he walks away rite, Im sayin 'fucken commercials' Ha Ha."

I testified at Marlene's dangerous-offender trial, and our last correspondence was related to that terrible ordeal. "You looked so brave, but alone, and my heart, as always, went out to you," I wrote. "I really appresheate you goin to kort, thanx millions," she answered. "Maudie, Pleeze take very special care, stay strong & walk proud. You are a fine lady & Im glad we've had the chance to meet each other. If everything else in this life is screwed up, this time they made no mistake."

Marlene's condition deteriorated steadily after that. She was in segregation almost all the time near the end. According to a report of an inmate committee of the time, segregation at P4W still had no hot water, cells had only concrete flooring, toilets were rusted out and putrid, and the bars were painted black in keeping with the punishment theme. "It is straight torture for any human person to be subject to cages such as these," the report said.

Marlene had to wear a urine bag so the staff could monitor blood clots from her slashing. "I'm wetting all over the place," she wrote to another inmate. "I dont feel good at all. Im sorry you guys I dont mean to wet — I cant stop. Bag or no bag. Im reelly embarrest. ashamed. hurt. I began to hate myself, ya no. Cuz I think whod want a person like me around. you no what I mean. I isolate myself cuz of this. . . . My greatest mistake was to be born." On December 3, 1988, Marlene Moore hanged herself with a bedsheet in the segregation unit of P4W.

It was for Marlene Moore and the other women inmates with whom we worked at P4W that a group of women calling ourselves "Women for Justice" launched a landmark case with the Canadian Human Rights Commission against the Federal Penitentiaries Service. Some other members of the group included my sister, Christie Jefferson; one-time coordinator of the federal program for female offenders, Lorraine Berzins; criminologist Brigid Hayes; and several women who worked for the penitentiaries service itself and who helped us gather the data for our case. These data were used to compare what was available to the male and female populations of the federal prison system.

The statistics astounded everyone. Women received far less counselling for drug and alcohol abuse than men, if they received any counselling at all. They had no access to training, with the sole exception of assistant hairdressing; the men had extensive options open to them. Women were even given less money at the prison gate (a practice to allow newly released prisoners to buy food, take a bus, and look for shelter). One official at P4W told me that was because women could "hook" for cash.

We argued that because the Prison for Women was the only federal penitentiary for women (women commit such a small percentage of serious crime, hence a single prison for them), female prisoners had far less access to training and rehabilitation programs than male inmates; they were more likely to be far away from home; they had no chance of being upgraded to a better institution for better behaviour; and they were all housed together as maximum offenders, even if they were classified minimum or medium offenders. "An Inuit woman from the Northwest Territories, a Native woman from Saskatchewan, a graduate student from Vancouver, and a grandmother from Newfoundland have little in common except that they are all prisoners at P4W and they are all women," we pointed out, and added that it seemed women were being penalized for not committing enough crime.

The Canadian Human Rights Commission agreed with us and, on December 14, 1981, ruled that the inmates at the Kingston Prison for Women were victims of discrimination, and the commission appointed a conciliator to assign remedies. Over the next several years, some real beneficial institutional changes, such as drug counselling, employment training, and improved living conditions, were mandated. The old building was virtually condemned; in 1994, the government shut it down and moved the women to new institutions closer to their homes.

More important, however, was the fact that the ruling addressed *systemic* discrimination and found that Correctional Services Canada, as a whole system, discriminated against women. The entire institution, from top to bottom, had to be overhauled, and employment and pay equity were eventually mandated within the entire system itself. The backlash was pretty strong. Even our father took some direct heat over "Bill's girls," which, of course, he loved. This is what he had taught us to be.

My last visit to P4W was for a five-year celebration of the case. Christie and I were invited to inspect the new computer training facilities at the prison and say a few words at the event, which they called, without a trace of irony, "Career Day for Lifers."

Amen, sisters.

3

IN THE EYE OF THE FEMINIST STORM

"The rising of the women is the rising of the race."

"Bread and Roses"
Union song

When I was a young stay-at-home mother, I had a neighbour, a sweet and gentle woman from a close-knit immigrant family. She had five children and spoke little English. One day, she came over to my house, bleeding profusely from a wound to her head, and asked me to look after her children while an aunt took her to the hospital. I brought her kids to my house so that I would be home when my own came home from school, and it was only when she came to fetch them that I noticed the bruises all over her arms and face. A couple of days later, I got up the courage to go across the street and ask my neighbour if there was "anything wrong." She said no, and closed the door gently in my face. Now and then we would have coffee and I would help her with her English, and from time to time she would have new cuts and bruises. I never asked again and she never offered an explanation.

Then one day, she was taken to the hospital so badly beaten that she almost died. I tried to talk to the aunt, who told me it was none of my business. Shortly after she left the hospital, the family moved away and I

41

never saw her again. I have thought of her so many times since then. Why didn't I persist? Why didn't I call the police? Could I have made a difference? It is so difficult to explain the code of silence that existed about wife assault in those days. With time, I vowed to make it up to her by taking a stand for other women. I was about to enter a phase of my life where this and other challenges would lead me through a trial by fire. The memory of my neighbour's suffering and my own inaction would see me through some difficult days ahead.

In 1980, I left Women Associates to become the director of the Office of Equal Opportunity for Women at the City of Ottawa. Most municipal governments in Canada at the time were notorious for their paternalistic hiring and employment practices. Ottawa was no different. Nepotism was entrenched. Years of habit had produced a system in which supervisors, foremen, and managers hired their friends and family. The only rule was that the hiring of blue-collar workers had to alternate between French and English persons. There was no human-resources manual, no hiring or employment procedures, and no job-interview panels. The city's idea of equal opportunity was to move the sole black police officer on the Ottawa force around, directing traffic in different spots during rush hour, so it would look to the public as if the city had an ethnically diverse workforce.

The woman who had held the directorial post before me had been fired for noisily pointing all this out, and the climate was very sour. I had two very big pluses on my side. Marion Dewar, public health nurse, feminist, and passionate advocate for the underdog, was mayor and insisted I report directly to city council and not the personnel department, as my predecessor had had to do. Her support was crucial and allowed me a great deal of flexibility.

As well, the office secretary, Doreen O'Hearne, was a long-time employee of the city and knew the ropes. She also was (and is) one of the kindest people I have ever met. Together, we hired my executive assistant, Bonnie Diamond, with whom I became close friends and would share many political adventures in the future. Bonnie went on to become a leader in the field of criminal justice, worked with the federal Canadian Panel on Violence Against Women, and is now executive director of the National Association of Women and the Law.

The first thing I did was meet as many of the municipal employees as was humanly possible and conduct my own informal survey of where the tension points were and where we had to begin. It soon became clear that there was little sense of solidarity among the women employees themselves and not much of a feeling of their entitlement to equality. So we developed a Friday "brown-bag lunch" series to introduce the issues I felt they needed to embrace as their own before we could proceed. Ageing, sexual harassment, pay equity, work sharing, day care, body language, you name it — we had a different topic and a different speaker each week. The word started to spread, and pretty soon our events were packed, and not just with women.

We also set up what we called our "Liaison Committee" made up of women from every department, elected by their female co-workers, to help us do our research and establish priorities. I felt that if I was to deliver a program for the women of city hall, I was working for them. This committee set the direction for our program and gave us a way to report back to our "employers." Its very existence unleashed an enormous amount of energy in these women: for years, they had bottled up not only their talent and initiative, but their anger about the obvious sexism that was built into the very structures of their workplace. Friendships developed immediately, and we formed a kind of support network for one another that stayed in place long after I left city hall.

One of the first problems they identified was that I was barred from the weekly meeting of the senior commissioners (department heads), where all the important decisions about staff were made. My predecessor had fought to be included, and won. But, after one of her first meetings, she gave a story to the local newspaper about what had taken place in it, and the invitation to future meetings was revoked.

It took me four months to earn their trust, but finally, at the last meeting of the year before my first Christmas with the city, I was sent an invitation by the chief commissioner to attend. Moments before leaving my office for the meeting, a young female lawyer who was articling for the city came into my office and shut the door. "I could lose my job for telling you this," she said, "but my boss [Don Hambling, the senior legal counsel for the City] is dead set against you and wants to prove you have no sense of humour. So he's going to give you a 'Christmas present' —

a little statue of a woman golfer holding a golf club that has been cut off to make her appear to be holding a penis. Under her is a drawing of a toilet, with the words: 'Women's Lib. Stand Up for Your Rights.'"

I thanked her profusely and vowed to keep her secret. On my way to the meeting, I worried. If I don't laugh, if I get upset, I'll prove his point. But I can't laugh at something this dumb. Then it came to me, and I walked into the meeting with a smile. Everyone was tense, particularly the only other woman, Evelyn Cooper, the city clerk. Clearly, they all knew. I said hello and sat down. Don Hambling pulled out his gift, put it in front of me, and said, "Merry Christmas." Total silence. I looked at the statue; everyone looked at me. Finally, I said, "Oh, Don, I didn't know we were to exchange presents, so I don't have one for you. But I do have a card." And I reached into my wallet and handed Don a little card I had kept for just such an occasion.

It read: "You have just insulted a woman. This card has been chemically treated. In three days, your prick will fall off." Don turned a funny shade of green and tried to put the card in his pocket, but I insisted on sharing it. John Cyr, the personnel commissioner, who was to become a real friend, laughed so hard he staggered out of the room. Poor Don. For weeks after, people would say, "How are you, Don?" and their gaze would not be cast towards his face.

One of our most controversial projects was an affirmative-action program to bring women into the "wage sector" — labourers, arena attendants, heavy-equipment operators, grounds workers, asphalt-repair workers, and sewer-maintenance workers. We had several hundred applications, which, after a rigorous interview process, we narrowed down to the six we hired. They then went through a week of intensive assertiveness training to get them ready for their adventure. I was quoted in a local paper at the time: "I wouldn't have wanted to go through what they went through. They were really put through the grinder — we don't put men through that." Then we sent them out to work in teams of two, the first women in the blue-collar workforce in our city.

These poor women were watched like rats in a maze by the press, city council, their supervisors, other women, and, of course, the men. Every mistake was amplified, every action analysed. They would come back to us with dreadful stories. One female snow-removal worker was forced to do double time outside the vehicles until she started to turn blue, despite the fact that regulations said workers were to trade off walking outside. Another found notes taped to her locker, warning her to go home. Several on the night shift had to stay in their trucks while some "colleagues," who were supposed to be working, visited prostitutes. The six wouldn't let us say anything, of course, because they were being tested and knew that whether they could take this treatment without complaint would form part of their "marks."

In the end, all six of them left, and, although we knew the real circumstances, officially and publicly the women gave the kinds of traditional reasons that confirmed every stereotype about women in the book. One said the work was too hard; another moved out West to follow her husband; a third got pregnant; another had "female" problems and had to stop lifting heavy objects. These women were genuinely surprised by the treatment they received at the hands of their male co-workers. One, a lesbian, was so sure she was going to be accepted by her male co-workers, she invited them to her wedding to her female lover and couldn't understand their horrified rejection.

Bonnie and I can laugh about it now, but it was very difficult at the time. The first of anything is always the hardest; the next group of women we brought in worked very well, and with time the wage sector started to reflect a slightly more diversified character.

It remained an uphill battle. In 1982, we undertook a major study on the status of women at city hall and found that the situation was still deplorable. We found, for instance, that women made up only 22 per cent of the workforce; a man with a grade-eight education made more money on average than a woman with a university degree; women with equivalent experience and years of service made close to 30 per cent less than their male colleagues; and the higher women rose in the organization, the higher the discrepancy.

We did make some concrete changes. We worked with the personnel department to help design a human-resources manual so that mandatory fairer hiring and employment practices were implemented. We designed a pilot program on job sharing and issued a feasibility study on a City Hall day care centre. We implemented one of the first by-laws on workplace sexual harassment in the country, setting out policy and protocol in these cases and establishing the culpability of the employer if it failed to act. And we developed an extensive career and life-skills training program for women employees that was widely attended and that played an important role in changing the attitude problems I had identified when I first arrived.

These programs and rights are taken for granted now and it is hard to imagine both the excitement we felt in creating them and the backlash they caused. There was such tremendous hope and enthusiasm in the early women's movement. We were out to change the world, not only for women, but for everyone. There were such clear, unequivocal injustices that the fights themselves, no matter how tough, were always exhilarating.

Now that our world has changed so much, it's easy to forget that change came one person at a time. There was the talented woman of colour who was without doubt the object of racial discrimination at work, as well as the victim of severe battering by her partner. We helped her to leave him, lay a complaint against her employer with the Human Rights Commission, get a better job, and go back to school. There was the woman lawyer whose boss tried to fire her because, after many years with the city, she had no experience representing the city in court. I took on the whole city council for that one; it turned out a former boss forbade her from going to court as he said it was no place for a woman. He'd made it impossible for her to *get* experience. A group of women in one department were sexually harassed by its supervisor. I brought him into my office and read him the riot act. The harassment ceased. One timid secretary became a feisty and feared union organizer. A whole group of women were underclassified, and Bonnie and I got them upgraded.

In many ways, the most important work was done when women came together to name for the first time the discrimination or violence they were experiencing. They would describe the problem and we would help them practise how they were going to deal with it back in the office. One woman, who went on to form her own successful consulting firm, had lost her temper in front of her (powerful) boss and knew she had to apologize. She was very young and very emotional about this and was afraid she would break down in tears. I helped her formulate her words and we wrote them on the back of her hand so she would get it exactly right. She bounded into my office moments after with the news that all had gone well. Sometimes, all a woman needed was a safe haven, and our office became a gathering place and a life support system for many, many women blazing a new path in a still-hostile world.

During these years at city hall and with the council's blessing, I also served on the board and then became president of a women's drug and alcohol centre called Amethyst. We brought a feminist approach to the issue of substance abuse, dealing with the woman in her family and social setting, and concentrating as much on her work and personal life as on her addiction. The courage of the women I met at Amethyst — both the clients and the staff — was inspiring, and the centre's work continues to this day.

When a report was tabled in the House of Commons in 1982 that said one man in ten beats his wife, MPs roared with laughter. Ignorance of the severity of the problem was general. Doctors regularly refused to report what they saw as a private matter; neighbours turned up the television to drown out the cries of domestic violence in homes or apartments nearby; co-workers pretended not to see the telltale bruises and cuts; and social workers who would never ignore the signs of an obviously beaten child considered it an invasion of the family to get involved in a situation between adults.

One day, a group of battered women came to see me, sent to my office by Marion Dewar. They had approached her with tales of the deplorable state of services and lack of police protection for abused women in Ottawa and asked for her help in addressing this issue. After a talk, the mayor and I approached the Police Commission (on which she sat) to recommend a joint assessment on the situation. The police chief (thankfully about to retire) was rigidly opposed. He said that his men had the domestic-violence protocol down pat. They would take the husband for a long walk around the block to help him cool off and stay to make sure the couple "made up." He made it clear that he saw the woman as equally responsible for any violence, and that under only very rare circumstances did he recommend further involvement on the part of the justice system.

Writer Barbara Amiel summed up the prevailing views of the day in one of her column for *Maclean's* (although she kept these antediluvian views when most of the rest of society advanced) when she called wife assault "domestic strife between consenting adults" and claimed that some women willingly consent to an element of violence in their relationships. "The sado-masochistic relationship is another petri dish for violence. Some people have a psycho-sexual orientation that requires pain for full satisfaction."

Following a report I prepared for city council, I was mandated to set up the Ottawa Task Force on Wife Assault, which brought together the police, family services, the hospitals, the Crown Attorney's office, defence lawyers, the family court, the Canadian Advisory Council on the Status of Women, and the Ottawa Board of Education. For almost a year, we studied what happens to a woman from the moment she is assaulted — the role of the police, the hospitals, the schools (who have to deal with children who have witnessed violence), the courts, and social-service agencies.

Everyone in this group worked hard, but three stand out: the new police chief, Tom Welsh, who was a breath of fresh air; Andrejs Berzins, the empathetic Crown Attorney and husband of Lorraine, with whom I had worked in Women for Justice; and Joan Gullen, an exceptional community activist who was then with the Family Service Centre. Joan soon became my co-chair and, when our work was done, stayed to run the Ottawa–Carleton Coordinating Committee on Wife Assault.

Our task force heard directly from battered women in closed hearings. Their stories were not new to some in the room; others, overcome by emotion at the testimony, had to leave the hearings from time to time. One woman who deeply affected the group had married an older man at sixteen to escape an abusive father, and moved into her husband's farm in a remote part of the Ottawa Valley. She had six children in rapid succession. Her husband, kind at first, started to get possessive, jealous first of her attention to the kids, then of anyone with whom she had contact, including neighbouring women.

He cut her off from everyone, including her family, and kept her locked in the house. He beat her if she looked at him the wrong way. In time, he permanently disfigured her face. After the children moved out, he kept her tied to her bed and wouldn't let her wash. He took clean hair as a sign of an affair, and would punish her for days. Her ordeal ended when her children, as a group, rescued her and set her up in a safehouse. When we met her, she said simply that, if he found her, he would kill her, so she lived her life one day at a time.

We made sweeping recommendations to council, many of which were implemented. This was a very proud moment for me personally and for all the women who worked so hard to make it happen. The report was well received by city council, the press, and my colleagues; most important, the small group of women who started it all the year before loved it. They brought a bottle of champagne to my office and we toasted all the women who had been silenced by domestic violence for so many years. No more, we vowed.

But the enduring legacy of that group was the coalition building that took place among all the various players in the system, people who had not worked together before. Many communities have gone on to institute similar cross-sectoral committees on wife assault, and the practice of this kind of cooperation is now standard. I continued with my own interest in this field for many years, speaking out at conferences and hearings, and, from 1985 to 1987 I worked with the committed and tireless Dr. Pat Kincaid at the Ontario Ministry of Education to design the ministry's family violence guidelines, curricula, and professional development program for teachers and administrators.

It was while I was working at the City of Ottawa that the issues around sexism and pornography in the media started to warm up. I had been following these issues for a long time, ever since my first phone call about the movie ad featuring the chained-up woman. In 1976, I appeared before the Ontario Royal Commission on Violence in the Communications Industry, chaired by Judy LaMarsh. Only months before, an Ottawa high-school student had brutally murdered a young woman and then killed himself. When police searched his room, they found nearly three hundred hard-core sex magazines as well as bondage photos, handcuffs, and a large box of women's underwear. His victim's horrible death was an exact re-enactment of a ritualistic murder depicted in the student's porn collection. The murder was widely covered in the press.

When I scanned the local newspapers for the week after the murder, I found more than a dozen different movie ads showing some form of bondage, torture, or mutilation of women. I made them into slides and showed them at the LaMarsh hearings, inviting us as a society to look at the link between violence against women as entertainment and the real thing. As time went on, I devoted more of my energy to this issue. I appeared for the Ontario Advisory Council on the Status of Women before the 1979 Task Force on Sex-Role Stereotyping in the Broadcast Media, set up by the Canadian Radio-Television and Telecommunications Commission. And in 1981, I helped found a national women's organization to monitor the portrayal of women in the media, and I served as Media Watch's Ontario representative for two years.

National attention to the issue intensified in 1980 when Barbara Schlifer, a young feminist Toronto lawyer, returned to her apartment one evening after celebrating her call to the bar with friends, and was murdered by a man hiding in the lobby of her building. Pornographic magazines were found surrounding her body. A group of women, including Helen LaFountaine, Barbara's close friend, set up the Barbara Schlifer Commemorative Clinic to help women victims of violence in her name.

The issue of the portrayal of women in the media got even more serious for me when, as the equal-opportunities director for the city, I publicly complained about an ad for Sanyo depicting a semi-nude woman that was carried on the sides of the city's buses. I convinced the Regional Transit Commission to adopt a set of non-sexist advertising guidelines for its buses after that incident. I also got into a major dust-up with a local video-store owner when he set up a display in his store window to advertise *The Texas Chainsaw Massacre*. The display showed the top half of a female mannequin, severed at the waist, propped up in a blood-stained white T-shirt on a red-soaked sheet, a bloodied chainsaw placed beside her. When we organized several protests outside the store, the manager responded by covering the store window with peep-holes and putting a hard hat, moustache, and plaid shirt on the model. The press had a field day.

However, it was the fight with First Choice, the first licensed pay-TV channel in Canada, over their proposed contract with *Playboy* to air soft-core pornography, that ignited what journalist Allan Fotheringham would come to call the "porn wars." Several women's groups had gone before the CRTC to ask the commission to set conditions around the granting of these licences as they were concerned about the proliferation of porn on American pay-TV.

First Choice assured the commission and reporters that it had no intention of airing anything resembling pornography. President Don MacPherson said that his company would air only "special events of extraordinary value." No sooner had it been given the go-ahead for the licence than the company, whose parent firm was Eaton's, announced its $30-million deal with the men's magazine. To add insult, it announced that it would get around its Canadian-content commitments by hiring some Canadian women to take their clothes off.

The date was Wednesday, January 12, 1983, and within an hour of the announcement, we had convened a meeting. We sat down together — Doreen, Bonnie, and myself; my friend, Rose Potvin, who now runs a bed-and-breakfast with her husband in Nova Scotia; Cindy Wiggins, now with the Canadian Labour Congress; artist Sasha McGinnis-Haymon; and Pat Masters, a human-resources trainer who had previously worked with my predecessor at city hall. We decided to hold a rally on Parliament Hill on January 19, thinking we could bring out a couple of dozen women. In my monthly-planning calendar for that date, I later wrote the words: "The decision that changed my life."

A friend with connections got CBC's *As It Happens* to call for a comment. On air that night, Mary Lou Finlay asked what we were going to do. I told her we were going to stage a rally; before I could add "in Ottawa," she said, "National?" and I answered "Yes" without blinking. The next day, the story was front page across the country, and the calls started pouring in. "Who is organizing in St. John's?" asked Dorothy Inglis, a wonderful activist from Newfoundland. "Guess what, honey . . . You are!" "Who is in charge of Toronto?" asked Helen LaFountaine, my old friend from Women Associates. She laughed with delight at the answer.

Within twenty-four hours, we organized a nationwide protest and boycott of Eaton's, and only days later we held events attended by thousands of women in sub-zero temperatures in nineteen cities across Canada. Every organized women's group in the country and many municipal governments endorsed our fight, and we made national and international headlines.

After the Ottawa protest on the Hill, we marched inside Parliament to meet with Liberal Communications Minister Francis Fox and Status of Women Minister Judy Erola and, as we were walking to the meeting, which would be covered by the press now chasing behind us, we decided that we had better form a group. On the spot, we launched the formation of the Canadian Coalition Against Media Pornography (CCAMP), which eventually had six hundred member groups and would lead this fight at the national level. The federal government was already inundated with letters and calls for action.

Within days, we had obtained footage of a typical night's viewing on the U.S. *Playboy* channel and screened it for MPs, the CRTC, and the media. Graphic scenes of gang rape, oral sex, masturbation, whipping, sado-masochism, and ritualistic murder were interspersed with nude Playboy bunnies doing bicycle exercises to Rod Stewart's "Hot Legs." In one film, *Malicious,* a black slave is explicitly gang-raped in a saloon by a group of Confederate soldiers, who leave her for dead. "I hope the black don't rub off," one says, then laughs.

The effect of these images was galvanizing. Critics who had said that we were overreacting and that the TV version would be "soft" like the magazine backed off. Members of Parliament, particularly the women, claimed the issue as their own. (I also learned that it was important to show these images to people, not just talk about them in an abstract or intellectual way. CCAMP developed a slide show for our presentations and asked a bright young colleague, Alison Kerr, now a Toronto women's therapist, to produce a film showing images of violence against women in mainstream movies. *Just Entertainment?* is still used in high school and university classes today.)

Initially, First Choice haughtily refused to budge. It claimed its viewers wanted more sex, not less. "There is an incredible demand for pornography, and the steamier the better," said the company in a press statement, and it claimed the publicity had helped it sell subscriptions. However, the pressure built steadily, with church groups, the federal NDP, unions, and others getting involved. The feisty head of the Canadian Union of Public Employees, Grace Hartman, who would be on the founding board of the Council of Canadians with me years later, issued a strong statement of support.

Then the actors' union, the Association of Canadian Television and Radio Artists, publicly disclosed that female Canadian performers auditioning for First Choice at the Baton studios in Toronto were being given a "modesty" test. If they weren't prepared to strip to the waist and audition half-naked, they weren't even being considered for parts in the company's productions. ACTRA condemned this as a form of government-sanctioned prostitution, and the publicity for First Choice was very damaging.

The federal government debated the issue in the House of Commons. At first, Francis Fox refused to take action, hoping public opinion would sway the broadcaster. The CRTC took the same position. But eventually Fox gave in and ordered the CRTC to meet with the pay-TV operators to establish voluntary guidelines. The company's competitors were furious. They felt that First Choice had given the whole fledgling industry a bad name. "They started the whole mess, so it's their problem, not mine," said Ed Cowan, the head of C Channel. "I don't need a code of ethics, but they sure do." Added Superchannel President Steven Harris, "It would be difficult for us to agree with them on a common set of principles, considering what they've shown their principles to be."

In the end, First Choice backed off and cancelled its contract. *Playboy* stayed south of the border. Eventually the company, deeply hurt by the publicity, was taken over by Superchannel, which later became Super Choice.

It was a win, no question. But the "porn wars" were nowhere near over. Women across the country formed local anti-pornography coalitions and held high-profile events. Municipal by-laws to have porn magazines put behind barriers and out of reach of children proliferated. The issue was debated in federal, provincial, and municipal legislatures, in the media, and in universities.

When Jimmy Pattison, the west coast media baron and devout Christian, refused to stop distributing the lucrative porn-trade portion of his magazine empire, women in Vancouver photocopied pictures from some of the hard-core material he sold and placed it, with an explanation of its connection to the good Mr. Pattison, under the windshield wipers on the cars of his fellow Sunday-morning churchgoers while they were all attending service together.

Evidence of child pornography crimes started to surface. Police and children's aid workers were already well acquainted with this growing industry. I saw my first images of child pornography with Project "P," the Ontario Provincial Police unit responsible for tracking the purveyors of hard-core materials. By now, I had seen many, many scenes of women being raped, tortured, and murdered; I had even viewed a real "snuff" movie, in which real women were actually killed.

But the images of four-year-old babies being penetrated by men were so unspeakably horrifying that I still have nightmares about those pictures all these years later. They led me into a long relationship with children's aid societies across the country as we collectively tried to address the effect of the media on the growing violence of young males towards women.

Over the next few years, Canadian feminists like Toronto writer Susan Cole and Calgary lawyer Cathleen Mahoney joined our American counterparts, led by Catherine McKinnon and Andrea Dworkin, in putting forth a feminist analysis of the issue, differentiating us from the religious right but running headlong into former allies — men and women — in civil liberties. Bonnie Klein and Dorothy Henault produced the controversial and provocative film *Not a Love Story* for the National Film Board, and it showed to packed houses across the country. Toronto journalist Michele Landsberg wrote many columns on the subject. She had an answer for those who said you can't legislate morality. "Nonsense. All law is an attempt to legislate morality. Our laws are an expression of society's definition of what is human and right."

In another important battle, I testified as an expert witness in a widely publicized case against *Penthouse* in 1985 which showed women, several very young, trussed up in severe Japanese-style bondage scenes, hanging on ropes from trees or thrown, as if dead, over jagged rocks. That edition of *Penthouse* was removed from Canadian shelves.

Our very success provoked a backlash. We were accused of being "anti-sex" and of promoting censorship, both of which were untrue. What we were calling for was a change to the Criminal Code to include women as a category under the "Hate Law" provisions and to differentiate between consensual and non-consensual images of sex.

Writer June Callwood, who testified for *Penthouse* in that case, spoke out strongly and emotionally on this issue. *Chatelaine* featured the "great pornography debate," Callwood vs. Barlow, and Callwood wrote an article attacking me personally in the *Globe and Mail*. She called my views "apocalyptic" and said I was using the issue to downplay other issues of concern to women. "A government that doesn't want to take any meaningful action to help women needs all the Maude Barlows it can get," she said. I was very hurt at the time. (My mother told me not to take it too personally. "Serious people have serious enemies," she said. "Take it as a compliment.") But I can now see Callwood's position more clearly. This issue was so controversial and of such interest to the media that, for a while, it took on a life of its own and overshadowed some other important issues of concern to women.

Nevertheless, I stand by my position on this issue to this day. This is not the place to go into the intricacies of this debate. But I was then, and continue to be, convinced that there is a clear link between the treatment of women in the mainstream media and their treatment in society. The American Medical Association, the American Academy of Pediatrics, and the American Psychiatric Association have stated categorically that there is a link between violence in the media and violence in society, and have published hundreds of studies to back their position. Says the American Medical Association, "The scientific debate is over."

In response to the recent rash of shootings in American schools, an expert on the psychology of killing, Lieutenant-Colonel Dave Grossman, accuses the networks of denying these studies and says they have blood on their hands for the steady diet of violent, misogynistic material they feed to young people on a daily basis. "We have raised a generation of barbarians who have learned to associate violence with pleasure, like the Romans who cheered and snacked as the Christians were slaughtered in the Colosseum."

Linda "Lovelace," the famed star of the cult porn film *Deep Throat*, had been a guest on my series on women for CJOH just months before the *Penthouse* trial. She told the real story of that "classic." She was drugged, terrified, beaten up, and bruised while she made it. She had, only days before, been forced to make a film with the same men who held a gun to her head just off camera while she had sex with a dog. In her years in the business, Linda had been kidnapped, assaulted, bought, and sold.

She said that most women in the porn industry, like prostitutes, die young. The image that they are glamorous, wealthy businesswomen exercising their lifestyle "choices," instead of, say, brain surgery or law, is pure nonsense, she said. Linda introduced an analysis of class that had been missing in the debate and tended to be overlooked by the lawyers and intellectuals that make up the civil-liberties movement.

Now Linda Marchiano, she was married with two children and spent her life talking to young women to keep them out of the "trade." It enraged her that the film was still being shown in New York theatres; she had gone to court to have it stopped, but lost to the dictates of so-called free speech. She had never seen one cent of profit from that movie. I remember how the male camera crew and technicians reacted to her visit. "Deep Throat" was coming to their very own station! You could hear the snickers and feel the thrill of anticipation hours before she arrived. When she walked in, no one recognized this very ordinary, unsexy woman who looked like any tired working mother on the road. The boys were disappointed, to put it mildly.

Bonnie and I got a small taste of the violence Linda described by speaking out on this issue so publicly. Men would call our office and scream at us, and we received hate mail. One man sent me vicious pictures of women being tortured; he had cut out the faces of the women and substituted my face from pictures he had found in newspapers or magazines. "You're next, bitch" was the charming warning that accompanied most of them. At one point, it got so frightening that I carried the private phone number of a senior detective of the Ottawa police force with me day and night.

One man, who changed his name every time he called the office, would sound perfectly normal until it was clear he was masturbating on the phone. We called him Harry and soon learned to recognize his voice and hang up on him. One day, I was on an open-line talk show in Ottawa and "Harry" came on the air. I wrote a quick note to the host, saying "Cut this man off. He's going to start to masturbate." Harry was sounding quite normal still and the host looked at me as if to say, "Lady, don't kid your-self, you're not that hot." However, it didn't take the mortified host long to hang up when Harry proved true to form live on air.

The floor director for my CJOH series didn't like my stand on violence against women and was very rough with me on the set. He was rude to me and my guests, especially feminists, and would leave hard-core porn on my chair just before we were to go live on air. No one at the studio would do anything about it because he was a superb techni-cian, and I would come home upset and talk to Andrew and my kids about it. One day, my boys, then fifteen and sixteen, but big and strong, and very protective of me, asked if they could watch a taping of my show. "Sure," I said. "Tomorrow night." On the set, they casually asked me which man was the floor director. I pointed to him and, busy, thought no more about it until I saw them walking with him, one on either side, their arms draped around his shoulders. On the way back from the taping, they insisted they had said nothing unusual to him and I let it go.

Oh, what a difference. "Can I get you a glass of water, Maude?" "Are you sure you and your guest are comfortable?" For the remainder of the taping, the floor director was courteous professionalism personi-fied, and we finished the series without incident. One day, months later, I told Charly that I knew they had said something and asked him to tell me what. "Oh, nothing too heavy, Mom. We just told him if he didn't change his attitude towards you, he would soon find himself floor-directing for God."

In the spring of 1983, Justice Minister Mark MacGuigan mandated a comprehensive study on pornography and prostitution that came to be known as the Fraser Report, after its chair, Vancouver lawyer Paul Fraser. The study tackled the questions we had raised from a feminist perspec-tive and looked at pornography and prostitution, not from the perspec-tive of public morality in the traditional sense, but as a question of the human rights of those caught in the sex trade, and by extension women in general. The report called for sweeping changes to the Criminal Code and helped to change the nature of the debate in Canada.

But, by the time the report was issued in February 1985, the govern-ment had changed hands, and the new Conservative Justice Minister was one John Crosbie, a man whose path I would cross many times in the next decade. The Tories did recommend some changes to the Criminal Code, but they were trying to please members of the religious right as well as the women in their own caucus. As I said at the time, they were having a hard time distinguishing between sex and hate. In the end, no compromise was found, and the proposed changes were dropped.

As I look back on this fight now, I ask myself what we achieved. The old, regressive legislation is still in place. You can buy hard-core porn everywhere. Child porn has proliferated on the Net. I do feel, however, that we accomplished much. For one thing, the feminist community came of age and had a good old-fashioned ideological debate. Up until then, we had agreed on just about everything and had presented a pretty united front on poverty, reproductive rights, and equal pay. This was an important milestone for us.

For another, we collectively forced a debate in mainstream society, which has changed for the better. You won't find as many of those bondage images in the movie ads, and the role of women in film has improved. I actually think we made it uncool for a man to leave porn lying around on the coffee table, or worse, in the bathroom (always an image that, for me, proved what porn was really about). As a button of the time said, "Real men don't buy porn."

We also encouraged a healthy debate on the meaning of erotica and pornography in our society and identified that the issue of power is the essential feature that distinguishes them. We dealt with the fact that gays and lesbians were feeling, unfairly, the brunt of this cause, the police sometimes using our concerns to deny them rights and harass them for producing their own literature. Lesbian issues came to the forefront of the women's movement in these years partly through the need for dialogue on this matter, although it is still not entirely resolved, and lesbians and gays are still routinely targeted.

(I spoke, on invitation, to an Ottawa gay businessmen's group on this subject, where I argued, to some effect I think, that it was the same pervasive sexism in our society that produced the need both to subjugate women sexually and to foster hatred against gays. A man who doesn't fit the masculine stereotype is an object of scorn because he is "effemi-nate," defined by the dictionary as "womanish and unmanly," and, therefore, linked in the public mind to the lower status of the female sex. I told the group that progress on gaining their human rights would go hand in hand with the fight for full gender equality and that we had to work together to fight discrimination in all its forms.)

We are still considered "anti-sex" and pilloried by some. But these people have to understand that, when we undertook this fight two decades ago, the world was a lot different for women. "Sexual liberation" really meant that women took their clothes off in the movies and men didn't. Real liberation, sexual and otherwise, was still a long way away. I applaud young women today who are exploring issues of female sexuality and I see their work as a natural legacy of ours.

In 1983, my time at the City of Ottawa was coming to an end. My high profile was making some of the councillors distinctly unhappy. A staff person is not supposed to have a stronger public presence than an elected person, and I understood that. I had been catapulted onto the national stage and it was a natural step to move on.

Before I left the city, they gave me a "Roast, Toast, and Boast" — a wonderful celebration with speeches, tributes, music, and stories. A horse-drawn carriage picked up Andrew, my boys, and me, and drove us to the National Arts Centre, where several hundred women (and a few men) waited to greet me, and I was led in to the head table under a bower of roses. The speeches were full of energy, hope, and humour. Charles and Will (as they were now calling themselves) enchanted the audience with their tales of living with a feminist mother — "Maude Barlow, a relation? A distant cousin of my quiet, stay-at-home mother, sir." Marion Dewar, who was introduced as "Maude's boss," assured them there was no such thing.

The women presented me with a bouquet of roses and a loaf of bread, and we stood and sang that moving union anthem, "Bread and Roses," whose words so capture the spirit of promise, excitement, and anticipation that characterized those early years in our struggle. We were out, after all, to change society.

As we go marching, marching
We bring the greater days

The rising of the women
Is the rising of the race
No more the drudge and idler
Ten that toil where one reposes
But a sharing of life's glories
Give us Bread but give us Roses

My mother's speech brought the house down. "When Maudie told me you were going to honour her this way, she was unsure of how to react. She felt that this was more like a retirement party, something you have at the end of a long career. 'Well, dear,' I said, 'I think you should grab it. At the rate you're going, getting everyone so mad at you and all, you might never get another one.'"

My mother, the prophet.

4

TRUDEAU'S FIGHTER

"I am a realist, but somehow, optimism always keeps
breaking out."

Pierre Trudeau

The call came as a complete surprise. One day in May 1983, while still at
city hall, I received an invitation to have lunch with Tom Axworthy,
principal secretary to Prime Minister Pierre Trudeau. Now, as I look
back, it shouldn't have surprised me. I had been contacted by the
women's commissions and caucuses of all three national parties to speak
at party events and had met with both NDP leader Ed Broadbent and
veteran PC Flora MacDonald about running for office for their parties.
David Peterson, then leader of the opposition Liberals in Ontario, had
also approached me about running provincially. But Pierre Trudeau was
another matter. I was in awe of him.

I had never been a political partisan, although I had worked for
several women NDP candidates I admired on particular election
campaigns. My goal was the advancement of women in all walks of life,
from the boardroom to the shop floor, and I wanted to see women

advance in all the political parties. (My view on this was to undergo a substantial change with time.) I had not thought about any political future for myself and went off to the first of several meetings with Tom and others in the Prime Minister's Office for what I thought were simply advisory sessions on current issues of concern to women. I talked to him openly about poverty, equal pay, wife assault, incest, and violent pornography. (In a note following our first lunch, Tom said "The Château Laurier Grill may never recover from the subject matters we were discussing!")

On the last Friday of that June, Tom Axworthy caught me completely off guard by asking me to join Trudeau's PMO team as the first ever adviser on women's issues to a prime minister. I said I'd heard that Trudeau might have been planning to retire. Tom acknowledged that this was a possibility. However, if Trudeau were to stay and run again, Tom was going to design the platform around women's equality, with a slogan saying that Trudeau had spent many years fighting for the minority that is a minority (francophones) and now he would fight for the minority that is a majority (women). I would be central to a team that would write that platform.

"What should I say?" I stupidly asked Tom. "Well, you have to say yes or no," he answered. "Yes or no," I said, surely making him doubt his judgement about me. "Ah, Maude . . . you have to choose one or the other of those words, not both," Tom said kindly. The opportunity he had just offered me was awesome. Without pause, I blurted out an unqualified "Yes!" but added, "Shouldn't I meet Mr. Trudeau?" Tom assured me that all had been arranged. I was to present myself the following Wednesday at 3:00 p.m. When I hung up the telephone, I asked myself what in heaven's name I had got myself into.

For people of my generation, Pierre Trudeau was *the* dominant political figure. The 1968 election that first brought him to power was also the first election in which I was eligible to vote. Like all Canadians, my faith in him ebbed and flowed in time to his changing policies and peccadilloes. But federal politics for all my adult life to this point had been characterized by the very *presence* of this extraordinary man. To meet him for the first time at an honest-to-God old-fashioned job interview was intimidating, to put it mildly. I fussed about what to wear, finally choosing a tailored teal blue suit and (I admit with contrition and full recognition of the contradictions this poses) a deliberately short skirt and matching high heels.

My interview took place in the historic Langevin Building, across from Parliament Hill (where Trudeau had his other, parliamentary, office) that houses the prime minister's staff. To get to Trudeau's office, I had to ascend a huge red-carpeted staircase to the second floor and was escorted down to the prime minister's personal suite. His own office was framed by huge windows looking across Wellington Street to the Senate building, and occupied by imposing mahogany chairs and the biggest marble desk I had ever seen. Pierre Trudeau came out behind it like something out of central casting. He was smaller than I imagined, but more attractive, his lips set in a half-smile, his famous eyes boring into me as if he could read my every thought. When he said hello, he was so much the caricature of the man I had seen from afar that I thought that maybe this was really Rich Little and that the real Pierre Trudeau was hiding in the back.

"I understand if we don't fight in the first twenty minutes, I'm going to offer you a job," he said. Without thinking, I replied, "Well, then, I had better be pretty provocative, because I'm not sure I want to work for you." This slipped out spontaneously, but it was not without logic. At some elemental level, I guessed that Trudeau was surrounded by people who bowed to him, and if I wanted to carve out a space to promote an agenda for women, I had to be seen to have my own power base.

Indeed, we spent a fair amount of the interview talking about the state of the women's movement in Canada. As I suspected, Trudeau had little time for collective grievances. Present a woman in a position of power and he would treat her as an equal. But he remained suspicious of any ideology that he felt affirmed the rights of the collective voice over those of the individual, and he viewed affirmative action and pay equity with equal scepticism. However, it also seemed that he would trust his senior adviser, Tom Axworthy, who was younger and more in touch with these matters, and we agreed that I was to start my new job in the fall.

As I walked out of the PM's office, a startled Judy Erola, then minister responsible for the Status of Women, now the chief mouthpiece for the pharmaceutical transnationals in Canada, glared at me. I didn't realize that she hadn't been warned of my appointment or that she had been left cooling her heels in the waiting room for a now-delayed meeting with the PM. Behind me, Pierre Trudeau chuckled and said something about a "cat fight." I had entered the world of partisan politics.

I started work on September 12, the day the brand-new leader of the Progressive Conservatives, Brian Mulroney, first took his seat in the House of Commons. My office in the PMO was a cubbyhole down the hall from both the PM and Tom Axworthy. I had been given a choice of a bigger office on another floor, but I remembered reading that one of President Kennedy's young advisers had been given a similar choice. "He who pees with the President has his ear for at least those few minutes every day," he was quoted as saying. I obviously didn't have the advantage of a shared washroom with these two, but I felt it important to be close to the action. My only condition for accepting the job was that Bonnie Diamond come with me, and she occupied another cubby hole across the hall. There was no job description and no one had time to help me develop one. So I promptly got myself into trouble.

In an interview with Canadian Press about the nature of my new job, I explained that I hoped to bring a feminist vision to issues concerning women to the PMO. I particularly singled out the issues of poverty and child care. The reporter suggested that Mila Mulroney would perform the same task for the Tories, and I said that Mila, with multiple staff to look after her home, her children, and her office, could hardly be considered a spokesperson for the average working woman. The media had a field day. "Trudeau's fighter," as the *Toronto Star* called me, was attacking the "innocent" wife of a political rival. Tom firmly suggested a note of apology, which Mila graciously acknowledged. From this experience, I learned to guard my tongue and choose my issues more carefully. I was being watched now, and I couldn't afford to waste any "political capital" on my personal opinions.

I had a lot to learn. The atmosphere in the Liberal camp appeared to me to be one of an armed encampment. The long Trudeau era was winding down, even if no one in the PMO wanted to admit it; a new breed of Conservatives with fire in their bellies and winning on their minds was closing in. Pierre Trudeau had resigned once before from politics, months after his loss to Joe Clark in 1979, and only returned, under great pressure from his party, to lead the Liberals back to power in 1980 after Clark was ousted in a vote of non-confidence. Trudeau wanted to spend more time with his boys and was demanding more and more private time away from his political duties. While he was still popular in parts of Quebec and Ontario, he was alienated from the West, and the love for him that had once existed across the country (and would resurface when he retired) was largely dissipated.

As well, a concerted assault on the welfare state had been launched in the last few years by the big-business community in Canada and was growing. Corporate leaders had become convinced that Canada's social security system was undermining their profits and they were charged with U.S.–style free-market evangelism. Through their lobby groups and think-tanks and their increasing control of the print media, they were bombarding Canadians with negative messages about our social programs and the need to get mean and go global. The Liberal Party was by now dividing on these issues; a sea-change in the political culture was taking place in Canada, and the Liberals were caught in the tide.

Pierre Trudeau was not immune to this ideological tug-of-war. His public musings were all over the map: he was for corporate taxes and against corporate taxes; he defended social programs and cut social programs; he lectured the business community for being greedy and told Canadians that "survival of the fittest nations has become the rule of life." In this last term, he retreated from his 1980 budget attempt to close some tax loopholes for the rich under intense pressure from the business community and, in 1982, implemented the controversial "Six & Five" legislation that capped public-service wages, provincial transfers, and social-security payments, and brought down the wrath of the labour movement on his head. By 1983, the Liberal Party was a party without direction. The one bright spot was its strong desire to reach out to women. This was probably a survival tactic, but it was real, nonetheless, and I was ready.

At eight o'clock every morning, Tom called his senior staff together for a briefing and we would all report in. The "optics" of the latest issues would be put under a microscope. Any potential problems on the horizon would be identified. Opinions of political pundits would be analysed. Michael Valpy then had the cherished *Globe and Mail* spot on the editorial page now held by Jeffrey Simpson, and every morning we would discuss what he had to say as if we were reading tea leaves. I was shocked at the small-mindedness of some of the issues raised in those briefings. One report had to be scrapped and entirely reprinted because the cover was Tory-blue, not Liberal-red. Sometimes, though, the reason many of these people, now pretty jaded, had entered politics in the first place would surface, and we would have a real, even idealistic, discussion of the issues facing the country.

After my first foray across Canada in this position, Tom asked me at our early-morning staff meeting what women's groups were saying about the Liberal Party. I sat there silently and blushed. It had never entered my head to ask. I realized I had made a big blunder and knew I had to smarten up. (I didn't think this was a good time to tell him that at one event I was introduced as Trudeau's "adviser on women's affairs," and that I blurted out that I was, in fact his "adviser on women's issues" and "he looks after his affairs himself.")

Even more difficult to get used to (in fact, I never did) was being seen by women's groups as not only partisan, but close to the ear of the PM, when I saw myself as the same independent feminist fighter I had always been. At one conference on child care, I said, "Women's groups need to put pressure on the government. We need to write letters and there should be pressure from groups other than the day care community, like nurses, and teachers." I felt this was exactly what I would have said had I not been working for the Liberals, but I was chastised and told it was my job, not theirs, to get the government to shape up. I was hurt, but I knew they were at least partially right.

Eventually I found my political sea-legs. This was a heady time for women in politics. Never before (and not since) did women have the political muscle as a group we had in those few years. Women's issues were at the top of the agenda in the country and in politics. Our groups, from teachers to seniors to government bodies like the Canadian Advisory Council on the Status of Women, were at their most powerful. Membership in the National Action Committee on the Status of Women, founded in 1972, had doubled since 1980 and was a voice all politicians listened to, whether they liked it or not. Canadian women had just won, in a harrowing national fight, the constitutional guarantee of equality in the Charter of Rights and Freedoms. The first woman and a feminist to boot — Bertha Wilson — was sitting on the Supreme Court. And Canada had its first woman governor general — Jeanne Sauvé. Between 1980 and 1984, the number of women elected to the House of Commons doubled. My role was to assist women in reaching the next level of political power.

The "gender gap" had been discovered and we exploited it for all we were worth. Women actually thought differently *as a group* than men on some vitally important issues of the day, like war and child care, and could effect the outcome of an election. Politicians were openly courting "the women's vote." Headlines of the day tell the story: "Women Grits hang tough: Address issues or lose our vote" (*Toronto Sun*); "Politicians are learning peril of ignoring women" (*Ottawa Citizen*); "Gender gap gives women clout at the polls" (*Montreal Gazette*); "Wooing the women delegates" (*Maclean's*). Women's magazines all carried high-profile features on women in politics. "Make your opinion count," *Canadian Living* exhorted. "Maude Barlow, Doris Anderson and Judy Erola tell you how to speak up and get things done."

(In a note to the PM, I pointed out that women's support for the Liberal Party was substantially higher than men's. Trudeau returned the memo to me with a note that read: "Women are so much more sensible.")

The Mulroney camp, not to be outdone, cleverly appointed career public servant Jocelyne Côté-O'Hara, as adviser on women's issues. She got her party to adopt a policy whereby companies getting federal contracts would have to hire a quota of women. She also worked to promote women in winnable ridings in the party with Kay Stanley, president of the party's women's caucus, and Kay's sister, Marjory LeBreton, who would become Prime Minister Mulroney's trusted appointments adviser and, later, a senator.

I worked closely with Iona Campagnolo, Liberal Party president; Lucie Pépin, head of the Canadian Advisory Council on the Status of Women; Lauris Talmey, president of the National Women's Liberal Commission; and Chaviva Hošek, then head of the National Action Committee on the Status of Women (NAC), now a senior adviser to Jean Chrétien. (In meetings with politicians, NAC members were — and still are — well-known for their honesty, combativeness, and, on occasion, heckling. In one memo, Trudeau asked me if NAC members were the same "wild, wild women I met in Toronto a few years ago." If so, he cautioned, another meeting might be "counterproductive.")

So sure of the emerging power of women were we, that, in a feature interview on women in politics, both Jocelyne and I claimed political neutrality. "I'm not here as a Liberal," I declared. "I'm here as a feminist." "I have no [Tory] pedigree," said Jocelyne. "I'm a woman and I'm a feminist, unequivocally."

This strong spirit of feminist cooperation prompted a multipartisan group of women which included myself, Tory Libby Burnham, prominent New Democrat Michele Landsberg, writer Christina McCall, and journalists Rosemary Speirs and Judy Steed, to launch a group called the Committee for '94, whose goal was a Parliament that was 50 per cent female in a decade. Local groups to promote women in politics sprang up all over the country.

Finally, women's issues had come of age politically. Women from the NDP, the Tories, and the Liberals worked with NAC to host the first (and, to date, last) political leaders' debate in the weeks before the 1984 election. There, in a nationally televised Toronto hotel room jam-packed with feminists, Brian Mulroney, John Turner (who had just taken over as leader of the Liberal Party in the wake of Trudeau's resignation), and Ed Broadbent were forced to address exclusively the concerns of Canadian women for almost three hours. The women in the audience were not the polite "ladies" often found around political parties; they yelled and booed when they didn't like an answer, and stood to utter great long cheers when they did. It was a wild night.

Broadbent was the obvious favourite going into the event because his party had taken the best positions on women's issues, and the women in the room wanted to acknowledge this, but none of the leaders shone. Broadbent was stiff; Turner, clearing his throat every couple of seconds was even stiffer and reluctant to make any detailed promises because he was sure he would be forming the next government; and Mulroney was terrified. He kept Mila close by his side for advice, and, standing behind him, she would whisper answers in his ear. At the end of the event, the organizers presented the three leaders with flowers, and Mulroney, not used to receiving such a feminine gift, handed them immediately to his wife, who handed them right back to him with a stern look on her face. The debate was a high point in the women's movement in Canada and I sat in the audience fiercely proud of what we had accomplished.

Feminist cooperation also crossed national boundaries. I travelled to Washington in early 1984 and met with the National Organization for Women, the League of Women Voters, the Business and Professional Women's Association, the National Women's Political Caucus, and the wonderful Bella Abzug. Gender-gap politics were everywhere. Democrats were so far ahead in the polls with women, they were openly courting women's groups. Pressure for one of the main Democrat contenders to choose a female running mate was at fever pitch. *Time* magazine had a cover story featuring Congresswoman Geraldine Ferraro (who would become Walter Mondale's running mate in the 1988 presidential election) and San Francisco mayor, Dianne Feinstein. "And for vice president . . . WHY NOT A WOMAN?" the headline boldly demanded.

Not all American women shared our views. I met with my counterpart in the Reagan White House. Caroline Sundseth, a member of the Christian Right dressed all in pink, told me that she was forging an alliance of "women against feminists and Christians against liberals" and that anyone who didn't support her was a "lesbo." She was working on a task force to reinstate traditional family values, take sex education out of the schools, and put prayer back in, and she informed me that the pay gap between men and women is due entirely to women not wanting equal pay.

At that moment I was very grateful to be a Canadian and couldn't imagine any party in Canada putting someone like that in such a public position. (I still can't imagine it; even the Reform Party would know better.) Needless to say, we didn't have a lot to talk about. I thanked her very much and, even as she was still preaching at me, bolted out the door of her beautiful Capitol Hill office and ran down the steps into the Washington sunshine. I had taken my son Will on this trip, and we went to a little Italian restaurant near our hotel that night and laughed about my day and Caroline Sundseth over a bottle of Chianti.

I worked with some extraordinary women and men that year in Trudeau's office. The elegant crusader for Native women, Mary Two Axe Early, now dead, became a mentor and friend in this time. Mary, a Mohawk from Quebec, was one of the women who had lost her Indian status when she married a white man — as then dictated by the Indian Act. Mary believed that this law was profoundly discriminatory and worked all her life to regain legal standing not only for herself in her own community, but for all aboriginal women who had lost their status as well. I worked with Mary, women in other parties, and members of Parliament, NAC, and the Native Women's Association for an amendment of the Indian Act in order to reinstate the rights of these women. We were eventually successful. Mary regained her status and moved back to her reserve just before she died at the age of almost eighty-five.

The plight of First Nations' women was terrible and one I wanted to help publicize. There were many stories to learn. On a particularly moving trip to Happy Valley, Labrador, to help the Mokami Status of Women get funding for a battered women's shelter, I was taken into an inner council of women elders who told me stories about their lives that haunt me still. One had had an abortion by having her two grown sons hold her down on the kitchen table while her husband performed the "operation" with a stick.

The distinguished Robin Badgley, seconded from the University of Toronto's Faculty of Medicine to head up a major government study, put the public spotlight on the terrible reality of sexual child abuse in Canada. His *Report of the Committee on Sexual Offences Against Children* was tabled in the summer of 1984 and sparked a national debate. It was my privilege to be the political contact in the PMO for Dr. Badgley, and, right up to the time I left, I was trying, with the child-welfare community, to establish a high-level office with exclusive authority to review and implement the recommendations of the report.

Judge Rosalie Abella's ground-breaking royal commission report, *Equality in Employment,* was published just before the 1984 election and I helped with advance publicity. I had shared with Rosie stories of my Washington trip, and told her that American women were using the term "pay equity" instead of the more cumbersome "equal pay for work of equal value." She loved the sound of that and wisely decided to replace the American-sounding term "affirmative action" with "employment equity" in her report. The term is now part of the lexicon of our movement.

The 1983 Throne Speech was the highlight of my year with Trudeau. I wanted many things included and one left out. I was encouraged by a memo from Trudeau promising to "work it all in somehow." Women's groups were particularly worried that Trudeau was going to keep a spontaneous promise he had made to the Real Estate Board to amend the recently passed Charter of Rights and Freedoms so that it protected private property rights. The fear was that men whose name was on the family property would use their Charter rights to override provincial family-law rules that forced equitable sharing upon divorce. There was also concern about giving private corporations the same rights as individuals to use the Charter to challenge affirmative-action legislation, minimum-wage laws, and labour-arbitration awards.

In the December 7 Throne Speech in the House of Commons, the PM addressed a wide range of the issues I cared about: sexual harassment, violence against women, pornography, child care, parental leave, part-time workers, survivor benefits, and International Women's Year. He announced to my delight the historic bill to amend the offensive section of the Indian Act that discriminated against women and left out his promise to include property rights in the Charter. Although I knew the fight was just beginning, it was significant progress.

But amid all this seeming progress, I was becoming uneasy. This position of mine opened doors. I was treated as royalty right across the country, whether I liked it or not. I was asked to speak as a role model to students as if my proximity to power gave me special insight. (Glashan, an Ottawa public school I had attended, asked me to come back as a "VIP" and address the student body. One teacher had her class write me letters after my presentation to tell me how they felt about it. One grade-eight boy wrote, "Oh, Ms. Barlow. I . . . I think I'm in love with you. Now I can see why Mr. Trudeau wanted you to be his secretary!")

I began to understand the sweet taste and siren call of power. Every morning, at our senior staff meeting, the national press would yell questions to us as we silently (and arrogantly I sometimes felt) entered the meeting. We were clearly powerful insiders and I began to see how you can get cut off from the world and start to believe that you have an inherently special place in the scheme of things. I now believe that power corrupts most people when they get near it and I'm deeply grateful to be far removed from it. But at this time, it was all new. I was still fairly young and the possibilities seemed endless.

Trudeau launched his famous peace initiative in the year I worked for him. I believe he wanted to leave this legacy for his sons and he decided to try to cool down the Cold War rhetoric escalating under U.S. President Ronald Reagan. His project took him to capitals around the world to talk to peace activists and heads of state, and he also called together leading peace activists and thinkers in Canada to advise him. He asked me to contact some key women in the movement and this led to a friendship with one of my heroines, the writer Margaret Laurence.

In January 1984, I wrote to invite her to a luncheon at 24 Sussex with other peace activists to advise the PM on his project. She was unable to attend but was excited that Canada was to take this international stand and invited me to visit her at her home in Lakefield, Ontario. Helen Porter was already a good friend; her father and his wife were Margaret's Lakefield neighbours. So Helen came with me to introduce us and the three of us passed a sunny winter day in Margaret's kitchen, where, after explaining that she had no time for "domestic tasks," she served us canned rolled ham, stale baking soda biscuits, and unripe tomatoes. It didn't matter. We talked for hours about everything from children to writing to violence against women. Margaret was immensely interested in politics and fascinated by my involvement at such a senior level. She was also very excited about the PM's peace initiative and signed a statement of support. We parted with real warmth and corresponded by letter and telephone for several years.

In one very-late-night phone conversation (her emotions a little raw from wine), Margaret wept with despair about the possibility of nuclear war. The next day she sent me notes for a speech called "My Final Hour" that I cherish still.

> Can we conceive of a world in which there would be no succeeding generations? A world in which all the powerful works of the human imagination would be destroyed, would

never again be seen or listened to or experienced? We must concede that this is now a possibility, and one not too far in our uncertain future, either. We must not, as artists, or so I feel, stand by and passively allow this to happen.

The death of the individual is the end which we will all one day meet, but in the knowledge that our children and their children will live, that someone's children will go on, that the great works of humankind will endure in art, in recorded history, in medicine, in the sciences and philosophies and technologies that our species has developed with devotion and a sense of vocation throughout the ages. The individual is the leaf on the tree. The leaves fall but the tree endures. New leaves are born. This concept has been the mainstay of our species from time immemorial. Now the tree itself is threatened.

On the morning of February 29, 1984, Bonnie and I and the rest of the PMO staff were rounded up without warning by an RCMP guard and ushered into the Cabinet boardroom. There, flanked by his loyal supporters, Pierre Trudeau announced to us what he had only told his family: he was retiring, permanently this time, from politics and would be informing the House of Commons within the hour. The place was deathly silent as the reality of this news sank in. He thanked us for our hard work and loyal support, particularly singling out Tom Axworthy and his parliamentary procedures adviser, Joyce Fairbairn. Then, in a tight cocoon of security, he was gone.

I turned to a PMO veteran who had been around the last time Trudeau retired and asked him what this meant for us. "Oh, it's business-as-usual for us. People just won't answer your phone calls as quickly, if they answer them at all."

The race to replace Trudeau was on immediately, and the front runners were crown prince John Turner pitted against Trudeau loyalist Jean Chrétien. Both had been ministers (and friends) in an earlier Trudeau Cabinet, but John Turner had resigned in 1975 after a disagreement over the future of the party, while Jean Chrétien stayed on, eventually serving in almost every major post in government. The public reason for Turner's resignation was a dispute over policy direction. Business Liberals were pressing the government hard on everything from wage and price controls to corporate tax cuts, and they had found an ally in John Turner. The trigger for resignation was a last-minute reduction by Trudeau to promised cuts of almost $2 billion in government spending.

What was less commonly known was that the personal animosity and rivalry between the two men had grown to the point that one of them had to leave, and Turner went back to Toronto to practise law. There, he became the great hope of business Liberals for the future of the party and they bided their time. Chrétien was very bitter that someone who, in his opinion, had deserted the party and missed all of the events of the intervening years, including the repatriation of the Constitution, would be considered a returning hero, and said so. Writer Ron Graham, now a professor at Ryerson University, quotes Chrétien talking to Quebec ministers during the leadership campaign in his book *One-Eyed Kings*: "I don't understand those of you who are supporting a guy who's made a career out of knocking Trudeau in the last eight years. You guys owe everything to Trudeau. When I leave politics, I'll leave by the front door. Nobody will ever be in a position to say that Chrétien's a prostitute."

The staff in the PMO were given a clear choice. If we wanted to work for a candidate, we had to resign. I chose to remain with the PMO team putting together the briefing notes for whoever would form the new team. My contribution was a detailed twelve-point plan for the new leader, which included employment and pay equity, a national child-care program, pensions for homemakers, a program to prevent women from being further ghettoized by the new technology in the workplace, protection for part-time workers, and a national campaign against family violence. At a breakfast sponsored by the Liberal Women's Commission, the organization that promotes women's issues and women candidates in the party, I outlined this platform and warned all the candidates, including John Turner and Jean Chrétien, who were sitting in the front row flanked by their supporters, that abandoning women at this point could cost them the election.

I knew that the dispute between Turner and Trudeau was long-standing and personal; however, I failed to understand that this competition and animosity extended to their teams. My platform, along with the larger transition program from the Trudeau PMO, was ignored and eventually shredded by the new Turner team, who also unceremoniously dumped me without warning. I found out I'd been fired when Bonnie and I came in to work one morning only weeks after Turner's win at the Liberal convention (where Iona Campagnolo told second-placed Chrétien that he was "first in our hearts") and found our offices occupied and our papers out in the hall.

Our ouster caused a strong backlash from the women's movement and hit headlines across the country. Minister Judy Erola jumped in immediately to say that she would take over advising the new leader on these concerns on top of her current responsibilities. When it was pointed out to her that Brian Mulroney and Ed Broadbent had advisers, Erola snapped, "The other two leaders are just that, leaders, so they have to have a women's adviser. Who does Turner have? The minister responsible for the status of women — me. I sit at the Cabinet table. I see him daily." Questioned whether she could handle the advisory role along with her role as Minister of Consumer and Corporate Affairs and MP, Erola boasted: "Yes, and like any good woman I can handle all three of them very well."

Against seasoned advice and before it even "found out where the washrooms were located," noted Tom Axworthy, Turner's team went with an early election on September 4, 1984, and, of course, lost massively to Brian Mulroney's Tories. A new political dynasty had arrived. Over the next decade, a small, select group of women would play a significantly increased role within the power structures of Ottawa and in the boardrooms of the nation's corporations. Most other women would find themselves on the losing end of a neo-conservative agenda and the all-out assault on universal social programs to follow.

I now had a decision before me. Thus far, I had not considered myself a partisan Liberal. It was clear, however, that if I were to have a political future ahead of me, I would have to commit to help rebuild the party. I had mixed feelings about this. I knew that most women still had a very rough time inside the power structures and were still segregated in female ghettoes. One long-serving female MP from Toronto told me that, after being defeated in an election, she applied to the federal government for a job. She was sent for a typing test.

Nor was the work of women generally credited. The men in the PMO regularly left the office for extended lunches and were not missed. But if the support staff — all women — wanted to have a Christmas lunch or other special function together, they had to do it in shifts, so much did the running of the whole place depend on their steady work.

Early on in my days at the PMO, having observed this power imbalance between male and female staff, I put up two cartoons on a central bulletin board. One showed a man and a woman at work. Under the man, the caption read, "Think." Under the woman, the caption read, "Do." The other showed a very tough-looking boss growling the words "You *can* fight an idea whose time has come." The cartoons kept disappearing off the board, but mysteriously, they would reappear, the women having made a raft of copies in case they were needed. I was discovering sexism and sexual harassment were widespread, particularly among political staff who were not protected by the Public Service union.

I was also beginning to see (though my political naïveté, or stupidity, prevented me from seeing too much too soon) that partisan politics in the two old parties was an incestuous cycle of donations in, and rewards — in the form of appointments and contracts — out. I would not have used the term "corporate influence" at the time, but I was becoming puzzled that groups advocating for the poor, women, peace, or the environment had to seek appointments and accept whatever precious moments a politician would give them, while persons of money and influence just seemed "about the place" as if they belonged. With time, recognition of this reality would be one of the reasons I would leave the party and would spend much of my life trying to limit the role of big business in politics.

Nor could I figure the role of "politicos" like the one who occupied the office next to me in the PMO. Gordon Ashworth, who would later be accused by the press of accepting favours when he was adviser to Ontario Premier David Peterson, sat with the television and the radio on all the time, while he simultaneously read newspapers and talked nonstop on the phones — sometimes two, one in each ear, at a time. He didn't have a job title as far as I could tell, never wrote briefs like the rest of us, and never seemed to attend meetings. When Tom invited me into his office about a month after I had been hired to ask me how things were and if I had any questions, I had one that made him roar with laughter. "Yes, Tom. What does Gordon Ashworth *do?*"

The influence of insider politics and of money was somewhat revealed to me when I received an invitation from a senior Liberal politician to come for "tea" in the dying days of Trudeau's regime. He gave me the grand tour of his magnificent office suites, which were filled with artwork and gifts from visiting dignitaries from around the world. As an assistant (male, the politician was pleased to note) served us tea and biscuits, he asked me to consider being the Liberal candidate in a riding he had formerly held.

He was looking for a "pro-development" candidate for the riding. Much to his dismay, both the NDP and the Tory candidate were "greens," he said. He assured me that he knew a political career could be costly and so, he said, if I would consider being his candidate in the riding, he would "see what he could do" to help me find financial stability through his "modest" real estate holdings in the riding. I said that I was supporting another candidate for the Liberal nomination. She happened to be a woman of colour and it was immediately apparent that he knew this. "It's not that I'm bigoted. It's just that I know the riding. They're not ready," he said solicitously.

When, clearly shocked, I turned him down flat and bolted for the door, the angry politician (who had recently been charged with sexual harassment by a female assistant and later settled out of court with an undisclosed payment), grabbed my face and kissed me. He immediately drew back and said, "I didn't mean to do that." I left his office immediately, told very few people about this incident, and made light of it to those I did tell.

Looking back on this now, I realize that I reacted in a classic way. For one thing, I didn't have a witness and I didn't think anyone would believe me. For another, I felt (and still feel) that the first two incidents were more offensive than the clumsy kiss, and neither of these was grievable. Mostly, I was part of a "team" and didn't want to cast a negative public spotlight on the party months before a federal election. (As I watched Kathleen Willey years later describe her encounter with President Clinton in the White House on *60 Minutes,* I believed her. And I continued to believe and understand her when it came to light that she had continued to be in contact with Clinton for months after.)

On the plus side, however, I had made some very good friends in the party. Tom Axworthy was consistently fair to me and his politics were genuinely progressive. I greatly admired his brother Lloyd and Herb Gray, both of whom I would work closely with in the coming years. Many women, including Sheila Copps, were very supportive, and we all had started to form a bond to help promote each other in the trenches.

Then there was Pierre Trudeau himself. From the day I started to work for him he gave me genuine freedom to speak publicly about my concerns without requiring that my statements reflect well on the party. I spoke often about injustice to women, and even once got an agitated call from Finance Minister Marc Lalonde when I hit the front-page condemning the lack of public and political concern over older women living in poverty.

Trudeau was unfailingly kind and encouraging to me. (In one delightful conversation early on in my time with him, I urged him to become knowledgeable about what his children were watching on TV. He told me that he didn't think they watched any, that they read books, skied, and hiked together instead. I said, "Well, Mr. Trudeau, I'm sure that's true. But they have another parent who is, how shall I say it, perhaps more in touch with 'common culture' than you are and who probably lets them watch it from time to time." He thought about this a minute and then asked me what he should watch. I suggested *Mr. T.*, a popular program for kids of the time. Pierre Trudeau said, "Mr. T. Is that not me?")

On his last night as prime minister, Trudeau's staff held a farewell party for him and Tom Axworthy at a smoky little rock-and-roll club in downtown Ottawa. It was a steamy June night and the place was packed. Some female staffers, including the now-distinguished author of *The Concubine's Children*, Denise Chong, belted out 1950s and '60s "girl band" hits like "Leader of the Pack," to a raucous and appreciative crowd. Normally staid female Ottawa journalists and senior civil servants acted like schoolgirls, flirting and dancing for the man who could still turn heads and stir hearts.

In his *Maclean's* column several months later, Allan Fotheringham said that that evening marked the end of an era. The funky little club had by then been demolished to make way for a big office tower at the same time that the Tories were moving into 24 Sussex. The heady days of youth, optimism, and confidence in the future that the Trudeau era personified — rightly or wrongly — were over. A new breed of political corporate managers was taking over, and Canada, as we knew it, was about to go the way of that club.

As he was leaving the party, Pierre Trudeau gave me the rose from his lapel. "Are you planning to stay in politics?" he asked me and I said, "Probably." "That's too bad," he said. "I don't think you belong in partisan politics. You will not be able to make the necessary adjustments." And then, swirling his cape dramatically around him, he was gone.

It would be several years before I recognized that he was right.

5

THE POLITICS OF
DISILLUSION

"One cannot be both powerful in the state and unlike
it in character."

Plato

The first adjustment I had to make was working with the man chosen to
replace Pierre Trudeau. Soon after John Turner became leader, Ottawa
teemed with stories about how badly out of touch he was with the issues
of the day. It had been almost a decade since he left Ottawa and returned
to Toronto, where he lived in an elegant Rosedale home, worked in a
gleaming bank tower at the corporate law firm McMillan Binch, and
dined so often at Winston's, the posh restaurant in the heart of
Toronto's financial district, that he had his own table and a salad named
after him.

In this rarefied atmosphere, Turner, the business-Liberal-in-exile,
had avoided all the major social upheavals of the decade. He called
women "girls," and slapped them in places he should not have.

Reporters were the "gentlemen of the press," "guys," or "boys." In his first briefing session on aboriginal issues, he asked enthusiastically after the infamous 1969 White Paper that had called for assimilation of First Nations peoples into mainstream society and was so hated by Natives that it spawned the Red Power movement and massive demands to settle land claims right across the country. Turner hadn't given the issue one thought since he had left politics and had missed the whole thing.

He was, however, totally up-to-date on what the big-business community wanted from Ottawa. For me, this posed an enormous problem: just as I was getting ready to commit myself to the Liberal Party, John Turner, with (I thought) a totally different set of values from mine, was elected to the party's helm. I was becoming intensely involved in the fight against Brian Mulroney's proposed free trade agreement with the United States and was on the founding board of the Council of Canadians, the group that would lead the fight against it. John Turner looked like a Mulroney clone to me.

Situated on the right of the party, Turner, in both the leadership race and the election of 1984 ran as a fiscal conservative, concerned most notably with reducing the deficit. At the time of his loss to Brian Mulroney, he represented the longing of many Liberals to re-establish the link with the business community that the party had had under St. Laurent and C.D. Howe during the 1950s. Many, including myself, saw Turner's leadership as a sign of the decline of "social" Liberalism. But I was wrong about John Turner.

He entered politics because he believed deeply in the notion of public service to one's country. As author Ron Graham explains so well in *One-Eyed Kings*, John Turner was "the sum of every summer-camp, private-school, varsity, junior-bar, model-citizen, and parish-church virtue he had ever been taught." Turner himself said, "Life is a trust and one has a fiduciary obligation toward one's country to put back into it what one has received. I've received a great deal, and I believe that a free society only operates properly if the best men and women offer to serve."

For Turner, Canadian business served a role in nation building and had a responsibility to give back to the country in equal measure what it secured from the privilege of operating here. Invited as a peer into the inner-boardroom councils during their early deliberations on free trade in 1986, Turner became convinced that the big-business community no longer had the best interests of the nation at heart. He heard business leaders from the Business Council on National Issues talk openly about moving their production and jobs offshore in a post–free-trade era and came to passionately believe that the trade deal posed a threat to the nationhood of Canada.

Many of my friends in the NDP and the growing anti–free trade movement were highly sceptical about the position Turner eventually took on the Canada–U.S. Free Trade Agreement. But I knew his opposition was genuine. The passionate defence of Canadian cultural and economic sovereignty by Turner and others in the party like Lloyd Axworthy, Sheila Copps, Herb Gray, and then president of the youth wing, Richard Mahoney, was the single biggest reason for my eventual commitment to the Liberal Party. As John Turner matured as a politician, his positions on a host of related issues, including culture, women, social security, the deficit, jobs, and the role of government, began to change as well.

Slowly, and in large part because of our converging position on the free trade deal, my nasty parting with the Turner camp healed and I was invited in to advise the leader on women's issues as well as the social impacts of free trade. John Turner's long years out of politics had left him rusty and awkward in dealing with the women's movement, and Bay Street didn't exactly offer a daily course in Feminism 101. I drafted background notes for various speeches and briefed him in person, particularly on child care and the feminization of poverty, two issues I was pushing him to highlight. In March 1988, I was named as Turner's social-justice adviser and helped to draft the party's policy on women for the upcoming election.

I had also become closely involved in policy development at the party level and co-chaired, with rising Liberal star Paul Martin (who had become a friend), one of three major policy conventions called the Canada Conferences held in late 1987 and early 1988 to form the party's platform. My friendship with Martin then wasn't as bizarre as it might appear now, given our current radically different political perspectives. His father, Paul Martin, Sr., who served four prime ministers, was one of the architects of our national social programs. Paul Martin, the son, was very proud of this legacy. He spoke passionately about the need to preserve and expand social programs and campaigned in 1988 for a national child-care program.

Martin also opposed cruise-missile testing, the GST, and the Bank of Canada's high-interest-rate policy. The Mulroney free trade deal, he said in a speech to the Council of Canadians in 1989, was "unilateral trade disarmament . . . a terrible, terrible deal." Martin attacked Mulroney's obsession with the deficit ("I believe the way you reduce the deficit is by increasing revenue") and his budget cuts, which he said were "ripping the heart out of democracy." He said the cuts to seniors' pensions and unemployment insurance were "theft" and called for increased government spending to deal with poverty. "We need a new social contract in this nation, one that recognizes that a dollar spent today reduces poverty and despair and gives us much more in the future."

I also came to be a close colleague of Lloyd Axworthy's, the standard-bearer for social Liberalism in the modern party. After the 1984 Liberal defeat, Axworthy would urge Liberals to go home and build a Liberal Party that "cares," and not to abandon "the middle ground" in the political stampede to the right. He played a pivotal role in the party's stand on both the Canada–U.S. Free Trade Agreement and the North American Free Trade Agreement, and was the acknowledged expert on their substance. Axworthy attacked the Conservatives for ignoring the growing level of child poverty while giving tax breaks to big corporations.

At a 1990 conference on globalization, he said: "The view of the Conservative government is that the public interest is served by the accumulation of private interest. They have retreated back into a form of government that belongs to the nineteenth century, where all the decisions related to the needs of human beings will be decided by private decision-making and there will be no attempt to establish a public purpose." Lloyd Axworthy spoke out strongly about the undue influence of corporate money in the political process, saying that politics was becoming a high-stakes poker game in Canada. He would call for limits on corporate donations to leadership contests when he, himself, would have to back out of the 1990 race to replace John Turner for lack of funds.

With colleagues like this, I felt totally comfortable in laying out my strong views in my keynote speech to the Canada Conference on Social Policy, which were very well received by my peers, including Paul Martin. I sounded a strong warning about the growing gap between rich and poor, the feminization of poverty, and the rise in child poverty, and called for a new social contract in Canada. "At the root of the problem is the commonly held notion that economic concerns for creating wealth are somehow at odds with the social concerns of spending it. . . . Foremost among our immediate priorities is the need for government to start planning economic growth in tandem with progressive social policy to reverse the growing inequities among us. . . .

"The answer lies in sharing — sharing our resources, our ideas, and power. In our current system, power is used as a means of control. This must change. Power is the ability to effect change and can truly revolutionize our society if we broaden the base of those with access to it. . . . People are not units of production. We are citizens of a sovereign nation. The wealth and opportunity of Canada must exist and flourish for the benefit of all Canadians — not just the privileged few. Only then will we have the social consensus to be truly great."

I tell myself now, in light of where these very Liberals eventually took the party, that there must have been opposition to such sentiments and to me, but I can honestly say that it didn't surface in any way that I could see. The desire to win caused the right and left of the party to unite in a way that looked fairly genuine to me and, in fact, probably was genuine as long as it was out of power. Paul Martin was able to convince himself that he was a champion of social programs because he was a long way from being finance minister and I am sure he believed what he was saying at that time. And the rivalry between Chrétien (who had left politics in anger after his defeat) and Turner — a rivalry I would get caught up in — was still underground and not yet causing big waves. We seemed to me to be united in a progressive and attainable platform.

In the summer of 1986, Richard Mahoney took me out to a little vegetarian café near the University of Ottawa and urged me to run for the Liberals. He knew my politics and smartly introduced me over the next few months to a wonderful group of young people with progressive politics, including Teri Kirk, Atul Sharma, Kim Doran, Judy Pfifer, Shyle Gautama, Mark Resnick, and Jim Oldham (who became a speech writer for Jean Chrétien and died tragically young in 1998). They were wonderful people and offered to play key roles in my campaign. I was truly touched by their proposal, and after many long talks with Andrew, who was very supportive, I said yes.

On July 17, 1987, I was nominated as the Liberal candidate in Ottawa Centre, where I lived and had grown up. The decision to run for office was hard for one reason, and that was that I would be running in the election against Michael Cassidy, the NDP incumbent. Friends in the NDP could not understand why I was involved with the Liberal Party, and I came in for criticism that would take years to fade among colleagues in the labour movement and social groups.

In the end, there were several reasons why I chose to run. While I deeply admired the NDP, and particularly its founders (especially Tommy Douglas), I wanted to be part of a party that would become the government and therefore have a real chance at effecting change. (I have since changed my view on this. I now feel that it is far more important to seek influence than raw power.) I also felt that my progressive views had found a solid home in the Liberal Party — a naïve view, as it turned out, but it didn't seem so at the time, given the support I had for them.

Most significant, though, was Ed Broadbent's weak position on the FTA. Compared to John Turner, he seemed unconvinced that it was a problem, and he was unconvincing in his opposition to it. I remember watching the evening news on TV with a group of labour leaders just weeks before the 1988 election. To a person, they bemoaned their leader's campaign performance on this issue and grudgingly praised Turner for his passion. I felt (and still feel) that I was on the right side of history in that campaign.

Lloyd Axworthy spoke at my nomination meeting, which was filled with music and celebration, and he brought everyone in the room to tears. He talked about how lonely it was to sit on a plane late at night, flying away from his home and family, and said that it was in just those times that he had to look into his heart and figure out why he had committed his life to politics. No greater answer existed, he said, than this fight against the Mulroney free trade agreement and for Canada.

One day, he explained, no matter what else he did in his life, he would be able to look his children in the eye and tell them he had been there for his country when he was needed.

I was ready to run. But before I could even start putting my platform together, a minor glitch threatened my chances. At first it affected my life negatively, but in the long run, infinitely for the better. The federal-riding boundaries were redistributed and I had to stand for the nomination all over again. This time, I was contested by a right-wing city alderman named Mac Harb, and he turned the next year of my life into the most difficult one yet. It was practically hand-to-hand combat as I fought to keep my hard-earned right to represent the Liberals in the riding in the upcoming election. The insurrection against John Turner was in full swing by now, the Chrétien forces lining up to be ready to take power if and when Turner lost the fall election. Harb was a long-time Chrétien supporter and, since I was one of Turner's so-called star candidates, I was high on the Chrétien hit list.

Harb's people, backed by Chrétien, ran a ruthless campaign. They turned it into one of the most hotly contested ethnic battles in the history of the party to that time, signing up people who had never been in the slightest bit involved in politics before. One faction of the Lebanese community was pitted against another. Vietnamese Canadians battled Chinese Canadians. My Jewish husband was the subject of a racist whisper campaign. Between us, Harb's team and mine signed up more than eight thousand members eligible to vote at the nomination. I had a wonderful campaign team, young, idealistic, and hard-working. They were led by John Brooks and my devoted friend John Walker, who is now with the federal department of the Solicitor General. But they weren't nasty and they wouldn't stoop to the kinds of tactics our opponents had no trouble using.

My second bid for nomination was held a year after the first. All the sense of joy was gone, and in its place was a brutal contest of nerves. Someone on Harb's team took busloads of my Vietnamese supporters to a deserted suburb and let them out to find their (long) way home. Harb supporters closed all the elevators but the ones they were using in seniors' homes so that they could ensure all the seniors got on only "their" buses to take them to the nomination site. I will never forget hundreds of old people being herded into the voting booth flanked on either side by a Harb supporter saying his name to them over and over, like a mantra. We found out later that some seniors were told if they didn't vote for Harb, they would be on their own to get back home that night.

Harb's people, contrary to the agreed-upon rules, managed to put their people almost exclusively in charge of the voting booths. One woman, an immigrant from Vietnam, had her ballot torn up in front of her at the booth when it was seen that she had voted for me. She was led out weeping, saying that it had never been this bad in her country.

It was a show of raw power, and Harb won the contest. It was common knowledge in the party that many rules had been broken that night, but no one seemed willing or able to stop it. My loss was reported on national television that evening and clearly caught John Turner off guard. When confronted by a CBC reporter who asked him how he felt about losing one of his star candidates, Turner stuttered and mumbled and finally said that he would try to find another riding for me. His inability to intervene or to protect me, and the fact that it was the CBC, and not his staff, who informed him of my loss, was a harbinger that he would lose his own upcoming battle with the seasoned street fighter Jean Chrétien.

(I was the least surprised person in Canada when Chrétien throttled a Canada Day protester in 1995 or when, at the 1997 APEC Summit, he joked about the pepper spray that had been used to brutally subdue peaceful student activists.)

After the loss, my supporters were in tears. By the end of the night my teenage sons were ready for violence themselves. I, however, felt enormously calm, as if some weight had been lifted from my shoulders. I went to the podium and asked the delegates to make Mac Harb's nomination unanimous and wished him well.

Andrew and I attended a gathering of our supporters later that evening and I thanked them with all my heart for their faith in me and their hard work. Many of the people in that room that night, particularly young people, have since left party politics, deeply disillusioned.

Over the next few days, so many flowers and notes came to my door that my house looked like a funeral parlour. People were very generous with their sympathy and support, and I deeply appreciated their kindness.

A sad-sounding John Turner called to assure me they would find me a safe seat somewhere else and to say how terribly sorry he was. (In 1998, when CBC's *The National* interviewed Turner for a ten-year retrospective on free trade, I left a message on his voice-mail at his law firm in Toronto praising him for an excellent interview and for staying the course in his analysis and his principles. He phoned me back and left a message on my voice-mail. "Do you remember when I tried to get you into Parliament, Maudie? Maybe it turned out better this way. Heh, heh.")

I didn't realize it then, but that night in the Ottawa Civic Centre was the beginning of the end of my career in the Liberal Party. I would continue to help John Turner in whatever small way I could up until the election. And I would work in concert with Liberal and NDP colleagues through the upcoming NAFTA fights to defeat the Mulroney Tories.

But something had been broken. I wouldn't be able again to be part of an institution capable of such conduct. Over that last year, I felt myself changing in ways I didn't like. I started to take the "edge" off my views to make them more palatable. I "lunched" with people I couldn't stand and wouldn't have spent time with under any other circumstance. A left–right split was beginning to emerge in the party and I was finding the compromises necessary to form a consensus between the "social" wing and the "business" wing more and more difficult to make.

Already there were signs that the Liberal Party was about to go through a profound transformation over the next decade. The contest between Turner and Chrétien, I now believe, reflected the growing influence of big business in the back rooms of the Liberal Party and was the mirror opposite of the earlier bout between them. In 1984, big business had backed John Turner for leader, connecting Jean Chrétien to "big-spending" Pierre Trudeau, the National Energy Program, and the screening of foreign investment. But as his colleagues in the business community came to see it, Turner had betrayed them. The Business Council on National Issues' Tom d'Aquino said Turner's policy conversion was "disturbing and sad." By 1986, the knives were out for him, and the right of the party was rallying around a bitter and determined Jean Chrétien.

One of John Turner's last acts in power turned out to be the performance of his career. In the leaders' debate in the 1988 election, he routed Mulroney with his superior debating skills and his detailed knowledge of the free trade deal. I visited him at Stornoway on the afternoon of the debate to go through a few last-minute questions he might encounter about the effects of the FTA on women. He could hardly walk, so stiff was he from a bad back. He looked easily a decade older than his fifty-nine years. But miraculously, on television that night, he stood straight and dignified and looked, I thought, every bit like a prime minister.

However, a combination of factors conspired against Turner. He headed a bitterly divided party (I now believe Chrétien's people were prepared to lose the 1988 election so their leader could replace Turner and start preparations for the next election), and there was an unprecedented media campaign by the big-business community to support Mulroney's free trade deal. Ed Broadbent refused to join Turner in targeting the FTA for an all-out campaign, and chose instead to join some members of the Liberal Party, the big-business community, and the Tories to single him out for destruction. It was the final straw. John Turner lost the election, giving Brian Mulroney's Tories a second term. In May 1989 he announced his resignation as Liberal leader.

In July, the day before Turner left Ottawa, Mel Hurtig, Edmonton publisher and founder of the Council of Canadians, and I had a long, private lunch with him at Stornoway. He spoke openly about the price his stand on free trade had cost him, and speculated that it would continue to haunt him in private practice. But not for one moment, he said, would he ever regret the "fight of his life," and always he would feel he had upheld the best traditions of his party. He was particularly puzzled and still saddened by the fact that Ed Broadbent had spent more time attacking him than Brian Mulroney during the campaign and mused about how things might have gone if they could have found a way to work together to defeat the FTA. In 1990, Jean Chrétien became leader of the Liberal Party. Soon after, John Turner returned to private life.

(Several years later, to thank him for his unswerving loyalty to Canada, the Council of Canadians honoured John Turner with our Distinguished Citizens' Award. Not long after, as I was riding in a Toronto taxi-cab on a warm spring day, I passed him on the street. He was walking with his head down as if in a hundred-mile-an-hour wind, clutching a stack of papers, intensely focused on some private thought. Not one person he passed on the crowded street seemed to recognize him or turned to look at him. I felt very, very sad.)

Under Jean Chrétien's leadership, the Liberal Party would turn its back on decades of Liberal policy and mutate into what one journalist called "Libertories." As Bruce Campbell and I wrote in our 1995 book, *Straight Through the Heart*, "Within two years, the party that came to power [in 1993] on a pledge of jobs, social security, and preserving the nation-state would gut Canada's social programs, break the collective agreement with its public sector workers, privatize its transportation system, commercialize its cultural sector, abandon its environmental obligations, endorse world-wide free trade, sever trade from human rights, promote deregulated foreign investment, yield control of the economy to global investment speculators, and become apologists for the corporate sector it had once vilified."

I now wonder what would have happened if I had chosen to stay with the party during those years. It would have been fairly simple to find another, more "winnable" riding and run again, and I was certainly given that option. I do believe that I would have been deeply unhappy with the shift in political direction in the party and either left politics or defected to the NDP if they would have had me. But one never knows these things for certain. Power has a way of seducing people and of helping them come up with the most amazing rationalizations for their choices.

I believe that some of my one-time colleagues on the left of the party, like Lloyd Axworthy and Sheila Copps, have used such rationalizations to justify their continued presence in and support of the current Liberal Party. They carve out special progressive projects and tell themselves that, without them there, the field would be left to the party's right wing and things would be even worse.

But Plato's dictum that introduces this chapter speaks a powerful truth. "One cannot be both powerful in the state and unlike it in character." When you represent the government in power, you represent it in its entirety. The Liberal Party, under Jean Chrétien, has demonstrated breathtaking hypocrisy in every facet of public policy, reversing the position it held in opposition on social programs, environmental stewardship, and economic and cultural sovereignty. It has picked up the policy torch of the Mulroney Tories and carried it further than Mulroney ever dreamed possible. Not even a special fund for filmmakers or a global landmine accord, no matter how satisfactory such victories might be in themselves, can make up for the fact that government under these people has exposed Canadian culture to raw global competition and turned Canada's foreign policy over to the forces of unregulated global competition.

With time, I would come to be one of the most vociferous critics in the country of the Liberal Party and its policies. And with time, the rift would become bitter and personal, and I would find it very painful to have to criticize these former friends publicly.

However, all I knew that hot July night in 1988 in the Ottawa Civic Centre was that one chapter of my life was closing and another was about to open. Competing for my attention with politics over the last three years had been my growing involvement with the Council of Canadians and a dream to build a non-partisan citizens' movement from coast to coast. As life inside partisan politics became more ugly, my work outside of it had become more and more inviting. Now I would have the chance to follow my heart, returning to activism outside of party politics, but around a whole new set of issues and with a whole new set of players. The truth is, I was calm that night because I was relieved. Pierre Trudeau had been right. I didn't belong here.

Just before leaving the Civic Centre, my beloved friend Helen Porter, who had driven in just to be with me for this event, put her arms around me and said, "Now, this is the beginning of your true career." I would never look back.

6

THE FIGHT FOR CANADA

"We have only been in power for two months, but I can tell
you this: give us twenty years, and it is coming, and you will
not recognize this country."

Prime Minister Brian Mulroney
November 7, 1984

On a crisp day in early fall, 1988, Mel Hurtig phoned me to ask me to
become the chair of the Council of Canadians. For the past three years,
I had become deeply immersed, when not working in Liberal politics, in
the growing movement against Brian Mulroney's plans for free trade
with the United States.

Still fresh from the pain of my nomination loss, I was reluctant to take
on such a difficult task. Not only was the council flourishing, and therefore
demanding, but the coming election was shaping up as a contest around
the FTA and Canadian sovereignty, and it was clear the council would be
playing a pivotal role in the debate. I wasn't sure I was up to it.

But Mel gently persisted. Phone calls from friends on the board
came rolling in and my personal friends and family knew it was just the

thing I needed. "Okay," I told Mel. "But don't leave me. I need you to be my mentor and guide or I won't do this properly." Mel promised.

Mel Hurtig had entered my life in February 1985, when he phoned to invite me to a meeting in Toronto to discuss strategy around Brian Mulroney's interest in pursuing a free trade agreement with the United States. More than eighty of the smartest people I had ever met were gathered in one place to share information and to plan what was to become a national movement to protect Canadian economic and cultural sovereignty.

Bob White, then with the Canadian Auto Workers; Grace Hartman, of the Canadian Union of Public Employees; Gerry Caplan, then principal secretary to Ed Broadbent; the environmentalist David Suzuki; writer and passionate cultural nationalist Pierre Berton; Peter Herrndorf, then with the CBC; the distinguished fighter for Canada, Walter Gordon; political scientists Mel Watkins and Stephen Clarkson; feminist icon Doris Anderson; and politicians Marion Dewar, Sheila Copps, Herb Gray, and Paul Martin, Jr. were all there. One after another, they stood to speak about their love of Canada, the threat to Canada's sovereignty represented by Brian Mulroney's free trade flirtation with the United States, and their determination to fight to preserve Canada's culture, social programs, and economic integrity. I was hooked.

Stephen Clarkson gave a brilliant history of Canada and talked about the constant battle of succeeding generations to maintain its independence in the face of the fierce pull of economic continentalism. He also recalled how Brian Mulroney had grown up in a U.S.–dominated one-company town and gone on to work for the Iron Ore Company of Canada, controlled directly by an American corporation that in turn controlled Canada's largest reserves of ore.

Bob White, fresh from his battle to take his Canadian workers out of its U.S.–based parent union, the UAW, gave a passionate defence of Canadian unions and workers and the threat free trade would pose to both. Academic activist Robin Matthews told about the growing dominance of American researchers and professors in Canadian universities. Pierre Berton provided the staggering numbers on foreign domination in the cultural sector. David Suzuki sounded the alarm about the growing domination of large foreign corporations who were being given unchecked access to our forests and our energy reserves. I sat and drank it all in.

This event was a turning point in my life. Like many Canadians of my generation, I had taken my country and all it had to offer for granted. I am of the generation that has had it all. We grew up in the postwar boom of the late 1950s and 1960s. I have benefited from universal social programs not accessible to either my parents or my children. Family allowance that helped both my parents and me raise our children is gone. Medicare was my birthright; but my parents did not enjoy it and my children are inheriting an impoverished shadow of this once-universal program. Old Age Security and public pensions may be a thing of the past for the next generation. I had easy access to university. That was not true for my parents or my children; for their children, post-secondary education will be a lottery.

Although I couldn't see it in 1985, there was already evidence that this social infrastructure was beginning to unravel. While subtle, there were in the early 1980s signs of what would become an out-and-out assault on these precious programs and on the very role of government itself. In the dying days of his regime, Pierre Trudeau established the Royal Commission on the Economic Union and Development Prospects for Canada, chaired by former Liberal Finance Minister Donald Macdonald. The commission published its report in 1985 for the Mulroney government and it was just what they wanted to hear. Macdonald called for major "contractions" of government in order to foster business competition, claimed that the welfare state subverted the "genius of the marketplace," and, in effect, laid the groundwork for continental free trade, planned high unemployment, and the assault on universal social programs.

As well, big business in Canada, as in every country in the world, had set up a political lobbying arm to counter what it called an "excess of democracy" represented by social programs, job creation, and progressive taxation. The Business Council on National Issues, established in 1976, set out to conscript politicians, universities, think-tanks, the media, and the public to its world view and created a kind of shadow Cabinet to influence every government portfolio, from energy to trade to social policy. Along with corporate-funded, right-wing think-tanks like the C.D. Howe and the Fraser institutes, the BCNI under Tom d'Aquino set the stage for Canadian economic globalization, starting with free trade with the United States.

Immersed as I was in the politics of equality, I had been only vaguely aware of these issues. I realized in that Toronto hotel room that I had a great deal to learn. It was the beginning of a journey of discovery that would lead me, in the process, to fall in love with my country. I read voraciously and talked to everyone I could find who could help me learn its rich history. My schooling had not provided me or anyone I knew with the kind of historical analysis or framework from which even to approach these questions. History as taught in Ottawa public schools in the 1950s was a catalogue of facts about early explorers, battles between the French and the English, and the names and political affiliations of successive prime ministers.

I now had to learn about the terrible struggles for self-determination of a nation small in numbers but vast in size, living next to the biggest superpower in the world. I read about the herculean efforts to set up a public broadcasting system, farm marketing boards, a full employment policy, and national social programs based on the principle of sharing for survival and a culture of interdependence. I read about those who were beaten up, jailed, and even killed for establishing decent working conditions and pay for working people. I read with such pride that I might have been there, of the great "march on Ottawa" and the creation of collective bargaining for workers. I discovered that great citizens' movements have played a major role in every progressive policy that governments have ever adopted in Canada and that there was a rich history here on which to build.

From the 1930s League for Social Reconstruction, with such outstanding Canadian academics as Eugene Forsey, King Gordon, Frank Underhill, and Frank Scott, to the 1970s Committee for an Independent Canada, founded by Mel Hurtig, Abe Rotstein, Walter Gordon, and Peter C. Newman, Canada's best and brightest, I learned, fought to keep a distinct society on the northern half of the North American continent. This was no small-minded, xenophobic movement, I found, but a gathering of like minds, progressive in domestic policy and international in vision. Nor were these people anti-American. Many admired the great qualities of our vibrant neighbours to the south. But, they stubbornly insisted, Canada has its own history and culture that must be preserved for all generations to come.

I was tapping into a social movement with a rich history and a body of thinkers, writers, and activists that would serve as my guides in my journey ahead. I discovered George Grant's *Lament for a Nation* and Kari Levitt's *Silent Surrender* — two anthems of the movement. Kari's father was the influential Karl Polanyi, who wrote *The Great Transformation* in the 1940s. More recent writers such as Christina McCall, James Laxer, Leo Panitch, Mel Watkins, and Duncan Cameron also inspired and taught me.

I learned the negative lessons as well: that Canada is the most foreign-controlled country in the industrialized world. That we have hardly ever been allowed our own defence or foreign policy. That our economy is deeply intertwined with that of the United States and that we establish independent economic policy at our peril. That our writers and musicians and artists have had to struggle for every bit of space they get on our airwaves or in our magazines. That much of our rich natural-resource heritage is leased to foreign corporations who often call the shots on our resource and environmental policies.

Most of all, I learned how fragile and precious our social programs are to us all, and this concern formed the link between the work I had done in the women's movement and the work I was to do in the Council of Canadians. For any threat to universal social programs is also a threat to the hard-earned equality gains women have made. And it wouldn't be long before I came to believe (correctly) that free trade and economic globalization would pose the greatest threat to our social programs since their creation.

Canada's universal social programs were born of the "twin crucibles" of the Great Depression and the Second World War. During the Depression, the federal government paid out large amounts of money for social welfare. In fact, it would not be until the 1960s that it would again spend as much on social programs as a percentage of overall government spending. But the system was based on the notion of charity for the "deserving poor," not universality, and help for Canadians became lost in a patchwork of inadequate, badly managed, and punitive programs.

This system could only react to sickness; it could never prepare families for health. This system could only react to the worst excesses of unemployment; it could never help create desperately needed jobs. It was the utter failure of this formula for social welfare that inspired the great social reforms of the 1960s, all the more so when Canadians could see in hindsight that the same government that had not been able to feed, house, clothe or employ them during the Depression could suddenly find all the money it needed to send them to war. A sea-change in the political culture of the country was born at the end of the Second World War. It was now understood that, to be effective, social programs had to be based on national standards that would give a sense of continuity and security to social funding, allowing people to plan ahead.

Universal social programs were created to establish the notion that Canadians have equal social rights no matter who they are; what their ethnic, gender, socio-economic background; or where they live. They were based on an approach to society that included everyone. The Canadian definition of social welfare concerned itself with the well-being of the whole community; one major goal of social programs was to narrow the gap between rich and poor — still a crucial component for women.

For women remain poorer than men, earn less than men, are more responsible for child bearing and rearing, are still the dominant care-givers in their families, and live longer. Women are, therefore, more dependent than men on universal social programs and, in fact, have made great strides because of gender-neutral accessibility of universal programs. (This is one major difference between American and Canadian women. Poor American women have far less access to social assistance and health care than Canadian women, although this is changing rapidly as we hurry to replicate the worst of American society.) I vowed to fight to preserve these sacred programs so that all the work I and others had done to advance the rights of women would not be lost.

It is ironic that it was two men, deeply opposed in their views, who inspired me to take up this fight. One was Brian Mulroney, whose pre-election promise to profoundly change the country if ever he got a chance came true with a vengeance. Only months after beating John

Turner in his 1984 landslide victory, Mulroney made some of the most important policy announcements of his career to the prestigious Economic Club, the cream of corporate America, in New York. There, not to Canadian CEOs or, heaven forefend, to the Canadian Parliament, he announced the end of the Foreign Investment Review Board and the National Energy Program, new tax breaks for foreign-based energy companies, new ties in military cooperation with Ronald Reagan's administration. From now on, Canada was "open for business."

In a nine-page supplement placed in the *New York Times* that same week, Canadian corporations and the government declared together: "Canada is under new management, a marriage of government and business." From now on, it promised, Canada would be "a cheap place for Americans to invest in" and "would lay out the welcome mat for foreign investment." The supplement promised policies in tune with the new "market-oriented" style of the new Conservative government, like allowing corporations to take 100 per cent of their profits out of the country. Wage settlements were being "dramatically" decelerated in Canada, the ad boasted, and Canada would "look to move the Canadian dollar 'gently higher' against the American, with further measurable upward appreciation to follow in 1986 and beyond."

The ad brightly pointed out the advantages to American business of the fact that Canada sells raw resources and then reimports the American processed goods, thereby creating millions of American jobs. "For every dollar's worth of steel Ontario producers ship to Pennsylvania, they buy back $1.25 in iron, coal, and other related products." The ad reminded its readers that the first entrepreneurs in Canada were American and encouraged even more American investment, with the assurance that, "with as much as 60 per cent of the manufacturing sector and 70 per cent of the mining and petroleum sectors under the control of foreign companies, Canada has been more dependent on foreign investment than any other industrial country."

Peter Lougheed, premier of Alberta, promised to "sell" his province to the world, and invited American private investment into Alberta's health-care sector. Lougheed is a passionate Albertan and felt (with some justification) that eastern Canadians had taken his province and its energy resources for granted. He had become a strong proponent of provincial

THE FIGHT FOR CANADA

rights, particularly over resources, and had been a thorn in the side of centralist governments for years. When Pierre Trudeau's government introduced the National Energy Program in 1980 to keep the price of oil and gas, which was soaring on the world market, affordable for all Canadians, Lougheed was furious and (right beside the big energy multinationals) accused the federal government of "occupying" his home. When world prices unexpectedly fell soon after, the NEP was allowed to ebb, a bit at a time.

But Lougheed never forgot the NEP; for him, free trade with the United States would provide a free market for his province's resources and a guarantee that no future government in Ottawa would ever again introduce such legislation. (In recent years, Lougheed has softened his position considerably. He now worries about what he calls the "Americanization of Canada," and concedes that free trade opponents had some valid concerns.)

The supplement also helpfully pointed out that the Reagan administration, displeased with former "narrow, self-styled" concerns about too much foreign control, had made it clear that Canada would have to prove itself trustworthy in this area and be the initiator in a free trade deal. The Reagan administration, said the ad, kindly let Canada lead the "pas de deux."

I was shocked. But those were just the opening shots. In preparation for his free trade agreement with the United States, (a concept he had opposed during the 1984 election campaign), Mulroney dismantled Canada's energy security, gutted foreign-investment screening, gave the giant drug companies new patent rights, moth-balled promises to improve Canadian access to film distribution, started the gutting of Canada's social programs, privatized much of our transportation system, attacked farm marketing boards, and deregulated much of our natural-resource protection.

Mulroney's deep and subservient ties to the Reagan and Bush administrations and to corporate America have been well documented in several excellent works by Mel Hurtig, Linda McQuaig, and Marci McDonald, among others, and it is, therefore, not necessary to repeat that story here. Similarly well documented now are the unprecedented business coalitions that formed in both countries and coordinated their well financed campaign to push the free trade agreement through both political systems.

For my first book, *Parcel of Rogues: How Free Trade Is Failing Canada*, published in 1990, I cross-referenced the six hundred corporations and industry associations that made up the American Coalition for Trade Expansion with Canada with its Canadian counterpart, the Alliance for Trade and Job Opportunities, and found that many members of the former were directly involved, financially and strategically, with the latter. I also got the list of corporate donors to the Conservative Party for 1987 and 1988. Industry leaders like Shell, IBM, Weyerhauser, Allied-Signal, AT&T, Cargill, General Motors, and Dow Chemical (to name just a few) not only spent millions of dollars promoting the free trade deal in their own country, but joined the Canadian Alliance and, through their subsidiaries, gave money directly to the Mulroney Tories.

Then I cross-referenced these names to those corporations, particularly in defence, that had received Canadian and American government contracts in those years. What emerged was an incestuous little clique of political and corporate friends working on either side of the border to promote their own interests by scratching one another's backs.

For instance, General Motors belonged to both the American Coalition for Trade Expansion with Canada and the Canadian Alliance for Trade and Job Opportunities; its Canadian division was, and remains, a top contractor in Ottawa and Washington. Imperial Oil gave $200,000 to the alliance and $46,000 to the Tories, and is a major Pentagon contractor. AT&T was a major donor to both the American and Canadian coalitions, and is a major recipient of contracts from both governments. Boeing Corporation, the Seattle-based U.S. aerospace giant that was given a grant of $161 million by the Canadian government to take over de Havilland Aircraft of Canada in 1985 (a move the Council of Canadians fought vigorously), was a charter member of the American Coalition for Trade Expansion with Canada and a major contractor with both the Canadian government and the Pentagon.

Mulroney pals like James Robinson III and Harry Freeman, chairman and vice-chairman, respectively, of American Express founded the American Coalition for Trade Expansion with Canada because they had been trying unsuccessfully to get free trade in financial services at the General Agreement on Tariffs and Trade so their company could go truly global. To them, the Tories were a godsend. Not only would they now have the prototype they needed in this bilateral deal with Canada to open these markets successfully at the GATT, but Mulroney would hold a private Cabinet meeting on voting day — November 21, 1988 — where it would bend Canadian law and grant American Express banking rights in Canada.

(In 1996, at a Washington teach-in sponsored by the International Forum on Globalization, John Cavanagh of the prestigious Institute for Policy Studies, Indian physicist and populist heroine Vandana Shiva, and I debated Harry Freeman, now a private consultant, Joe Cobb of the ultra-right wing Heritage Institute, and Paula Stern, a Clinton legal adviser on trade. Freeman didn't know me from Eve, hadn't prepared for the debate, and spoke in generalities about the unlimited "benefits" of globalization. I, on the other hand, came prepared to do battle with a man I considered to have been one of the chief architects of a deal that had deeply compromised my country and handed it over to big corporations like American Express.

I quoted Harry Freeman's own speeches extensively and outlined the now well documented leadership role he and James Robinson played in the free trade talks. I quoted Linda McQuaig quoting Tom d'Aquino that Robinson and Freeman "stood out head and shoulders above everybody else, and had the highest profile in terms of marshalling the forces" and that he remembered many strategy meetings between top Canadian and American business leaders to promote the deal where the two were present in leadership roles. I pointed out that David Culver of Alcan (a Canadian), who was also on the board of American Express, became good friends with Robinson and Freeman and ran the Canadian Alliance, which led the lobby effort in Canada, out of his offices in Montreal.

Freeman and I got into a shouting match. He denied any influence in Canadian politics and said I was promoting a conspiracy theory. I answered that it was not a conspiracy, but organized greed. I did, however, remind him of the two cows on the hill. One says, "Oh, you and your conspiracy theories." The other is not listening, however, because she is engrossed in a pamphlet entitled "Where Beef Really

Comes From." The audience loved it and Freeman stormed out.

Not long after, I received a letter threatening a lawsuit. Freeman said that he had spoken to Canadian colleagues who urged him to sue me, as I had gotten away with such accusations for too long and "it was time somebody took me on." He demanded an immediate apology. I sent him stacks of material backing my charges, but on the advice of my lawyer-husband, who said we could lose our house if we had to hire a Washington law firm, apologized if what I said had appeared to be "personal." I never heard from Harry Freeman again, but a year later, he was interviewed for a documentary on free trade for the CBC's *National Magazine*. Freeman openly talked about his pro-active role in the free trade negotiations and how closely big business on both sides of the border had worked together to get their deal.)

The more I learned about Brian Mulroney, the more I disliked everything he stood for. I first heard about him when he ran for, and lost, the Conservative leadership in 1976. He flew across the country in a private jet, lavishing favours on anyone who would support him, and his appearances were accompanied by marching bands and beautiful, scantily clad young women. In power, he was the epitome of cronyism, having brought his extensive old-boys' network from his university days at St. Francis Xavier with him to Ottawa, where they ran the country as if it had been put there for their personal profit. His admiration for all things big, all things expensive, all things American was offensive to me. I used to say that what Brian Mulroney really wanted to be when he grew up was the president of the United States.

I vowed to fight him with every ounce of strength I had, and joked in many speeches for the nine years he was in power that I ate nails for breakfast every day so I would be tough enough to help defeat him. Obviously, I wasn't alone in my feelings.

One day, I was on an open-line talk show in Regina about Mulroney's record. Every single caller castigated Mulroney and his policies to the point that the host, in the name of fairness, set aside a whole separate line and said it was only for anyone who had anything good to say about the man. For the whole hour, the "Mulroney" line sat silent. Just seconds before the end of the show, it lit up. "Oh, good!" said the host. "A positive call on the 'Mulroney' line. Hello, sir. You're on the air.

Do *you* like Brian Mulroney?" "Hell, no," said the caller. "I hate the son of a bitch. I couldn't get through on the other line and I just had to say my piece before you end this program!"

My dispatches on Mulroney caught the eye of Peter Gzowski. His call led to several animated dinner conversations about Mulroney and the free trade agreement, and to some appearances on CBC's *Morningside*. As a result of these conversations, I would later be included in a very special list.

In one of his columns for *Canadian Living*, called "My fantasy dinner with ten women," Gzowski listed the ten women he would "like to spend an evening with" if he could have this dream come true. One of the women, Dulcie McCullum, a Victoria lawyer working with people with mental disabilities, decided it should happen, so, on July 13, 1990, Peter's fifty-fifth birthday, Dulcie and *Canadian Living* put on a surprise dinner party for him in their Toronto office boardroom, attended by all but one of his choices (Evelyn Hart was on tour with the Royal Winnipeg Ballet) and prepared by the noted chef Elizabeth Baird. The guests were a delightful mix: besides Dulcie and me, there was Dinah Christie, singer and comedienne; Debbie Brill, former Olympic high jumper; Mary-Wynne Ashford, then with Physicians for the Prevention of Nuclear War; Nellie Cournoyea, then natural resources minister for the Northwest Territories; Barbara McDougall, then minister of employment and immigration in Brian Mulroney's Cabinet; the incomparable writer, Alice Munro; and Margaret Somerville, director of the McGill Centre for Medicine, Ethics and Law.

Peter was truly surprised and speechless for at least the first few minutes. The menu was his favourite: roast beef, peas, and potatoes, and we all settled into it and the wine with pleasure. But it was soon clear these feisty women were impressed with each other and were going to let down their hair. Alice Munro was sitting beside me and quickly dispelled any stereotypes I had harboured of the quiet, retiring writer. She has a marvellous wit and started to goad a slightly unsettled Peter right away. Any wall that might have existed between Barbara McDougall and me came down when I mentioned that my mother had just started receiving a monthly war-widow's pension that had been cut off when she married my father so many years before, and what an incredible difference it was making to their lives. It turned out Barbara was the Cabinet minister responsible for restoring this pension to about 4,500 women in Canada and had quietly gone about this work without seeking publicity for it. I have been grateful to her ever since and consider this an example of how one woman can make a difference to the lives of other women.

After getting over his shock at his surprise party, Peter decided to start acting like the media host he is and started "interviewing" us. We were mostly polite until he asked Debbie Brill, "Tell me, what kind of a mother raises a Debbie Brill?" "Oh, fuck off, Peter," said Debbie to our loud applause. Poor Peter. He had chosen an unruly bunch. When it came time for the gifts, he turned deep scarlet. For her present, Debbie Brill had sat down nude, first in red watercolour paint, and then on a large white canvas; the "painting" was an imprint of her backside. Nellie Cournoyea presented Peter with a boiled ground-squirrel, twisted the tail off it, and said saucily, "Have some tail, Peter." Peter nibbled at it without much enthusiasm.

My gift in comparison was pretty tame — collectors' items like buttons and posters from the opposition to the Canada–U.S. Free Trade Agreement. But the talk around the table got increasingly hilarious and we had such fun, we all decided to meet again the next year without Peter (a promise we unfortunately didn't keep.) A reporter from *Canadian Living* was covering the evening for the magazine and kept muttering, "I can't print this . . . I can't print this either." It was a memorable night for us, but for Peter, it might have been an illustration of the old adage, "Beware of what you wish for. You just might get it."

The other man who inspired me, obviously in a very different way, was Mel Hurtig. An Edmonton publisher with a passionate love of his country, Mel had spent many years keeping the flame of Canadian nationalism alive. Mel could take the driest of statistics on foreign investment and corporate mergers and make an audience weep. He had crossed the country literally for years, fighting to have others see the threat to his beloved country through his eyes. Mel Hurtig's most important characteristic, for me, was his ownership of these issues. He practised what another colleague, Murray Dobbin, calls "intentional citizenship," living his politics and claiming a role at the centre of the great debates of his time.

I knew I was going to love working with Mel Hurtig when he rented a Twin Otter in the summer of 1985 and "bombed" the American icebreaker *Polar Sea* with a Canadian flag and a message as it entered Canadian waters in our North without permission from our government. The message he dropped on the ship read in part: "Canadians consider our Arctic waters, islands and ice to be Canadian territory under Canadian jurisdiction. Your failure to request advance permission to sail the Northwest Passage is insulting and demeaning to our citizens and a threat to our sovereignty." He urged the ship to return to international waters and respect Canadian sovereignty in the future. Pitifully, the Mulroney government handled the situation by granting permission for the voyage after the fact, permission the American government had never sought.

Mel Hurtig became my mentor and good friend. It was my great pleasure to support him and be part of the creation of the Council of Canadians. We held our founding press conference to coincide with Ronald Reagan's trip to Canada in March 1985. As Mel writes in his memoir, *At Twilight in the Country*, the release stated that "the COC does not support anti-Americanism or chauvinistic nationalism. Rather, the new organization will advocate positive policies in the national interest, similar to policies other nations around the world adopt in the best interests of their citizens."

The fundamental policy goal of our fledgling group was the "maximization of Canadian economic, political, social, and cultural sovereignty." High on our priorities was support for Canadian culture, copyright, film production and distribution, and broadcasting. We advocated a multilateral approach to trade; the development of well-thought-out national industrial strategies; more control over monetary policy, the Bank of Canada, and the activities of Canadian banks; reduced foreign ownership; and much better use of our natural resources. In foreign and defence policy, the COC advocated that Canada work for a strengthened United Nations, for the de-escalation of tension between our superpower neighbours, for steps to ensure Canadian sovereignty in the Arctic, and an activist role in world arms-control discussions.

The founding convention of the council was held on Thanksgiving weekend in Ottawa. Within a year, we had three thousand members. By the time of the 1988 election, we had more than ten thousand members and chapters across the country. Under Mel's leadership, we held town-hall meetings right across the country, wrote briefs, appeared before parliamentary committees, placed ads in newspapers, and fought the escalating takeovers of key Canadian assets.

Although I did a little of everything, including participating in some early debates with pro–free trade lobbyists like economist John Crispo (Brian Mulroney would reward him for calling the CBC a "pinko slag heap" by putting him on its board), Tom d'Aquino of the BCNI, and Gordon Ritchie, Canada's deputy chief negotiator in the free trade talks with the United States, I carved out two projects on which to concentrate. The first was a fight to stop the giveaway of Canada's energy sovereignty.

For me, one of the most egregious aspects of the Canada–U.S. Free Trade Agreement was that it wiped out the long-standing Canadian policy that sufficient supplies to serve Canadian needs had to be guaranteed before exports grants were authorized. The FTA forbade charging higher prices for American consumers than for Canadian consumers and outlawed taxes on energy exports. Most important, the FTA, and NAFTA after it, placed strict limits on the ability of our government to curtail energy exports in times of Canadian need or for environmental purposes. The deals say that Canada must maintain at least the same level of oil and gas exports to the United States as it has supplied for the past thirty-six months. Only if Canadian consumption is cut proportionately, and then only in times of crisis, could the Canadian government claim jurisdiction over its own energy resources.

Brian Mulroney didn't wait for the FTA to dismantle Canada's energy regime, however. He introduced the Western Energy Accord that deregulated oil and gas exports and stripped the National Energy Board of its powers. The government also dismantled the vital-supply safeguard that required there always be a twenty-five-year surplus of natural gas before allowing export grants, and dropped the only remaining regulatory test for gas exports that gave Canada the right to deny any not in the national interest. As a result of these moves, there is now no government or industry agency empowered to ensure that Canadians will have access to their own energy supplies in the future.

The Council of Canadians fought the Mulroney government at

every step of this process. Although we did manage to place some obstacles in the government's way and raised public awareness and debate on the issue, we lost every fight. Our most ferocious battle was over an application by three companies, Shell, Gulf, and Esso, to access and export 90 per cent of the proven gas reserves in the Mackenzie Delta region of the Northwest Territories. We argued that the sheer size of these reserves — 9.2 trillion cubic feet of gas — would give the United States a legal, binding claim to well over half of Canada's gas reserves.

My partner in this fight was Ken Wardroper, a fellow board member, a former ambassador, and a retired senior civil servant with a long and distinguished career in External Affairs. Ken was also a founding member of the council and served as interim chair for the last half of 1988, leaving his retirement home in Victoria, where he and his wife, Nancy, had just settled. At great personal expense and against Nancy's wishes, he relocated to Ottawa to keep the organization alive. Soon after returning to Victoria, Nancy, who had accompanied him to Ottawa in spite of her objections, died. I felt terrible for the price this man paid for his dedication to our movement.

Ken shone at the fall 1989 Energy Board hearing into the Mackenzie gas reserves. The room was full of high-priced lawyers for the government and the gas companies, all of course on the same side. We had no money for lawyers, so Ken and I had to put the council's case ourselves. At one point, the chairman of the Energy Board, Roland Priddle, took Ken to task for his adamant opposition to these exports. "But, Mr. Wardroper, what about the owners of the resource?" he asked, clearly referring, without saying it, to the corporations represented in the room. "Owners? Oh, you must mean the people of Canada," Ken replied. "Yes, they're why we're here." The media, many of whom were on our side in this David and Goliath fight, lapped it up.

"This is a tragedy," I said to *Maclean's* of the demand by U.S. multinationals to unfettered access to our resources. "We will lose control over our own energy policy." Roland Priddle curtly countered, "Now is not the time for energy nationalism. The NEB has become an agency that helps the market work." Couldn't be much clearer than that.

The other project I undertook, this time with another dedicated board member, political scientist John Trent, was the formation of a national coalition to fight the Mulroney trade deal. It was becoming evident that many social and labour groups were concerned about the FTA talks and starting their own campaigns. But it was also obvious that the business-community lobby for the deal was highly organized and hugely funded. John and I felt that, if we didn't coordinate our work, we wouldn't stand a chance of winning.

On April 4, 1987, to coincide with the famous "Shamrock Summit" where, arm in arm, Brian and Mila Mulroney and Ronald and Nancy Reagan crooned "When Irish Eyes Are Smiling," an unprecedented gathering of environmental, labour, women's, church, anti-poverty, seniors, farmers, nurses, teachers, cultural, aboriginal, and human-rights groups took place at the historic Château Laurier in Ottawa. We called it the "Maple Leaf Summit" to contrast with the spectacle going on just across the street. The energy in that room was electric; I will remember it until the day I die.

One after another, people from all walks of life and from all over the country committed themselves to building a citizens' movement unparalleled in our country's history. In spite of the daunting size of the task before us, there was enormous joy and great hope for the future in the hall that day. The front row displayed a who's who of the labour movement, including legends Grace Hartman, Madeleine Parent, and Louis Laberge. My dear friend, ninety-year old Walter Turnbull, who had served as postmaster in Mackenzie King's government and was an incorrigible flirt, sat up on the platform with some students to represent inter-generational solidarity. All day, he winked, grinned, and waved at a blushing Nancy Riche, the feisty, feminist vice-president of the Canadian Labour Congress.

At the end of the day, John and I led a march of the brand new "Pro-Canada Network" to Parliament Hill, where, in the pouring rain and in front of a wall of television cameras, we put our "Canada Declaration" on the doors of Centre Block. We said this was the modern-day equivalent of Luther nailing his demands to the church doors, but that, being good Canadians, we would use adhesive tape instead of nails so as not to harm the wood of those beautiful doors. The declaration demanded that no free trade agreement be signed by the government without being submitted to the people for their approval.

The PCN, with John and me serving as co-chairs at first and then under the capable hands of Tony Clarke from the Canadian Conference of Catholic Bishops, went on to play a crucial role in shaping public opinion over the FTA. Two million copies of a "comic book" titled *What's the Big Deal?* written by Rick Salutin and illustrated by Terry Mosher (Aislin of the *Montreal Gazette*) were inserted into major newspapers across the country and had an important impact on the views of many Canadians. The Pro-Canada Network, whose name would eventually be changed to the Action Canada Network to resolve a difference over the name with our Quebec allies, would flourish under Tony's leadership for almost another decade.

At the annual general meeting of the Council of Canadians held on October 15 and 16, 1987, we announced a public-relations blitz to turn the upcoming election into a kind of referendum on free trade. The *Globe and Mail* noted that the "weekend strategy session went from crescendo to emotional crescendo."

Magna's Frank Stronach gave a rousing denunciation of free trade, saying that, as a businessman, he would profit from it, but as a person who had carefully chosen Canada as his home, he had to speak against it because it would harm his adopted country. He promised that, if Canadians rejected the FTA, he would keep his plants in Canada, but if we voted for it, we would be changing the rules of the game and he would have to move his operations where the money is. Although the audience very much appreciated his position, many were smiling to themselves as Stronach's legendary ego (only months before, he had told me he would one day be prime minister of Canada) broke out every few minutes as he paused to tell us how great he was, how much money he had (lots), and what a towering figure he was in the world of business. Stronach has since moved many plants off-shore and moved himself back to his homeland, Austria.

Roy Romanow, then Saskatchewan NDP opposition leader, had the audience roaring with laughter when he compared free trade with the United States to a cattle rancher with a big spread and 10,000 head of cattle agreeing to take down the fence between himself and his neighbour, who has a spread the same size, but 100,000 head of cattle. "I promise," says the neighbour with the 100,000 head of cattle, "if you take down that fence, my cattle won't go onto your land, ever!" On a more sombre and poetic note, Romanow compared Canada to a string of ten pearls held together by a tradition of federal-provincial compromise that would be put in jeopardy by the free trade deal.

At this meeting, I was unanimously acclaimed as the new chairperson, a volunteer position I have held ever since. I was deeply honoured and promised the delegates that, no matter what the outcome of the election, I was going to devote my life to making the Council of Canadians a citizens' force to be reckoned with in Canada.

For the next two nights I took part in a historic two-part debate on the FTA on CBC's *The Journal,* pitting Bob White and me against Tom d'Aquino and Peter Lougheed. Bob and I were nervous and spent several days holed up with our advisers, Duncan Cameron from the Canadian Centre for Policy Alternatives, and Sam Guindon, Bob's research director at the CAW.

On the evening of the first debate, held in the Old City Hall in Toronto (because, host Barbara Frum explained, "the great debate about Confederation was held here and it is fitting that this debate, as key to the country's future, be held here as well"), the two teams and their advisers were separated in different rooms until just before we were to go live to air.

The hall was filled with just about every famous person in Canada, including actors Gordon Pinsent and Eric Peterson and playwright John Gray, and I said to Bob that maybe one of them would like to take my place as I was feeling distinctly not up to it. In a very short time, I had come to like and admire Bob very much and was touched as he turned to me just before we left our room and said, "I've only got my grade ten, you know."

I had been calling Mel for last-minute advice and, between his and Bob's counsel, I had developed a simple mantra to help me with my nervousness: "They're bad men. They want to hurt your country." I must have had this in my mind when Peter Lougheed, whom I had never met, approached me just before we went on air and said, smooth as butter, "Maude. I'm Peter Lougheed. How are you?" Without a pause and much to my mortification, I blurted out, "I'm nice!" Lougheed looked puzzled and walked away. I thought I was doomed.

But, miracle of miracles, we did our side proud. Lougheed and d'Aquino, who had obviously not prepared, wrapped themselves in the flag and spoke in generalities about how they loved Canada, and free trade would be good for us. Bob and I got right into the technicalities of the agreement, arguing about secure market access, American omnibus legislation, proportional energy sharing, national treatment (which requires that a country not discriminate between foreign and domestic investors and companies), and the threat to jobs, social programs, and the environment.

Where the other side praised the American dream, I reminded the audience that, although the United States is wealthy, among industrialized nations it has the biggest gap between rich and poor, the highest per-capita poverty rate, the most children living in poverty, the highest infant mortality rate, the most people without health care, the most homeless, the highest rate of adult illiteracy, and the poorest legislation governing working conditions. Mulroney's people were very unhappy with the performance of their "side." (D'Aquino sweated so hard on air that night, that the following evening the make-up people had to spray underarm antiperspirant on his forehead.) They sent a team from the PMO to Toronto to brief them for the next evening's performance and give them a crash course on the technical aspects of the deal.

The second evening was even better. D'Aquino and Lougheed were much more specific about the intricate details of the FTA, but gave up the passion they had displayed the night before. Bob and I decided this was our chance to speak from our hearts and we called for the preservation of Canada's unique social infrastructure and reminded the audience that our country had developed values of equality, tolerance, and compassion, of which the world was sorely in need.

Alas, it was all to no avail. Even though polls showed that our collective opposition had managed to change the hearts and minds of the majority of Canadians about free trade, and, although a majority voted for the two parties opposed to the deal, Mulroney's win in 1988 ensured the passage of the Canada–U.S. Free Trade Agreement and ushered in a whole new political and economic era in Canada.

As I look back on this loss now, I can say that I was not so devastated as alarmed by it. I was beginning to see that the FTA was not itself the central problem, but rather a weapon in the arsenal of the right. They wanted to change fundamentally Canadian society and the fight was going to be long and hard. I was either in it or I wasn't. An eighty-seven-year-old woman who lives on Vancouver Island and has been involved in social justice campaigns for over sixty years gave me a valuable lecture one day when I seemed discouraged. "Fighting for social justice is not something you do once and then forget. Fighting for social justice is like taking a bath. You do it every day or you start to stink!"

I thought of my father's battles over the years and took great inspiration from them. They were never "won" as such. Progress was made, but it was a constant struggle to stay ahead of the backlash. (In fact, even capital punishment wasn't beaten for good. In 1985, when the Mulroney government, under pressure from its back bench, announced it would allow a free vote on capital punishment, my dad and I worked together on a national campaign called the Coalition Against the Return of the Death Penalty. The coalition was made up of church, social-justice, civil-liberties, and human-rights groups, and our motto was "Why kill people who kill people to show that killing people is wrong?" My dad's history with and extensive knowledge of this issue was a real boost to our work, and, in 1986, the House of Commons again rejected the death penalty for Canada. Now, of course, there are members of the Reform Party who would reintroduce it, given the opportunity.)

One thing I knew for certain as I sat in a darkened CTV studio in Ottawa for hours on election night waiting to give my (sad) thoughts on the outcome: this was just the beginning of a long fight for the soul of my country.

7

NO PLACE FOR
THE CHILDREN

"But what about me?"

Begging Mayan street child
San Cristóbal de las Casas, Mexico

"The politics are over," the president of the American Association of
Exporters and Importers said with a sigh. "Now business will do their
thing. To say we're happy is an understatement." Another business
leader, American Express's James Robinson, called it a "historic breakthrough." No wonder big business was triumphant. It was now free of
political or social considerations in running its North American operations. The Canada–U.S. Free Trade Agreement was an important milestone on the road to economic globalization in which transnational
corporations would be able to get around nation-state laws that forced
them to pay taxes and to assume some responsibility for social and environmental conditions in their countries of origin.

But I knew this was only the beginning, and I was right. The moment corporate Canada got its trade deal, its public lobby switched to an all-out war on the federal deficit and universal social programs (which had already started and had already influenced government bureaucrats); this despite a major 1989 Statistics Canada study by government economists Hideo Mimoto and Philip Cross clearly showing that unemployment, high interest rate payments on the debt, and tax breaks for the rich and big business, not social programs, were the causes of our deficit.

The fallout from the trade deal was immediate and it was devastating. Only two days after the November election, the U.S.–based multinational, Gillette, announced it was closing its Montreal plant, moving production back to the United States, and laying off six hundred workers. We held a press conference and called for a boycott of Gillette products. When asked by the media to prove the connection to free trade, I said, "I can't give you a piece of paper, but I appeal to Canadians' logic: Do you think this is just a coincidence?" I added that if this was the only plant closing for the next couple of years, "then I guess I'm wrong."

Wrong I was not. Over the next three years, thousands of Canadian branch plants, including Inglis (870 jobs), Hershey (466 jobs), Mobil Oil (375 jobs), de Havilland (700 jobs), Burlington Carpet (450 jobs), and Eastman Kodak (450 jobs) would close operations, causing the loss of a quarter of all manufacturing jobs in Canada. When the restructuring was over, the workforce of Canada would be profoundly changed.

On January 1, 1989, the day the free trade deal actually came into effect, about twenty of us went up to Parliament Hill where we held up a sign that said "SOLD/VENDU." "What happened during the election was a corporate buying of votes. It was the politics of fear. Our job now is to keep the issue and its fallout before the Canadian people," our executive director, Catherine Morrison, and I said to the press that day. Over the next five years, the Council would count every job loss and plant closing, fight the invasion of American big-box retailers like Wal-Mart, oppose the takeover of dozens of Canadian assets and the privatization of public enterprises, and rally public reaction to the Mulroney assault on social programs.

We issued our first "report card" six months after the signing of the FTA, showing that 33,000 jobs had been lost in those months; six months later, our second report card showed a loss of 72,000 jobs. (The Canadian Labour Congress was closely monitoring the effect of the FTA on jobs and unemployment insurance and I was able, using their excellent research, to list the Canadian plants that had closed in the first year of free trade in my book *Parcel of Rogues*. The list was thirty pages long and included the names of almost six hundred companies.)

We slammed Mulroney's first post–free trade budget of May 1989 for its deep cuts to unemployment insurance, agriculture and grain transportation subsidies, and regional development. "This budget is way more than an individual set of catastrophes for seniors and for the regions and for farmers. It's the final deed of sale to our country, the final deliverance of the free trade agreement," I said to the press. These three specific programs had been the target of ferocious attacks from American administrations over the years and were targeted for extinction soon after the deal was signed. I felt, therefore, the worst had been done. If only I could have known then how much more there was to give away, perhaps I might have tempered my remarks.

In the wake of free trade, the country was in the grip of a series of high-stakes takeovers. *Maclean's* reported that during the first six months of 1989, foreigners spent $10 billion buying up Canadian companies — triple the total for all of 1988. The magazine identified a trend that was to intensify over the next decade; instead of building new firms from the ground up, the fastest way to make a buck was to take over another firm after it had become profitable. Thus, the vast majority of new investment doesn't create new jobs or produce new goods; it just trades domestic owners with foreign, making it harder for governments to maintain regulations benefiting citizens.

We fought as many as we could. One was the purchase of Consolidated-Bathurst (where Jean Chrétien's father, Wellie, worked as a labourer for many years and on whose board Chrétien himself now sat), by Stone Container of Chicago, with a consequent loss of hundreds of Canadian jobs. I blasted the fact that Maurice Sauvé, husband of Governor General Jeanne Sauvé, for a fee arranged the sale of this venerable Canadian company. "While she's representing Canada, he's off selling it," I pointed out.

Another was the sale of Connaught Laboratories, Canada's leading bioscience firm where Dr. Banting first produced insulin, to Institut Merieux of France, a company directly controlled by the French government.

Industry Minister Harvie Andre called me "Canada's answer to [Romanian dictator] Nicolei Ceaucescu" on CBC Radio for our stand on Connaught. To placate us, as public opinion was on our side, Investment Canada, the agency that had replaced the Foreign Investment Review Agency and has never, to the present day, turned down one request for a foreign takeover of a Canadian company, placed some pitifully unobservable and unenforceable conditions on the sale.

The day the sale of Connaught became final, I received a call from a senior bureaucrat in Health Canada. "Ms. Barlow," he said, "can you please tell the Canadian public and the press that now Canada won't have first call on these serums in time of crisis?" I said, "I will try but it would have a hell of a lot more punch coming from you." No such public statement ever came from the department.

When challenged about the sale of this important institution in the House of Commons, Brian Mulroney slipped into his usual banalities: "Our view is a confident, modern Canada building into the next century." But I knew otherwise. The only way you can guarantee our future in biotechnology is to not let these companies fall out of Canadian hands.

Next, the COC joined forces with the Energy and Chemical Workers' Union to buy shares of Consumers Gas to stop the giant British Gas PLC from buying this key Ontario utility and to back a Canadian consortium that had come forward with a competing bid. I testified at Ontario Energy Board hearings and was pounded by the board's lawyer, John Campion, who I felt treated me like a criminal on the stand. We called on Premier David Peterson to intervene to save Consumers. He had been very outspoken on the threat of free trade, but he didn't respond to our entreaties and we lost that fight too. This was becoming an all-too-familiar scenario and I was getting used to the battering.

As the effects of the free trade deal widened, there were many more fights to come. We worked through the Action Canada Network to build a national fight-back on the ground against the Goods and Services Tax. The GST was the hated consumer tax the Mulroney government introduced to replace the Manufacturers' Sales Tax (MST). We called it the "free-trade tax" because it didn't apply to exports and forced Canadian taxpayers to make up for the tariff revenue lost under free trade. It therefore shifted the burden of taxes from manufacturers to consumers in order to create a level playing field for business in North America, now that companies had the option to locate where they wanted.

We went before the Royal Commission on Electoral Reform, calling for strict limits on corporate donations to parties and candidates, and for full disclosure of corporate funding of political issues. We attacked the role played by the pro–free trade forces prior to the election and said the many millions of dollars they had spent during the campaign to promote their interests represented "a clear and present danger to Canadian social values and the democratic process." We warned that no one could become prime minister any more unless he or she was independently wealthy or backed by corporate sponsors who would inevitably come calling to collect their reward.

In 1990, I helped the truckers of southern Ontario to fight the invasion of their industry by giant American companies like J.B. Hunt. They were a diverse and independent band of individuals, and it was no easy task to discipline them to the job at hand. I attended the founding meeting of their group, Truckers for Canada, in Kingston, and had quite a time dealing with a plethora of political agendas. Several members wanted changes to the Young Offenders Act ("Lock them up and throw away the key!") and I had to point out that this issue was a little outside our mandate. There was a fair amount of hostility to immigrants from some (but by no means all) of the truckers and some pretty rough and racist language that I had to confront. We decided we needed some media coverage and I volunteered to help them do that with my press contacts. One said, "Go to the *Sun* first, because all the guys look at the Sunshine Girl first thing every morning and if you can get us an article just eye level from her tits, we'll reach everybody." I said, "I guess you don't know who I am." "No, ma'am," he smiled. I explained that I would be starting with the *Toronto Star*.

In the end, they put aside their competitive differences and rivalries to create a united front to fight the erosion of their rights through deregulation and free trade. That spring, "my mothertruckers," as I called them, brought downtown Ottawa to a standstill with a blockade that was backed up all the way to the 401. Leader Wayne Whitney told a huge gathering on Parliament Hill, "I'm a trucker, but I'm a Canadian first. I've paid a high price for being Canadian, and I have a promise for Brian Mulroney: you brought the fight to our doorstep. Now, we're bringing it to yours."

With Ian Morrison of the Friends of Canadian Broadcasting and Judy Darcy, president of the Canadian Union of Public Employees, we formed a coalition called *100 Days of Action*, to try to stop the drastic cuts to the CBC. Over one thousand employees and eleven regional production centres were to be cut according to the 1991 budget (which also announced cuts across the board to cultural institutions amounting to almost 40 per cent of their budget). We lobbied Tory MPs and were stunned at the antipathy toward the public broadcaster and the outright ignorance many of them displayed about Canadian culture. Some had no sense of the history the public broadcaster has played in shaping Canadian values and said the sooner Canadian culture was opened up to market forces the better.

Clearly, this assault was an ideological one to MPs like Mississauga's Don Blenkarn, who slapped me hard on the back in one television debate over the cuts and called me a "communistic socialist and a socialistic communist." I was reminded of the saying, "If you give money to the poor, you're a saint. If you ask why they're poor, you're a communist." This name-calling would become a familiar phenomenon in the years to come, and I would find it used especially when politicians or business leaders didn't want to (or couldn't) discuss the specifics of a particular piece of legislation or trade treaty I was criticizing.

The COC, meanwhile, was continuing to grow and become the grass-roots movement so badly needed to counter the sellout of our country. Under Mel's leadership, it had been mainly financed by individual members giving fairly large donations. Mel himself put money in, as did businessmen Bill Loewen of Comcheq Services and Wallace McCain of McCain Foods. Grateful as we were for this generous support, it was clear we could never reach critical mass (never mind stability) without a large membership actively and regularly supporting our work. We made the difficult decision to move to direct-mail funding and started the long, hard work of building a permanent membership. I took up where Mel had left off and crossed the country again and again over the next years speaking in public, building our chapters, meeting with local activists, and raising money to continue our work.

At our 1991 annual general meeting, we took a difficult decision on the question of the Canadian Constitution. Like many other national social organizations, we were very worried about the decentralizing aspects of the Meech Lake and Charlottetown accord. Our position was that decentralization would be the worst possible option for Canada, already one of the most decentralized federations on Earth, and that further devolution of federal powers would leave Canada without a centre, an international presence, or national cohesion.

We argued that, while the West wanted more *power* within Confederation, Quebec wanted more *autonomy* and that the "ten equal provinces" model would never satisfy both. A resolution was passed supporting a form of asymmetrical federalism and calling for a recognition that there are three founding nations — aboriginal, English, and French — in Canada, each with the right to protect its historical roots, sovereignty, and culture. Assembly of First Nations' Grand Chief Ovide Mercredi, with whom we were working closely, pleaded passionately at that meeting for us to take his quest for justice for his people to the Canadian public and used the powerful image of Canada as a ship, now flying three proud flags instead of just one.

I had long felt a keen sympathy for the aspirations of francophone Quebecers. I envied their passion for their own history and rich culture and wished that we in English Canada could discover some of the same passion for ourselves. I couldn't understand why someone waking up in Red Deer, Alberta, would care if someone waking up in Trois-Rivières, Quebec, had a different relation to Canada or identified first as a Quebecer. It wasn't an easy position to put before a group of Canadian nationalists, and I was proud of the step forward they took.

I took part in several of the five constitutional conferences chaired by Constitutional Affairs Minister Joe Clark and watched as the big-business community used them to promote decentralization, deregulation, and privatization. What started as a series of dry, tightly controlled gatherings of the country's anointed, turned into a boisterous and disorderly outbreak of democracy, as citizens' advocacy groups, coordinated under the Action Canada Network, turned back the corporate agenda so openly at work and demanded that a social agenda be placed on the table. In every session, we had our people lined up at the microphones to counter the smooth arguments being put forward by the many representatives of the Business Council on National Issues, and we refused to accept the preprogrammed "consensus" that the government workshop facilitator had been trained to seek.

Michele Landsberg, in her *Toronto Star* column, noted what she called a "sea-change, a well-spring of new energy" at these conferences, and said that her husband, Stephen Lewis, noted: "It's the women. They're turning it around." Landsberg praised Ontario Law Reform Commission chair Rosalie Abella for the fact that there were an equal number of women participants at the conferences (Rosie called for recognition of "the two founding genders"); Shelagh Day and Judy Rebick of the National Action Committee on the Status of Women for their arguments for asymmetry and an elected and equitable Senate; Rosemarie Kuptana of the Inuit Tapirisat for bringing bitter antagonists Joe Clark and Ovide Mercredi together; and me for "swaying the Montreal conference toward the social charter."

In 1991, John Trent, then head of Political Science at the University of Ottawa, invited me to be a scholar-in-residence to graduate students in his department for a term. I accepted with gratitude. I was often asked to speak to university students and faculty and had been a visiting women's scholar at Queen's University in Kingston a few years back. But that was only for a week, and I welcomed the opportunity to establish a more in-depth relationship with a small group of students. That year was a very happy one for me. The students were trying to find their way, not just in a tough job market, but ethically and politically in a world that was presenting fewer and fewer ideological choices to them. I wished I had had a similar opportunity to explore these kinds of ideas when I attended university.

Throughout all these battles, the Action Canada Network and the COC were gearing up to fight the next step in economic globalization: the North American Free Trade Agreement. Although Ronald Reagan had been honest in his desire to extend free trade "from the Yukon to the Yucatan," and George Bush was now prepared to extend such a deal to the hemisphere "from the Arctic Circle to Tierra del Fuego," Brian Mulroney and the Tories were still denying their interest in it as late as 1989, at the very time their bureaucrats were quietly laying NAFTA's groundwork.

When Brian Mulroney went to Mexico in March 1990, with representatives of the BCNI, he admitted for the first time that he wouldn't be "scandalized" by the prospect of extending the deal to Mexico. (On that trip, he told the Mexicans that 200,000 jobs had been created in Canada in the year since his government signed the FTA. I infuriated the Mulroney Cabinet by writing to President Carlos Salinas de Gortari and quoting to him the latest figures from the Canadian Labour Congress that showed a net job loss of 100,000 in that year. My letter was widely reported in the press here and in Mexico, but I never did receive a reply from Salinas. I did it, as I explained to the Canadian Press "because Mulroney is spreading more blarney.")

Two weeks later, the *Wall Street Journal* reported that the Mexican and U.S. governments were going to enter formal talks. On September 25, Trade Minister John Crosbie announced that Canada would seek full participation in the process.

The Coalition for Trade Expansion regrouped, and they and the political leaders of the three countries launched the "Enterprise for the Americas" agenda. Suddenly, the American and Canadian media were full of the wonders of the Mexican economy and Salinas, its saviour, a man who has since been discredited for his total mismanagement of Mexico's economy and has had to flee his country. The fact that the standard of living for most Mexicans had been dramatically dropping in the last decade while a small business and political elite was becoming more and more wealthy was somehow overlooked in the North American press.

The *Globe and Mail*'s Terence Corcoran, (Allan Fotheringham says Corcoran won't be happy until children are back working in the mines) had it right, even if he was being facetious: "Time for the nationalists to wheel out Maude Barlow, fire up Mel Hurtig, and stoke Bob White's engines. If they don't move fast, the free traders will have expanded the Canada–U.S. Free Trade Agreement into a continental agreement with Mexico."

By this time, the Action Canada Network had become a force to be reckoned with, arguably the most powerful coalition of labour and social groups in the country's history. Tony Clarke must be given much credit for this development. Trained at the University of Chicago where he received his doctorate in social ethics, Tony spent twenty-one years running the social justice office for the Canadian Conference of Catholic Bishops, where he became, with others like bishops Remi De Roo and Adolphe Proulx, the progressive and contentious conscience of the church.

Deeply committed to citizen politics, Tony had been instrumental in building various coalitions around social and economic justice issues over the years, and had played a pivotal role in both the Mackenzie Valley Pipeline hearings and in the blistering attack the Canadian Conference of Catholic Bishops had launched against the Trudeau government in 1983 for the crisis of unemployment. Tony's political advocacy is inseparable from his spiritual beliefs. As he says in his moving book *Behind the Mitre*, "The ancient prophets understood that life itself is a spiritual question. They knew that the injustices that divided humanity — poverty, hunger, homelessness, exploitation, slavery, and oppression — were all signs of the broken covenant between God and the people. For the prophets, we can come to know God more deeply by actively defending the rights of the poor, the marginalized, and the oppressed in our daily lives."

This belief led him deeper into the fight against free trade and economic globalization, systems that, by their very nature, are forced to sort winners from losers and abandon the latter to their fate. Tony and I became partners in our fight to stop NAFTA and led a noisy, spirited opposition that took us from the halls of Parliament to the slums, prisons, and low-wage factories of Mexico's infamous free trade zones along the Mexico–U.S border called *maquiladoras*.

I had numerous trips to Mexico, but two stand out in my memory. In October 1990, a delegation from the Action Canada Network held the first formal meeting with our counterparts in Mexico to share information and plan a joint strategy to fight NAFTA. Our *encuentro* (Spanish for "gathering") was the beginning of a process in which, every time governments gather to advance their free trade/free market agendas, a "Peoples' Summit" is held close by to spotlight the issues — poverty,

My mother's parents, Flora and Jack Wilkie, on their wedding day in Scotland in 1915. They emigrated to Canada when my mother was five years old.

My father's parents, Maude and "Big Bill" McGrath, in Pointe du Chêne, New Brunswick, 1953. Watching my mother look after her parents for almost 20 years made me understand that growing old and ill is a vital part of life.

My perfect 1950s family: Mom, Pat, me, Dad, and Christie in Digby, Nova Scotia, 1951. My family has been one of my greatest sources of inspiration and support.

First day out of bed after a year of near-death illness. My
teddy bear was my constant companion.
Digby, Nova Scotia, 1950.

Fall in the Glebe. This bike was my older sister's and I passed it
on to my younger one. Ottawa, 1956.

Me and baby Charly "raising each other," Toronto, 1968.

Heartstoppingly beautiful. My sons, Charly and Billy, in the Gatineau Hills, 1974.

The first woman to teach at the Canadian Police College. The photograph suggests what I was up against but it was a rewarding experience in the end. Spring, 1978.

"Women For Justice" takes on the whole penitentiary service—and wins! My sister Christie is right behind me to my left. 1980.

The women of Canada say no to pornography on pay T.V. *Playboy* protest, Parliament Hill, January 1983.

My boys meet my boss, Pierre Trudeau, 1983. He wows them.

Social Justice Adviser
to Opposition Leader
John Turner, 1986.

Parliament Hill, January 1, 1988. Lament for a nation — the day the Canada–U.S. Free Trade Agreement becomes law.

Terry Mosher (known as Aislin) catches my feeling for the Mulroney Tories.

CANAPRESS PHOTO SERVICE / FRED CHARTRAND

Railway Committee Room, House of Commons, December 7, 1992. We take over the NAFTA signing ceremony and hold up the American flag behind Mulroney. This photo is flashed around the world.

Mel Hurtig announcing the formation of the National Party at the COC Annual General Meeting, fall 1992. I am not amused.

In Baghdad, Iraq, meeting with senior officials of Saddam Hussein's regime. On my left is my dear friend Flora Abdrakhmanova and on my right our leader, Margarita Papandreou. I got home the day before the Gulf War broke out. January 1991.

Photographer Peter Sibbald captures the terrible lives of Mexico's *maquiladora* children.

With Bob White and Jesse Jackson at the Peace Bridge,
Niagara Falls, 1993.

One of the many NAFTA rallies, this one at the Ford glass plant in
Niagara Falls, 1993.

Fall 1997 was a non-stop round of protests. After speaking to a huge teachers' rally at Queen's Park, I wished OSSTF President Earl Manners good luck with his fights against the Harris cuts to education.

An enormous protest parade at APEC in Vancouver had come to a halt at the police blockade. We gave our speeches in spite of unprecedented security.

With Tony Clarke at the first annual teach-in on global corporate rule. Two thousand enthusiastic supporters packed Convocation Hall at the University of Toronto. November 1997.

Launching the COC pensions campaign in Ottawa in 1996. Over a million petitions went to parliament.

Conrad Black comes calling.

Cartoonists have been more supportive of me than columnists.

Friends for life. Helen Porter, Sheila Purdy, and I on the Pennine Way, England, June, 1989.

Andrew and Pasha, Goose Rocks Beach, Maine, 1997.

human rights, labour conditions, and the environment — our elected representatives refuse to deal with in their meetings. From the G-7, to APEC, to the World Trade Organization, wherever governments and their corporate advisers gather to plan the next stage of globalization, the emerging global citizens' movement is a heartbeat away and growing.

One of the rewards of my work is the quality of immediate friendship I am able to form with people who might otherwise be total strangers, but whose value systems and world view are totally compatible with mine. The Canadian delegation met the Mexicans in the modest headquarters of the FAT (*Frente Auténtico del Trabajo*, "Authentic Workers' Front"), the independent union in Mexico (the main union is government-controlled and does the bidding of the ruling party, the PRI, the Party of Institutional Revolution, which has governed Mexico for sixty-five years), and over the week, formed bonds that would last a lifetime. One was with economist Carlos Herédia, now a member of Congress working closely with Mexico City mayor Cuauhtemoc Cárdenas, who, when he was opposition leader, had his 1988 election victory fraudulently taken from him by Salinas and his paid thugs. In 1993, I brought Carlos to Canada to "testify" for me against NAFTA when CBC's *The National* put the deal "on trial" and I was defence for the prosecution. Another person we met in Mexico was Berthe Luhan, a vibrant and courageous labour leader, who would go on to become the first woman to lead the Mexican coalition.

Between our intensive meetings, the Mexicans showed us the reality of their lives. One-quarter of Mexicans, including most of Mexico City's indigenous people, live on the streets. If no one gives them money for food, they don't eat. Wages in Mexico dropped by 60 per cent since the country was first forced to undergo "structural adjustment" by the International Monetary Fund in the early 1980s. During those same years, Mexico developed twenty-four billionaires. No statistics, no matter how startling, however, can express the horror of seeing dead-eyed street children permanently stoned from sniffing glue, fighting one another for a scrap of food, holding terrified pigeons to kill later if nothing better presents itself, alongside the newly wealthy consumer class lined up at fancy night clubs and driving hot American cars.

We were taken to Tijuana for an intensive tour of the free trade zones — low-wage, industrial ghettoes used by transnational corporations to assemble components for cars, appliances, computers, and other goods for export. The factories were full of young women, mostly teenagers, who were worked so hard they usually only lasted a few years. We stood beside one fifteen-year-old who was handling DDT — long banned in North America — without a face mask. Another was making batteries; the acid produced by the process poured into an open bucket whose poisonous stench gave us headaches within moments. Human rights workers told us the women were sexually harassed regularly and raped by North American company executives who expect a "good time" when they come to inspect their operations in the area. In many factories, they had to show monthly proof of menstruation, or be fired — a humiliating experience.

Journalist Charles Bowden of *Harper's* magazine has recently published a photo-essay of another *maquila* town, Juarez, which depicts in stunning images the gruesome reality for the young women who work in the factories there. Adriana Avila Gress was a sixteen-year-old who worked in a plastics factory six days a week for five dollars a day. Each morning, she rose at 3:30 a.m., ate a cold tortilla, walked into the darkness with her few possessions — a pan, a plate, knife, fork, spoon, and cooking oil — and then buried them secretly in a hole (for otherwise, they were sure to be stolen) and then walked two miles to work. Every evening, she made the long trek back in the dark to her cardboard shack where she lived with her family of seven. One night, like 520 other inhabitants of Juarez in 1997 alone, most of them young women, Adriana didn't come home. She was found in the desert — raped, tortured, and murdered; Bowden's photo shows her now-mummified face contorted by the scream she had on her lips at the moment of death. Her murder was not reported in any press and no one was ever charged for the crime.

We were taken behind one industrial park where we saw bulldozers ploughing raw industrial waste into a toxic cesspool where it then was diverted into the local water supply. (This happens all over northern Mexico. Later that year, Stephan Chemical of Chicago was filmed by the AFL/CIO discharging the toxic poison xylene into the canals of Matamoros at 53,000 times the allowable limit in the United States.) We met families who lived along a stream that, only ten years before, was a pristine water supply for drinking, cooking, and bathing. Now it was an open sewer, filled with toxic sludge, and animal blood and carcasses from a nearby slaughterhouse, as well as raw sewage from the shantytown that had grown up to house the workers for the new factories. Now and then, local authorities came along to spray diesel fuel on the water to kill the mosquitoes that bred in abundance in such conditions.

Someone gave me a pencil and told me to dip it in the river: it came out stripped of its paint. Sitting at the edge of the water was a little boy, covered in open sores, drinking Pepsi out of a Pepsi-Cola baby bottle. This is a common sight in northern Mexico, where there is no clean water left and people can't afford juice or milk for their children. The cola wars are a reality in the Third World and are rotting the teeth of an entire generation. At least these children were alive. They took me to meet a woman who had become pregnant while working in a factory that makes pesticides; her baby was born with the not-uncommon deformity (for Mexico), anencephaly. Frog-like, with no brain, its internal organs encased in a liquid-filled sac on its back, the baby died within hours. The young mother buried it out back and reported to work the next morning.

At night, our hosts took us to the United States-Mexico border, where a terrible nightly ritual is played out. Thousands of young Mexicans try to enter the United States illegally to look for work. American authorities, outnumbered in men, but superior in technology, try to stop them.

The Tijuana strip is notorious. A six-lane highway — a dangerous crossing in itself — divides the city from a desolate belt of dirt where the men start to gather at dusk. A steep cement drop leads to a slow-moving river of chemical sludge and raw sewage about two feet deep. On the other side, the cement wall inclines at a 90-degree angle, fenced in at the top by a huge barbed wire, electric fence, and flooded with light like a football stadium at night. On the other side of this barrier is the United States.

The drama is always the same. On the Mexican side, the men wait all day for nightfall, drinking beer or sniffing glue. On the U.S. side, the helicopters, police vans, and dogs rev up. The stench along the strip is unbearable: human and animal excrement, used condoms and needles, piles of garbage, and the smell from the river of sludge mingle with the scents of fried tacos and meat from the little stands and roving food vendors. Boys walk the line, selling plastic bags to protect shoes from the brief, but unavoidable, journey through the little river of poison.

Suddenly, we saw a small group of men rush the border, run down the cement valley, through the river of sludge, up the cement wall, and into the police defences. Some were caught and sent back. But a rush like this keeps a lot of American officers busy and sure enough, another rush of about two hundred men hit the valley half a kilometre away. This time, some got through. All night, this scene was repeated.

We were told that, now and then, when the United States wants a certain number of workers for the fields, the lights and sirens are turned off, the dogs are muzzled, and a large hole is opened in the fence. The men are peacefully counted through until the required number has been met, and then the lights go on, the helicopters fill the sky, the dogs are unmuzzled, and the whole game begins again.

Once on the American side, however, the drama doesn't stop. The chase continues and men are rounded up and sent back. California has a new law, recently passed, that forbids arrest of the illegal aliens while they are on the state highway. The men are so desperate that sometimes as they are being chased, they run out in front of cars, causing accidents. But, as long as they stay in the median on the highway, they are untouchable.

For miles, all the way up to San Diego and beyond, men sit, sleep, or walk in the middle of this road. Helicopters fly up and down the freeway, monitoring their movement, counting their numbers, waiting for night to fall. As soon as dusk comes, the men vanish like ghosts into the fields and towns, hunted by the police who catch some and miss others. Those caught are back in Mexico by morning, where they rest during the day to prepare for the nightly drama to begin again. Those not caught head for the huge farms in California where they will work as scabs, sleeping in the fields, ingesting the pesticides, and dreaming of bringing their families over one day.

For the whole week, I kept my emotions in check. I did say in my closing remarks to the gathering back in Mexico City that I was leaving a piece of my heart behind and this was true. But it wasn't until I got on the plane to return home that the full impact of what I had seen hit me. I was sitting with Tony who could see that I was devastated and was helping me to comprehend what it all meant. I had seen poverty before;

what so upset me about this trip was that I had glimpsed a future the world was pro-actively and consciously creating. We were weaving a future out of extreme inequality and violence in order to service the growing consumer demands of the world's elite, many of whom lived in my country. The children I saw on the streets of Mexico would never be counted in the measurements I knew our government officials and business economists would use to "prove" that free trade was working for Canada. The twisted, deformed infant victims of the toxic *maquiladora* factories I visited would never show up as a negative factor in Mexico's Gross Domestic Product. I wept most of the way back to Canada.

The other unforgettable trip to Mexico took place a year later. I was part of a small delegation invited by Bishop Samuel Ruiz to visit San Cristóbal de las Casas in Chiapas, the southern-most Mexican state bordering on Guatemala. The area is breathtaking; the ancient town itself located high up in the mountains. We were picked up and taken to our destination in an old Volkswagen bus and the five-hour journey took us over one mountain pass after another as we travelled ever higher. The driver pointed out one particularly magnificent gorge that has great meaning for the local people for it is where a whole tribe of Indians killed themselves *en masse* by jumping off the mountain into the rushing water below rather than submit to Spanish rule.

The Catholic Church has a long history of protecting the local peasants from the brutalities of the state. Over four and a half centuries ago, the founding bishop of the diocese, Bartholomew de las Casas, built his church complete with gigantic fortress-like wooden doors inside which he hid the local Mayan Indians from the early Spanish conquerors; the same doors today protect their descendants from the Mexican military who are waging their own massacre of the Mayans.

The dark good looks of our host, Father Pablo Roma, confirmed his Spanish ancestry. He told us he had become a priest to atone for the brutality of his predecessors and had chosen this church because of its large Mayan population. He and Bishop Ruiz were already in great danger. Another priest, Father Joseph, had been imprisoned for "stealing chickens," a trumped-up charge laid because he stood up for the locals against the constant police harassment. Tony Clarke and I were taken to visit Father Joseph in prison.

It was a small, dark, and primitive facility on the outskirts of nearby Tuxtla, with security men who seemed slipshod and careless, but still capable of random violence. The soldiers who milled about in the courtyard surrounded by the little prison cells laughed and smoked and strutted about with huge rifles cocked and slung over their shoulders. We whispered to each other that they looked like they were in a "shoot-to-kill" mode. They allowed me to visit the prisoner in his little dirt-floor cell, but arbitrarily decided to keep Tony under armed surveillance in the courtyard. Father Joseph was a small, balding, dapper man, with dancing eyes and a gentle smile. I liked him immediately and asked him how he was doing. "Better than the Mayans they picked up the same day," he said gravely, but then brightened up and asked Pablo for all the news from home. Our hour passed before I knew it and I was so moved by his courage and unfailing optimism in that terrible place, I forgot he was a priest and gave him a big kiss when we all said goodbye. Tony and Father Pablo laughed all afternoon about that one.

Everywhere there were signs of growing brutality. Local peasants were jailed for burning firewood for cooking, while large transnationals were being given free rein to clear-cut the forests. We met a farm labourer in jail who was being held without trial because he had yelled at the landowner for feeding his dogs prime beef while the peasant's children were literally starving to death. We heard stories of horrific torture and of disappearances. In a report published that year, *Torture With Impunity*, Amnesty International said that torture in Mexico by police and military is so common that everyone arrested, even children and pregnant women, are at risk. "Torture remains endemic in Mexico. Amnesty International believes the principal reason for this is the almost total impunity extended to law enforcement officers who routinely act beyond the law without fear of punishment."

The visit wasn't all relentlessly dark. For one thing, the Mexican people have a great sense of joy and live life with passion and intensity. They are generous and kind and adore their children. I saw more character in the faces of the peasant farmers, Mayan Indians, and factory workers I met in Chiapas than I ever see on the faces I pass walking down Toronto's Bay Street. And we did see one very wonderful experiment that gave us genuine hope.

128

Nestled in the shadow of a mountain in Chiapas, the Catholic Church has set up a wonderful alternative model of economic development. The day we visited, the music of Beethoven filled the air from a central loudspeaker. Here, there were young people — smiling and well-fed — learning the ancient crafts of leather-making; children — fat and squealing with joy — in an outdoor school; farmers tending organic crops; workers learning how to rebuild automobile engines; and women weaving exquisite shawls and skirts. The air was clear, the water was pure, the land was abundant, the joy palpable. This was nothing less than a miracle and served as a sharp contrast to the soulless *maquiladoras* that form the basis of Mexico's new economy. To this day, when I am confronted with the argument that the global economy with its winners and losers is inevitable and has no alternative, I close my eyes and think of that lovely hallowed place, that paradise in the midst of misery.

But it *was* the exception. Because this project was supported by the international Catholic Church community, the Mexican authorities didn't dare touch it. Conditions for most Mexicans were bad and getting worse. Bishop Ruiz took us aside and warned us that NAFTA would make matters worse again as the few rights given to indigenous small farmers in the Mexican constitution would be wiped out, and huge agri-business farms geared for exports and run by transnationals like Green Giant, Campbell's Soup, and Monsanto, would be given total control of the local economy. Already, he said, there was a huge military build-up on the Mexico–Guatemala border because Mexico had to prove to the United States that it could keep refugees from South America from coming north through its territory. But the military was also being used to enforce "stability" in the area and protect American (and Canadian) corporate interests. He begged us to go back to Canada and sound the alarm.

Upon our return, we spoke publicly about the conditions we saw in Mexico and the Canadian corporations such as Northern Telecom, Mitel, and Magna that were taking advantage of them. I was shocked at our opponents' arguments. Michael Hart, then a senior bureaucrat with External Affairs, now a professor at Carleton University, said that the reason Mexican labour is paid less is because it is often "undisciplined and unproductive," so it takes twice as long to make some products. Added Steve Van Houten of the Automotive Parts Manufacturers

Association, "Their absentee rates are very high, their skill levels are very low. Sure wages are two dollars an hour, but you need five times as many people." Jim Moore of the Canadian Exporters' Association dismissed our concerns and said that discussions of "political" matters such as human rights violations had "no place" in a trade deal. I was beginning to understand that there was such a thing as economic racism.

This isn't to say that there was no support in the media. Quite a few individual columnists and reporters took our concerns seriously, and some independent newspapers like the *Toronto Star* even took an editorial position favourable to us. But the media and political establishment in Canada were closing ranks and joining the BCNI in covering up or glossing over the human fall-out from the first free trade agreement. Now, it was clear, we were going to witness an escalation of this coverup as NAFTA extended the free trade model throughout the continent.

Still emotionally raw from these trips, I was pretty upset to find how few people really cared what was going on in Mexico, especially since I knew it would one day have a direct impact on Canada. Not only would Mexico and the other countries of Latin America become a cheap labour pool for Canadian companies, but, more important, corporations operating in North America would use the threat of Mexico to force their workers to accept what they were already calling a "continental work week": competitive wages and hours. As well, we were predicting (correctly, it turned out) that corporations in all three countries would use NAFTA to strike down higher environmental standards wherever they existed. Mexico's practice of ignoring its own environmental laws to attract business would spread north; no reciprocal influence would encourage Mexico to clean up its act to match higher American and Canadian regulations.

Opposition to NAFTA was growing in labour, environmental, and social groups across the continent. A group called Common Frontiers brought Canadians, Mexicans, and Americans together to share common concerns, research, and strategy. A remarkable cast of Canadian activists and academics like Ken Traynor, Marjorie Griffin Cohen, John Dillon, Jim Turk, Monique Simard, Laurell Ritchie, and Joe Gunn worked tirelessly to forge a lasting continental citizens' coalition.

Our American counterparts included the writer and scholar John Cavanagh of the Institute for Policy Studies; feisty "trade warrior" Lori Wallach of Ralph Nader's Public Citizen and her team; Pharis Harvey and Thea Lee with the International Labor Rights Fund; and labour leaders like Ron Blackwell of the AFL/CIO. These and other wonderful Americans were to become good friends and allies and compelled me to confront any comfortable stereotypes I had nurtured that the United States was a monolithic culture uninterested in what happened beyond its borders.

As the NAFTA negotiations were being carried on in secret, we had to work together and share what little information we had. At the end of each day's briefings, the negotiators of the three countries would hold a "press briefing" in which they would, to the growing anger and frustration of journalists, give away nothing. Wherever the negotiators went, our three-country opposition was present. In Zacatecas, Mexico, local goons had ripped out the chairs in the hall where several hundred activists were to meet. Tony led the group to confront the negotiators at their posh hotel across town and forced the Mexican government to agree to a series of meetings with the Mexican anti-NAFTA coalition.

In a secluded retreat outside of Washington, United States Deputy Trade Negotiator Julius Katz was sent out to meet with us by the chief negotiator, Carla Hills. He was so angry that he hissed at us and threw a ball of paper right at our heads. In Montreal, we had a room full of textile workers who had lost their jobs under the FTA interrupt the negotiators' press conference with demands about the future of jobs under NAFTA. The press loved having us there, for we always gave them a good story, which meant their editors could move their reports from the business sections of their papers to the more political front sections.

We followed the negotiators to the infamous Watergate Hotel in Washington in the blistering dog days of August 1992, where they were working around the clock to put the deal to bed. Corporate North America was monitoring the process very closely. Stretch limos would come and go all day and late into the evening, bringing the cream of the business community for private briefings with senior government officials. Activists like us couldn't get anywhere near the delegates. One day, totally frustrated after being denied access to even low-level officials, Tony and I had a lovely lunch in the hotel's elegant dining room, and charged it, wine and all, to Trade Minister Michael Wilson's room.

That fall, the Senate finally held hearings on NAFTA, and Michael Wilson was the first witness to be called before the committee. Wilson was a former Bay Street financier and free-market ideologue (he frequently attended meetings of the ultra-right-wing World Anti-Communist League) who had served as trade minister in the short-lived Joe Clark government. A dry speaker, dour and plodding as an administrator, he hated to be publicly embarrassed and, if he had a sense of humour, I never saw it. At the hearing, we filled the place with students all wearing jackets or sweaters over T-shirts that read:

> Not
> Another
> F
> Trade
> Agreement

Just as Wilson was about to start his testimony, the students surrounded him, took off their outer garments, and displayed their T-shirts for all the TV cameras. Wilson turned white, then deep purple. This was the image that the press beamed all over the continent that night. (John Fieldhouse, a senior External Affairs communications officer who was with Wilson that day, appreciates a good media strategy. He said the shirts were terrific and asked me, in a whisper and when his boss wasn't looking, if we could send him one.)

In October, to aid President Bush's faltering re-election campaign, Bush, Mulroney, and Salinas held a trumped up "NAFTA signing ceremony" in San Antonio, Texas, which had no legal or trade significance (as the "initialling" of the deal had already happened two months earlier at the end of the Watergate talks) and was done simply to give the American president some badly needed press for his trade deal. The security was awesome: the compound where the signing took place looked like a war zone, surrounded as it was by thousands of fully armed police and army personnel. Michael Wilson, Industry Minister Gilles

Loiselle, and the Canadian ambassador to the United States, Stanley Hartt, held a briefing for the Canadian media.

For the reporters, this briefing was more useless than most. Negotiations were over and there was absolutely nothing of substance to report. Right after the politicians stepped down from the podium, Tony and I took their place and, using the government's technology, translation services, and against its backdrop of the Canadian flag, accused Mulroney of interfering in the American election and wasting taxpayers' money to rescue his good friend George Bush's campaign with a media circus. Our charges dominated the reports of the event back home. Michael Wilson was not happy.

We were clearly getting under the Mulroney government's skin. That fall, *Maclean's* published a transcript it had obtained of a telephone conference call involving more than a dozen senior Tory aides, including James Ramsey, Wilson's chief of staff; Marjory LeBreton, deputy chief of staff in the PMO; and Greg Ebel, chief of staff to Finance Minister Don Mazankowski, during which they planned a costly and extensive campaign to discredit us.

In the call, the advisers admitted trouble in the polls on NAFTA and expressed frustration at the failure of many Tory MPs to become active in selling the deal. They called NAFTA a "sleeping tiger" that could threaten the party's chances for re-election and expressed astonishing contempt for their enemies on the "looney left." Ramsey particularly singled out Bob White and myself for scorn, calling us "that old left-wing, crypto-communist, anti-free trade NDP-Liberal con group." (We had this quote made into a button — one of my favourites.) He sounded the call for battle. "There's no way to do it but to get out and grind it out with them toe by toe, riding by riding, paper by paper, outlet by outlet . . . we'll give them a real barroom brawl."

It came as no surprise to me to hear that the group targeted their big-business friends for help. They had already sent out "information packages" to 27,000 business associations and 1,000 CEOs across the country, said Ramsey, and been in touch with the BCNI, the Chamber of Commerce, the Canadian Bankers Association, and the Canadian Exporters' Association. General Motors had agreed to write all their employees to encourage them to support the deal. They were reminding their business friends that it was payback time. As Brian Mulroney was fond of saying, "Ya dance with the guy that brung ya." We didn't know whether to laugh or cry. This was such a pathetic exercise from people who were supposed to be serving the public; yet we knew it meant war and we got ready for the next battle.

It came in the beautiful Railway Committee Room of the House of Commons on December 17, 1992, when the three countries held a simultaneous trinational "signing" of NAFTA. The entire federal Cabinet, the NAFTA negotiators, ambassadors to Canada from all over the world, the top CEOs from Canada's largest banks and corporations (including the BCNI's Tom d'Aquino), and the national and international press were all in attendance. Because it had not passed through the legislatures of any of the countries, this signing, like the one in Texas, was largely for show and was broadcast worldwide from the three capitals by the satellite networks of CNN and the BBC.

As the ceremony got underway, six of us slipped past the security guards and took up seats in strategic locations around the room. As Brian Mulroney picked up his pen to sign the document, Tony Clarke rose from his seat and said, "Prime minister, with all due respect, sir, you have lied to the Canadian people about free trade!" Mulroney looked at Tony over his bifocals and snorted, "Too late, I've already signed it" to thunderous applause from the crowd. Then Jean-Claude Parrot from the Canadian Labour Congress jumped to his feet and begged the gathered assembly to address the plight of the unemployed, followed by Judy Darcy from the Canadian Union of Public Employees who spoke with great clarity about NAFTA's threat to public health care.

It was my turn. My heart was pounding. I closed my eyes and asked myself what on Earth I was doing there. As if I had been physically transported, I was standing on the banks of that river in Tijuana looking into the faces of the children and my heart stopped pounding. I knew exactly why I had to stand and take my turn. "Prime minister," I said, as I was being led out by House of Commons security, "You promised to protect basic democracy and the right of all peoples to determine their own lives. You have failed to keep your promise. Children are suffering."

Mulroney lashed out at us from the podium: "If you would stay to listen," he thundered (which, surrounded by guards showing us firmly out the door, was clearly impossible), "I would convince you free trade has been the best thing ever for Canada." To Mulroney's fury, Steve Shelhorn of Greenpeace was still in the room and stayed for Mulroney's remarks. "I stayed. I listened. I'm not convinced. NAFTA will hurt our environment," he said as he was whisked out of the room.

The carefully staged event was an international embarrassment. Not only was our protest covered around the world, but, unknown to Mulroney, Mike McBane from the Action Canada Network walked up behind him, Michael Wilson, and chief NAFTA negotiator John Weekes as they were shaking hands for the cameras, and covered the Canadian and Mexican flags with the American flag. The Stars and Stripes served as a backdrop for all the photos taken of the ceremony that day.

The Tories were livid. Transport Minister Doug Lewis cursed Tony on the Sparks Street Mall hours after and challenged him "to fight me . . . come on, fight me, here or in the next election." I was invited to "discuss" the event with Michael Wilson on *Canada AM* the next morning. When I got on the elevator at 6:45 a.m., who was there but a furious Michael Wilson and a bleary-eyed, very unhappy John Fieldhouse! The devil in me, never far from the surface, awoke. "Good morning," I said. Wilson growled. I looked at Fieldhouse and smiled sweetly. "Oh, John. I think I forgot to send you the NAFTA T-shirt you asked for. What size did you say you wear?" "Uh, large," he mumbled, looking down at the floor. Wilson glared at him as he stomped off the elevator as if to say, "For your big fat head."

I wasn't sure how my family was going to take all this NAFTA madness, but I need not have worried. Andrew thought it was great. My very proper mother said, "Oh good for you, being escorted out of the House of Commons for standing up to *that man*. All my friends have called to tell you they're so proud of you." It was becoming increasingly clear to many Canadians that politics as usual weren't going to address the growing injustices in our society. Citizen dissent has a proud tradition in Canadian history and has formed the backdrop against which our most important social reforms have been created. For me, citizen politics was becoming the most effective vehicle to confront the growing power of big business in every sector of Canadian society. I couldn't imagine being witness as I had, to the growing poverty in Mexico and now in Canada, and standing idly by while it got worse. Our invasion of the NAFTA signing ceremony was our way of "speaking truth to power."

Tony, however, paid a great price. Within the Catholic Church, a fierce backlash was growing. Tony had become too political, his stands on the economy and social programs too public. The same forces at work in government and business were also to be found in the higher echelons of the church. Tony was fired from the Social Affairs Office of the Canadian Conference of Catholic Bishops after two decades of loyal service — the first casualty on our side of the NAFTA wars.

8

A WAR FOR WOMEN TOO

"I know. I do not approve. And I am not resigned."

Edna St. Vincent Millay

On the eve of the Gulf War, and in the midst of the NAFTA fight, I received an invitation to be the Canadian representative on an international women's peace mission to Iraq. Of course, I said yes!

The invitation came through the Voice of Women, the venerable peace group filled with such legends of the Canadian women's movement as Kay MacPherson and Nancy Pocock of Toronto, and Betty Peterson and Muriel Duckworth of Halifax. The peace mission was organized by Margarita Papandreou, the American ex-wife of the many times prime minister of Greece, Andreas Papandreou, who had been involved for many years in the international peace movement through her group, Women for Mutual Security. Margarita had been trying to secure a meeting of women from the West, the Soviet Union, and the Middle East to form a united opposition to the growing atmosphere of armed conflict between American President George Bush and Iraq's Saddam Hussein. Only when war seemed imminent did the Iraqi government suddenly allow her to bring her mission into the country.

As a result, I received my invitation on January 3, 1991 and was on a plane bound for Greece three days later. I had to go to the Iraqi Embassy for my visa and was followed back to my office by an RCMP officer who didn't do a very good job of keeping himself hidden. Just as I turned to go into my building, I introduced myself and explained the whole story. He politely thanked me and walked down the street whistling.

My shocked family pointed out that war was about to break out in the region. My son Charles, now a captain in the Black Watch, wanted to come with me as a bodyguard. But I felt that anything I could do, however small, to try to avert this war was worth the risk, and I believed that I was going to be safe. I was shocked, as were many Canadians, at the sloppy last-minute way in which Brian Mulroney committed us to the war. Only after our troops were dispatched to the area and before the United Nations had decided to use force at the request of George Bush did Mulroney deign to hold a debate in the House of Commons on the issue. I felt I had to take this opportunity that had been handed to me. And, truth be told, I have never been able to turn down a chance for adventure. I wouldn't be disappointed.

The first stop was Athens, where two women met my plane and handed me a letter of introduction from Margarita and a lovely pin: the dove of peace. Margarita had got the Papandreou ancestral home in her divorce settlement, and I spent the day there marvelling at the exquisite artwork, ancient Greek urns and sculptures, and the breathtaking gardens. Margarita is tall and slim, with fine, chiselled bones, and a wonderful smile. She is as gentle and generous as she is beautiful and I fell in love with her at once. (I had packed lightly as I always do with one small soft-covered bag, not knowing where or for how long I would have to carry it. Margarita, used to having staff carry her baggage for her, packed two huge, heavy, hard-framed suitcases, filled with her suits and silks and gifts for our hosts. I had a very sore back for most of the trip from carting at least one of these monsters from pillar to post.)

We were joined during the day by the two American delegates, Joan Drake and Kay Camp, and a delicate little person from the Soviet Union named Flora Abdrakhmanova. "Oh," I said, "my mother's name is Flora.

It's an old Scottish name." "Really," replied Flora. "I didn't know that. It's an old Tartar name too. I was named for my Tartar grandmother." Flora and I would become very dear friends on this trip. (Bianca Jagger, who is a Nicaraguan feminist activist (and the ex-wife of Mick), was to join us, but got caught in a series of missed plane connections and gave up at the last moment. Similarly, Geraldine Ferraro was supposed to join us, but couldn't break away from other commitments at such late notice. Too bad on both counts.)

That evening, we flew to Cairo, where we met with representatives of Egyptian women's groups and spent the night. At five in the morning, I was awakened in my little hostel by the haunting Muslim call to prayer from the minaret that takes place five times a day. Throughout my trip to this region, I was moved to tears by this practice and the beautiful music that accompanies it. Imagine taking time out of what one is doing five times a day to contemplate God or nature or your own mortality. Imagine the New York Stock Exchange stopping mid-trade five times a day to think about something other than making money.

Here we picked up our Egyptian delegate, Nawal El Saadawi, doctor, psychologist, prolific writer (whose work is published in dozens of languages), and feminist activist who has spent time in prison for speaking out against the terrible practice of female genital mutilation. Nawal is a woman larger than life, with enormous courage and energy. She has a great mane of white hair that she attempts to tame every once in a while by talking to it as if it were an unruly child and then tying it violently in a big knot on top of her head. Nawal immediately took charge of our little party, and off we went to Amman, where we met up with our Jordanian delegate, a quiet doctor named Fathieh Saudi.

We spent the entire day in the airport, meeting with representatives of Jordanian women's groups and arguing with authorities about our visas. Finally, about ten o'clock at night, we boarded a plane bound for Baghdad (Amman was the only airport left that allowed planes to fly in and out of Iraq). The plane was filled with male delegates going to a high-level Islamic summit and they were very colourful: the men came from Islamic countries around the world, and were dressed in the various styles of their own countries. It was clear that we were the only women on the plane. I had dressed very conservatively in the longest skirts I owned and high-necked shirts and sweaters. Nevertheless, I boarded that plane with apprehension.

The plane appeared to be totally full with the exception of seven VIP seats at the front, which Nawal assumed were for us. No sooner were we seated than the party for whom the seats were really reserved boarded the plane. A strikingly handsome ebony-skinned prince from one of the Islamic African countries (I'm not sure which one; my lack of Arabic caused me to miss details), very tall and dressed in pale blue flowing robes, and his entourage emerged at the front of the aisle. Immediately, the (male) flight attendant asked us, in Arabic of course, to give up the seats and move to our own farther back in the plane. Flora and I jumped up right away; Nawal ordered us to sit. Then an unholy row broke out. Everyone was shouting. The pilot came out and begged us to move. The passengers got involved, about half, to my surprise, taking our side. Nawal said, "These are very brave women, who have come from all over the world to try to stop the war. We're not moving."

I whispered, "Nawal, I might die in Iraq, I expected that. But I don't want to die here." "Shut up," she said to me. "We were here first and we're staying." I was more frightened of Nawal than anyone on the plane and I stayed put. The prince, meanwhile, set his gaze at the back of the plane and never gave one indication that he saw or heard any of the fuss. Finally, his people decided enough was enough, and they took our seats at the back of the plane. We flew to Iraq in first class.

We were supposed to go to Baghdad, the capital, but it was badly fogged in and we were rerouted to Al Basrah, in the southern-most tip of Iraq on the border with Kuwait, and smack in the middle of the war zone. We had to leave all our bags on the plane and were taken by van to the Al Basrah Sheraton, where we stayed the night. The place was filled with military personnel, fully armed with machine guns. I shared a room with Flora and about 3 a.m., a knock came at the door. "Maude," said a terrified Flora, "I can't answer the door. I'm naked!" (Our nightclothes were in our suitcases on the plane.) "I'm naked too!" I said, and, wrapping my coat around me, I opened the door. It was a kind porter bringing us toothpaste — the brand name was Signal 2 — and badly made Iraqi toothbrushes, both of which I still have.

The next morning, the fog cleared and we flew to Baghdad. There we were picked up by the president's own bodyguard and escorted to the Al Rashid Hotel where we would spend the next four days — part guests part prisoners, of the Iraqi government. Each of us had our own car (Mercedes Benz), our own driver, and our own "minder," a person who was designated to know where you were at all times. My minder was a sweet young woman named Mina, whom, of course, I got to calling "Mina my minder." When we drove very fast in formation like a snake winding through the streets of Baghdad, it was clear that everyone knew what the president's fleet looked like and they quickly moved over to the side to let us pass, as we would for fire engines or police cars in Canada.

The city of Baghdad is a bewildering mixture of the ancient, the modern, and the military. Elaborate palaces, ancient mosques, and colourful markets stand beside soulless concrete towers and offices that have been hastily erected. Huge bronze statues everywhere glorify war and its dead. The city sits in the heart of ancient Mesopotamia, on the fertile land where the legendary Tigris and Euphrates rivers meet. This was the place where humans began cultivating and irrigating land, where writing was invented, where the first governments and laws were developed. It is filled with ancient art and antiquities, but much of its irreplaceable heritage has been plundered by thieves or destroyed in war. Standing on a hill overlooking the city one day, I felt that I was in the cradle of civilization.

Right next to my room was the American press war room, where CNN's "Scud Stud" Arthur Kent would bring minute-to-minute breaking news of the war to the world. On a table in their suite, which was always open, was a collection of the biggest bottles I had ever seen of scotch, rum, whisky, vodka, gin, and bourbon (with their caps off for immediate access). Every day, our delegation would go to meetings. Every evening, we would eat dinner (from rapidly diminishing rations) in the old hotel dining room that looked like something out of *Casablanca,* with its stately old furniture and cosmopolitan (but only male) guests dressed in everything from $2,000 Armani suits to flowing robes and head-dresses. The first people we would see in the morning were our minders who would be waiting for us with big smiles as the elevator opened, and in the evenings, our minders would escort us to the elevator before we retired.

The most moving meetings we had were with the women of the General Federation of Iraqi Women, a government-sanctioned organization, but one that had worked for change for women all the same. Headed by a compassionate and articulate leader, Manal Younis, they had just come out of the nine-year Iran-Iraq war and all had lost fathers, husbands, brothers, or sons. The women, like Iraqis everywhere, were terrified to speak openly in any way that didn't toe the party line. Iraqis are convinced that every word they utter is known to the government, and who am I to argue with this? In hotel rooms, people would talk only with the television blaring. In the streets, they would point to the street lights, as if to say, "Watch it, they're bugged." As a consequence, Iraqis watch their every word and repeat the official position on foreign policy. The whole country had their "side" of the conflict down to a science. I heard the same story of Iraqi victimization everywhere I went. It is little wonder, as the newspapers and the radio and television stations are government-controlled.

Iraq is a brutal dictatorship. Giant portraits of Saddam Hussein, a modern-day Caligula, are everywhere, and every home and shop has at least one, and usually several, smaller photos of him. This is a man who took power of the Ba'ath Party by hand-picking supporters of his rival at a leadership meeting for "martyrdom." (They were taken out and shot.) When the frenzied crowd suddenly backed him *en masse*, Saddam put his arm around his rival, and a handkerchief to his eyes. Crying, he told him it made him so sad to ask, but the only way he could be sure of his rival's loyalty was if he would step outside and finish killing his own supporters.

This is the man who orphaned children, then raised them to be his personal bodyguards and to do his violent bidding, including murder and unspeakable torture. This is the man who raised a son so violent, that, as a child, the boy went "fishing" by dumping live grenades into the water and scooping up the dead fish as they came to the surface. More recently, Saddam Hussein had two of his own sons-in-law and a number of his grandchildren murdered after promising them amnesty, when they fled the madman's reach with his terrified daughters. Yet, not one person I met in the entire time I was in Iraq said anything but that he was a saint, a wonderful husband (he'd abandoned his wife years before), and their great leader.

I said to Azza, one woman with whom I felt I had developed a bond, "Can I ask you a question, honestly?" "Absolutely!" she declared. "Ask me anything. I will tell you the truth." "Did Saddam order the gas bombing of the Kurds?" I asked. "I have seen terrible photos of dead children." Azza turned deadly pale, looked around as if she had seen a ghost, blurted out that this was a pernicious lie, and fled the room. We didn't speak of this again.

But bit by bit, I came to be friends with Azza and the others and I saw the women inside the armour. I also came to have a great fondness for the Iraqi people, surely among the most generous people I have ever met. They would have given me anything — the best food, the best room in their homes for the asking. I was appalled then as I am now by the Western powers' arming of Saddam and for ignoring his reign of terror for as many years as it suited them and then for punishing these people who had suffered so much when they decided he was no longer of use to them. While I hated Hussein, I found it hard to stomach that Canada was backing the abusive, dictatorial royal family of Kuwait who had helped impoverish the area and kept women, who had absolutely no rights, veiled by law, against a country where, whatever else was wrong, the women could vote, dress as they chose, and hold jobs. And where had Canada been when Hussein bombed the Kurds?

We begged our minders to take us to see the fabled monument to the dead of the Iran-Iraq war, off-limits to visitors and local citizens alike. They agreed. It consisted of two giant bronze statues on either end of a long tree-lined boulevard, and depicted Saddam's arms and hands from the elbows up holding crossed scimitars against the sky. At the base of the statues were a number of huge cornucopias, filled to overflowing. It was not until we got up close that we saw what they were filled with: the bloodied helmets of thousands of dead Iranians. Flora tried to take a picture of one cornucopia, but her driver grabbed the camera; her minder was visibly upset and frightened on the way back for allowing this breach of security to happen. We also visited a "peace camp" outside the city filled with a mixture of genuine peace activists from Europe, North America, and Australia, as well as every sort of bizarre misfit in the region, including some very scary mercenaries fighting with Saddam for money.

We had a number of high-level meetings with senior government officials, including Saadi Mahdi Salif, president of the National Council; Taha Yasim Ramadan, first deputy to the prime minister; Adel Abdel Karim, foreign affairs head of the National Council; and Latif Nusaif Jasim, minister of information.

Each, of course, gave the party line that Iraq was ready for war. But the mere fact that such senior officials would give this kind of time to a group of women on the eve of war told us they were looking for a way out. As Margarita said in an urgent letter to George Bush, "Reading between the lines, and sometimes from comments made more overtly, we understood that there is flexibility, and a willingness to consider other options along the lines of their proposed peace plan of August 12, 1990. We refer not to changes in the substance, but changes in the tone of their presentations. Clearly, they want to sit down and truly discuss the issues."

On Wednesday, January 9, a meeting that was described as the last chance for peace took place between Deputy Prime Minister Tariq Aziz and U.S. Secretary of State James Baker. Early radio reports from Jordan implied a *détente* and people were filled with hope. The Al Rashid had the feeling of a grand party. But soon, the truth of the complete breakdown of talks spread across the country, and a sea-change came over everything. The Canadian ambassador called and urged me to leave with them very early the next morning; they were not flying for fear of being stopped, but travelling across country by truck. The American Embassy was already deserted and the Australians were leaving the next day as well. I said the women had promised me safe passage and I would not leave until Friday. The ambassador asked me to keep the news of their departure quiet. Except for a *Toronto Star* journalist, I was the last Canadian to leave Iraq.

Thursday, we held a press conference with the Iraqi women, and begged both sides for one more attempt at peace. The room was packed with journalists. We spoke of our deep anxiety over the "notion that men and women may die to return to its throne the Al-Sabah royal family, a feudal, oil-rich oligarchy where male members treat women as play bunnies with no voting rights." We added, "In the name of justice and for the sake of humanity, we ask you to reject the rivers of blood that will flow in the Gulf region and find a political solution. This is the only solution in harmony with human intelligence and civilized behaviour." We were on the front page of the major Iraqi papers the next day, pictures and all, quoted as urging on the war against the "American running-dog imperialists."

The next morning, the women of the Iraqi delegation brought their daughters to see us off at the airport. I had lost my coat, a pretty pale-grey spring coat with a pastel-coloured scarf, probably left in one of our meetings of the last day. I didn't say a word, of course, as it was so unimportant in this situation. Sharp-eyed Flora noticed this at the airport and Azza got all bothered about it. "We'll find it and send it to you by mail. Or I'll give it to your embassy to send you." We looked at each other for a long time. I couldn't tell her that our embassy was gone. It didn't matter. She knew. We also both knew there would be no mail in or out of Iraq for a long, long time. Baghdad, in fact, would be bombed back into the nineteenth century. "Find the coat, Azza, and keep it as a gift."

We hugged and wept and said goodbye. I knew I could get on a plane and leave this terrible place. These women and their beautiful daughters, who looked just like my nieces, could not. During the war, when I would see the relentless bombing of Baghdad on television every night, I would have a recurring dream that my coat was keeping some little girl warm in one of those bomb shelters, and the pain would ease a little.

The plane we took to leave Iraq was taking the very same Islamic entourage we came in with back out of the country. They boarded us last (and under the tightest security I have ever seen, including female guards strip-searching us), and when we got on the plane, we understood why: our prince and his people were already seated in the VIP rows. As we passed, he momentarily lost his regal detachment and glanced up nervously at Nawal. "You may stay," she said to him magnanimously, "because it's your turn. It's called democracy. I'll be bringing it to this part of the world."

In Jordan, we held another press conference, saying that war could still be avoided and calling for a postponement of the January 15 deadline for Iraq to withdraw from Kuwait. I was quoted in the *Jordan Times* saying, "Only three days away from war, our message is that there are causes worth living, not dying for, and we still believe there is a way to avert this war. Our message to all the politicians and diplomats we met was the same, 'The bravest side in this is whoever blinks first.'" We said a sad goodbye here; the Americans were on their way back home, the others were going to Turkey where they would meet with officials there. I stayed in Jordan so that Fathieh and I could meet with officials there. If time allowed and the deadline was extended, we promised to meet in Washington and take our message there.

Fathieh and I and other representatives of her group spent Saturday in a whirl of meetings, including one with Hani Khair, secretary general of Jordan's House of Parliament, and another with Queen Noor's personal political adviser in her exquisite palace where we were served tea in gold cups by a man in full ceremonial dress, complete with a Madagascar sword in his belt. They were all desperate for a solution and begged me to take their message of peace back to "America." One said, "You're our last hope." Desperate indeed, I thought. On Sunday, I finally got a late plane to Cairo, where I was told that, yes, I had a ticket, but no boarding pass, and unfortunately for me, there was no opening to Europe or North America for at least ten days. "And don't try to bribe me," said the harried agent. "You Westerners always think we're for sale."

I had no Egyptian visa, so I had to stay at a hotel on the airport strip, called Caesar's Palace. The phones didn't work, there was no running water and no heat. This was the one time in the trip that I was truly frightened and felt very alone. I sat on the bed all night and, at the crack of dawn, returned to the airport. The same agent was just finishing his shift and I begged him to get me on a plane. He repeated the same message as the night before and I was ready to give up when I remembered that we had had a lot of press in the region and asked him if he knew about the women's peace mission of Margarita Papandreou. "Ah," he said, his face going soft, "Madame Papandreou is a saint. They were very brave women." I told him I was one of them and he laughed. So I pulled out my *Baghdad Observer* and showed him my picture with Margarita and the others.

Suddenly, I was a heroine. He called over his co-workers and they surrounded me with congratulations and asked me to please tell my country that they were terrified the war would spread to the whole region and to please try to stop it. I said I would love to but I couldn't do it sitting in the Cairo airport. In a wink, I had my boarding pass, and

I was on my way to New York and home, landing in Ottawa the day before the fighting began.

When I look back on that trip, I am filled with memories and questions. Could we have done something differently? Were we totally naïve to think we could have had an effect? There are no answers to questions like that, only more questions. I have learned in my life that you set yourself up for failure if you feel the only fights that matter are the ones you can win. I met wonderful women in Iraq who might one day help bring down the wall between our countries, and I helped Margarita Papandreou, in my small way, to build a truly international women's peace movement. It won't stop war in my lifetime, but it might lead to a very different future one day.

I gave a lot of speeches across the country upon my return and spoke about the pain of knowing real people living under those bombs and missiles. "The war we're watching on TV doesn't seem to have any people in it. I left people behind who are now my friends. They are in it." The Canadian media were very open to the human side of this story and covered my talks with fairness. I called for a deeper analysis of American history in the Gulf region, saying that the United States had no moral right to lead this war when it was their interests that helped destabilize the region in the first place.

I also castigated the Mulroney government for deepening our dependence on U.S. foreign policy with this war. Through both the free trade agreements and the growing integration of defence production between our two countries, we were creating an economic and political "Fortress North America," and were losing our autonomy to make our own foreign affairs decisions. I wasn't surprised that we didn't wait for the United Nation's decision about the use of force in the situation. We were dancing to George Bush's tune.

And what did the war accomplish? Kuwait is still run by a dictatorship that enforces rigid class and citizenship distinctions. Kuwaiti women are still arrested for speaking their minds. Saddam is more powerful than ever, the population still brutalized. After the war he stalked and killed many of his own people for aiding the American invasion. Meanwhile, many thousands of Iraqi children have died long, lingering deaths from starvation and preventable disease.

But the war was good for business. It was, as George Bush put it, "the first test of the new world order" and secured the dominance of American corporations over the world's two largest industries, oil and arms. Since the Gulf War, American arms sales to the Middle East have risen dramatically. "The peace dividend is replaced by a war dividend, the disarmament-development agenda eclipsed by resurgent militarism," said Douglas Roche, Canada's former ambassador for disarmament.

In no way do I want to diminish the human rights abuses Saddam Hussein has perpetrated and continues to commit in the region, but in the Middle East, everyone has blood on their hands, including Canada. Only reducing the glaring economic and racial discrepancies within the population and the region will bring peace to it one day.

One day, when the tyrant is dead, I hope to return to Iraq, surely one of the most beautiful places on Earth. Iraq will be free one day and its people will look to friends on the outside to help start the long process of rebuilding an ancient culture and society. It would be my honour to be counted among those friends. For Azza's daughters.

9

LIFE WITH LIBERTORIES

"I think the Liberals have crossed the great divide."

Tom d'Aquino
Business Council on National Issues

When Brian Mulroney resigned in February 1993, the country let out a collective sigh of relief. Many of us saw the end of nine years of Tory rule as a blessing. Canadians had come to dislike Brian Mulroney and to distrust his government, and a side-effect was that many people also became disillusioned with politics in general. But in the polite Canadian way, tributes poured in from all over the political spectrum. I was asked to go on the *Don Newman Show* on Newsworld and I didn't mince words. "It's not appropriate for us to start eulogizing this person. He's done terrible things to the country and it will take many years to undo them. He took every ribbon that bound us, north-south, east-west, and cut it. He said we're going to be part of a new highly competitive, win-or-die, dog-eat-dog North American system. We will be lucky if Canada survives in any form that we've known."

I was criticized by some journalists for the harshness of my reaction,

149

but I felt it was crucial to be honest about the destructive Tory legacy. The Liberals were starting to transmute in front of our eyes and a chill in my heart told me that the Mulroney agenda wasn't necessarily behind us. By now, it was pretty clear that the Liberals were going to win the next election and we started to turn our political attention to them. Mulroney's successor, Kim Campbell, briefly looked as if she might resurrect the flagging Tory fortunes; however, the party self-destructed before our eyes.

(I only met Kim Campbell once. In 1996, the BBC was doing a story on the countries of the "Empire," using former prime ministers to interview various players in their countries. Kim Campbell was hired to do the Canadian series and they told her they wanted an interview with me. Our office was all a-flutter, and the staff combed the walls to take down offensive posters like our 1993 election poster that showed a smiling Kim Campbell and Brian Mulroney with their arms around each other under a large headline of George Santayana's quote, "Those who cannot remember the past are condemned to repeat it." When she arrived, Kim was clearly unhappy to be there and acted very chippy and curt with the receptionist and me. But the election was by then long over, and, truthfully, I had always felt a little sorry for her and the treatment she received at the hands of the party, so I decided to be gracious and try to have a real conversation.

She is very bright; immediately upon starting the tape and asking me questions, she started to debate me. We got into a very serious and earnest discussion of free trade, economic globalization, social programs, and the role of women in politics. I could see Kim Campbell thaw before my eyes. She started to smile and nod her head and, a few times, said, "Well, I agree with you there." When she left the office, my open-mouthed staff were amazed at her cheery goodbyes and smiling face. A few weeks later on *Cross Country Checkup*, Kim Campbell surprised Rex Murphy when she praised me and said that my views needed to be given a voice.)

Since the 1988 election, we in the COC had worked closely with both the federal NDP and Liberal Parties to keep the heat up on the Mulroney Tories and had met regularly with Lloyd Axworthy, Herb Gray, and Sheila Copps. But there were many signs that the party was weakening its position on NAFTA and globalization, and we started to view Liberals less as allies and more as potential opponents.

The party had always been divided between "social" and "business" Liberals and a fierce internal battle had been waged between them in the last few years of opposition. Strongly fortified by the big-business lobby that had grown powerful in these years, and influenced more by the surging right-wing populism of the Reform Party than the waning left-wing populism of the NDP under leader Audrey McLaughlin, business Liberals were clearly in the ascendency.

Publicly, the Liberals continued to put forward a progressive platform on free trade, taxation, social programs, and foreign policy. But in the back rooms of the Liberal Party, the stage was being set for a radical shift to the right. The closer the Liberals got to power, the greater this shift became.

One of Chrétien's first acts as Liberal leader had been to bring a hand-picked gathering of "thinkers" together in 1991 to create policy direction for a floundering and divided party. The Aylmer Conference was the 1990s equivalent of Lester Pearson's famous 1960 Kingston Conference that laid the foundation for the social reforms of the next several decades. However, where the earlier gathering took the Liberal Party to the left, Chrétien's initiative moved it sharply to the right.

In a speech called "Nowhere to Hide: The Economic Implications of Globalization for Canada," banker Peter Nicholson, clearly the star of the event, set the tone for the convention and foretold the future direction of the party. "What seems beyond question is that the world has entered an era where the objectives of economic efficiency . . . will hold sway virtually everywhere." He called for a total reappraisal of the role of the nation-state, praised the "logic of global investment" and stated, "Today, there is no alternative and, like it or not, the world is in the thrall of global forces that cannot be defied by a relatively small, trade-dependent, and massively indebted country like Canada."

Nicholson laid out the blueprint for the party that Jean Chrétien, as prime minister, would follow to the letter: dramatic cuts to government spending; an overhaul of social programs to encourage the unemployed to "retrain and relocate to new opportunities"; the aggressive expansion of free trade; and the union of foreign as well as commercial policy with the private sector. (Nicholson was hired by Paul Martin when he became finance minister to implement the government's fiscal program and cure

151

for the deficit that would culminate in Martin's infamous budget of 1995, in which he cut social programs back to 1949 levels.)

In closing the conference, Chrétien gave an early warning of just whom he would serve as prime minister. He declared that left-right politics were defunct. Canada would have to adapt to the "inevitable reality" of the global economy, he said, and he gave no indication that he saw a role for government in helping citizens to deal with it. "Globalization is not right wing or left wing. It is just a fact of life," he said, ignoring the fact that there are many models of globalization and that governments can give shape and form to the process if they choose.

Jean Chrétien was the perfect candidate for a corporate community looking for someone to replace Mulroney. Chrétien had a reputation (largely undeserved) as a social reformer and played up his small-town beginnings, but he could be counted on to carry out the agenda of his big-business friends. (When he was finance minister in Trudeau's government, he recalled, "I never prepared a budget without seeking out the opinions of the Business Council on National Issues.) They helped him raise $2.5 million for his 1990 leadership bid — more than any other candidate. A self-made millionaire, he surrounded himself with business-oriented advisers with close ties to the corporate community.

His chief fundraiser was the wealthy and powerful Paul Desmarais of Power Corporation, a close friend and family member through the marriage of their children; John Rae, Power's vice-president (and brother of Bob Rae), was Chrétien's Quebec campaign manager. During his leadership bid, Chrétien attended several high-society fundraising events where invitees paid $1,000 each to rub shoulders with him. When confronted with criticism that this smacked of the same kind of patronage he had accused Mulroney of, Chrétien shrugged. "Millionaires vote." The business community, deeply unhappy about John Turner's position on trade, now put a full-court press on Chrétien, Martin, and other Liberals to reverse it.

In 1992, Chrétien appointed pro-free trader, Roy MacLaren, to be chairman of the Liberal Economic Policy Committee and the party's trade critic. MacLaren, who had recently called for a fundamental overhaul of "wasteful social programs," wrote a controversial paper, entitled "Wide Open," in which he called for the party to reverse its stand on trade and said that Canada should become the first country in the world to unilaterally take down all barriers to trade and investment whether or not other countries reciprocated. I called it "unilateral economic disarmament" in the *Toronto Star*. The war with the "Libertories" was starting.

MacLaren was pushing for a reversal of the party's position on NAFTA, as were Jean Chrétien's close advisers, particularly Eddie Goldenberg. In their well-researched book, *Double Vision,* which describes the backroom dealings of the Liberal Party, Ed Greenspon and Anthony Wilson-Smith trace the transformation, noting that Chrétien and MacLaren voted against the NAFTA bill the Tories introduced in the House of Commons in May 1993, knowing they would be supporting NAFTA when it came up for proclamation under a Liberal government. Chrétien couldn't be honest about his real intentions because, as poll after poll showed, NAFTA was very unpopular with the Canadian electorate. Only weeks before, the Canadian Labour Congress and the Action Canada Network held an anti-NAFTA rally on Parliament Hill attended by over 100,000 people.

I had two meetings with Jean Chrétien on the subject of free trade. In 1989, before Chrétien had become Liberal leader, Mel Hurtig and I met with him in his Ottawa law offices. He said that he was concerned about the free trade agreement, especially the energy giveaway, but that he was a "practical" person. The just-signed deal was like an omelette that "could never be unscrambled," he said, and cancelling it would be out of the question because the "monster would have had too many babies." I was invited to meet with him a second time, this time alone, in April 1993, in his Parliamentary office.

He talked for a good forty-five minutes, never really looking at me, hardly pausing to let me speak. He rambled on about free trade, how it had hurt Canadian culture, caused drug prices to rise, and threatened unemployment insurance, but would give no commitment as to what he was prepared to do about it. "It's a problem. It's a problem." He became very agitated over the GST, telling me that he was never in favour of promising to cancel the unpopular tax, but that he had been pressured by key members of his caucus when the party was low in the polls. Now that they were on the verge of winning power, he said, he felt boxed in because he knew as prime minister, he could never cancel it. Government had become too dependent on GST revenues to contemplate such a thing, he said, and he would never reintroduce a manufacturers' tax.

It was an extraordinary display of candour for someone he didn't know and probably didn't like (after all, he had helped defeat my bid for a seat in the House of Commons), and I left feeling enormously puzzled as to why we had met. I was not impressed with the man. He didn't seem at all introspective or in the least interested in my opinions. It appeared to me that Jean Chrétien was interested only in what political insiders call the "optics" of the issues he was dealing with, and not the substance. My opinion of him would not change with time.

By the lead up to the fall election, the Liberal Party had changed its official position on NAFTA. The *Red Book,* which set out the Liberal platform, promised to "renegotiate" the deal to protect labour and the environment, establish a common code on subsidies and dumping, and give Canada the same rights to protect our energy that Mexico had obtained. But the American government, now realizing that the Liberals would form the next government, were not prepared to renegotiate. It set out to smooth the way for a peaceful transition from the Tories to the Liberals, which included the passage of NAFTA, intact.

Greenspon and Wilson-Smith document how the American ambassador to Canada, James Blanchard, held a top-secret meeting with senior Chrétien adviser, Jean Pelletier, only days before the October 25 election. The week before, Chrétien had told a nurse in Vancouver who was worried about NAFTA that she should vote for the NDP. This pleased the Clinton Administration, Blanchard told Pelletier, but any talk of "renegotiating" the deal at this time would jeopardize its passage in the U.S. Congress, where it was already in trouble. Pelletier assured his visitor that the Liberal Party's pro-free trade position was solid — the concern was simply about the "optics" of explaining the new position to the Canadian people. As Greenspon and Wilson-Smith note, "Discussions with Pelletier and Goldenberg revolved around how to cope with the situation, not whether they wanted NAFTA." Chrétien dropped the term "renegotiation" from his campaign speeches.

Immediately after winning the election on October 25, Roy MacLaren and Chrétien's advisers set out to find ways to allow the new government to pass NAFTA in its entirety while appearing to have gained concessions from the Americans. "Side deals" on environment, labour standards, and subsidies were worked out. Canada asserted its rights over water and energy in an exchange of notes to the U.S. administration, an act utterly without legal meaning. Everyone in the circle of insiders putting together this political compromise, from politicians to trade bureaucrats, knew that unless the actual text of the NAFTA itself was changed, these side agreements and letters were meaningless window dressing. Tony Clarke and I even made public a letter we had obtained in which Clinton assured a U.S. senator concerned over the exchanged notes on energy that they meant nothing and that the access to Canada's energy the United States had established in the FTA would continue in NAFTA.

But the Canadian public was mightily weary of nine years of political brinkmanship with Brian Mulroney and the Liberals knew this. They gambled that Canadians wanted peace and quiet more than anything and that they would give the new government the benefit of the doubt. As well, Jean Chrétien had enormous personal popularity and, unlike Brian Mulroney, the Canadian people trusted him.

President Clinton was now able to say (correctly) that Canada had fully capitulated and was prepared to sign the deal without change. This removed a powerful tool NAFTA's opponents in Congress had been using to stall the vote. The deal was becoming very controversial in Washington. Clinton, who had been in power for less than a year, was also breaking an election pledge. Just as Jean Chrétien once promised he would never pass "Mulroney's NAFTA," Bill Clinton, in order to gain the support of labour and environmental groups, promised substantive changes to "Bush's NAFTA" before he would sponsor it. The battle in Congress pitted Clinton against the progressive forces in his own party and showed that he is a fiscal conservative on economic matters.

I went to Washington regularly throughout the months leading up to the vote in Congress, where, with other Canadians, I lobbied members of Congress and worked with our American colleagues to raise public awareness about free trade. We operated out of the offices of Congressman David Bonior, the Democratic whip, a fine man and the third-ranking Democrat in Congress. Because the race was very tight, the business community launched a powerful, well-funded campaign to ensure victory. While farmers and workers had to walk the halls of Congress looking for politicians or aides to lobby, Clinton secured a large suite to house the cream of corporate America in the days preceding the vote. Passing politicians and media were invited inside. "Would you like to meet the CEO of Ford? How about the chairman of General Electric?" asked beautiful young women sporting their big red-and-white "NAFTA-YES!" campaign buttons.

The historic NAFTA vote was held November 17 and I watched it from the gallery of Congress, where it passed 234 to 200. Only days before, it had looked as if it might not go through and would have posed the most serious challenge to date to the young presidency. For this reason, Clinton had staked a great deal on it. He had made so many promises to members who were undecided or opposed that activists quietly dropped dollar bills onto the floor of Congress just after the vote to symbolize how its passage was really secured. In a press conference with Jesse Jackson and Ralph Nader the next morning, I said, "When President Clinton couldn't sell NAFTA, he bought it." On December 3, 1993, Jean Chrétien's Liberals passed Brian Mulroney's two-thousand-word NAFTA without a single change to it.

"*Vaya con Dios*, Maude Barlow," crowed the headline in Terence Corcoran's *Globe and Mail* column. "And while we're in a celebratory mood, a hearty *Hasta la vista!* to Mel Hurtig, Tony Clarke . . . and all the other *gringos* who spent most of the past half-dozen years concocting preposterous claims regarding free trade with the United States and Mexico." This was a very painful defeat. Not only did the polls clearly tell us we had won the hearts and minds of the majority of Canadians on this issue (as we had on the FTA), once again it didn't matter. Once again, an agenda that superceded citizens' democracy had usurped the will of the people. After all, Canadians had just given a huge majority to a party that had worked against the FTA and NAFTA for almost nine years. What did these promises mean? Who was really calling the shots behind the scenes? I was to be in for a long period of reflection about the fragile state of democracy and the ability of any of us outside the business community to have any effect on the political agenda at all. But this had also been a painful time in another way.

In 1992, Mel Hurtig, after many years of thinking about it, decided to set up a new national political party and it led us into serious conflict with one another. After I took over the leadership of the council, I continued to confer regularly with Mel and he continued to work with us as our honorary chairman, often speaking in public and the media on our behalf. But when his *Canadian Encyclopedia* hit serious financial difficulties, Mel retreated from public life and started to distance himself from the council. We started to have some disagreements over policy, particularly over Canada's Constitution. Mel believed in the strict equality of the provinces and dismissed the sovereignty movement in Quebec as a communication problem.

Our biggest disagreement, however, arose when he assumed the council would convert itself into a partisan political machine to support the new National Party. I flew to Edmonton to talk to him about the formation of the party and to explain that the council would have to remain non-partisan. As our honorary chair, Mel was to give the keynote address to our 1992 annual general meeting. I was worried that he would take advantage of the fact that many like-minded people, all friends or admirers of his, were gathering there for our meeting and that he would announce the formation of his party. We had set up "The Great Trade Debate" between the Liberal trade critic, Herb Gray, and the NDP trade critic, Dave Barrett, and wanted to expose the weakness of the Liberal position in front of the national media. I was worried (justifiably it turns out) that if Mel made any kind of political announcement, his move would become the story of the AGM. A curious media would gobble up any hint of dissension between us, and I was anxious to avoid that.

After a difficult discussion, I gave Mel my blessing for his new political adventure and he gave me his promise that he would not launch the National Party at our AGM. When he rose on the Saturday evening, November 21, to give his (excellent as usual) speech to our AGM, he thanked me (as if my career was now finished) for all I had done for the council and said I should get the Order of Canada for my service to the country, noting that he would be home that Wednesday morning if anyone wanted to call him to see how to go about nominating me. Then, with at least four television cameras running, Mel Hurtig announced the formation of the National Party and walked, with media and nearly half our delegates in tow, across the street to the Château Laurier for its founding meeting. I was left sitting alone on the platform. A photo in the *Toronto Star* the next day caught my grim face at that moment.

Alexa McDonough, then leader of the NDP in Nova Scotia and a delegate to our meeting, was furious. She saw immediately the threat the new party would pose to the NDP if anti-NAFTA votes were split between the two parties in NDP-held ridings. Her father, Lloyd Shaw, now deceased, had been a founding member of both the Committee for an Independent Canada and with Mel, the Council of Canadians. Alexa told Mel as he was leaving the hall that she was glad her father wasn't there to see this "sad day."

I was very upset. No matter how I tried to rationalize it, Mel's action felt like a betrayal. I was used to being attacked by my political enemies and even by some people in other groups in our movement still angry with me over my former Liberal connections. All that I took (and take) with a grain of salt. But my friends mean a great deal to me and Mel had become a friend as well as a mentor. I couldn't believe he would do this to the group he had formed. And I was very worried that it meant the end of the Council of Canadians.

I found myself defending him to my family. My mother kept asking me to explain what happened (for it was all over the television) as if she couldn't fathom my account of the incident. Andrew was extremely angry. In the end, I drew on my Irish temper and my Scottish determination and decided the council and I were going to weather this storm.

Problems followed right into the election of 1993. To guard against a splitting of the vote similar to what happened in 1988 — which would allow the Tories a third victory — the council's campaign strategy during this election was a limited form of strategic voting. We supported all the NDP incumbents across the country plus a number of social Liberals, like Lloyd Axworthy, who had good track records on free trade. We asked Mel not to run candidates in NDP-held ridings as that party had taken such a strong and principled stand on NAFTA and it seemed odd that people so intent on defeating NAFTA would challenge allies. He didn't listen to us, and the National Party probably split the vote in at least three NDP ridings, giving the victory to a Liberal or a Reformer. The NDP won only nine seats, three short of the number needed for official party status.

Unfortunately, Mel and some other members of the National Party took the COC position very personally. I was picketed at a number of speaking events across the country. National Party supporters handed out pamphlets with headlines such as, "What is Maude Barlow Trying To Do?" and questions that verged on the conspiratorial. "Could it be that Maude Barlow has designs which go beyond the abrogation of the FTA and NAFTA? Designs which indeed make these awful agreements secondary considerations?" Another sheet held questions to ask me during public events. "Here are some suggested QUESTIONS to ask Ms. Barlow during the Q & A period: (Got stage fright? Just read it off the page.) 'Ms. Barlow, what is the extent of your involvement in the NDP (as it is now known)?' 'Do you intend to run for elected office in the NDP (or any future incarnation of that party)?' (If Barlow diverts the topic away from the question, e.g., to the piece of paper, the résumé of the person asking, etc., that's not an answer.)"

Mel wrote to a supporter in a letter, "Of course we very much regret the foolish move by Maude Barlow. It's beyond my comprehension how the COC could take such an action. It seems to me that what has happened is that the organization has been taken over by the NDP. . . What Maude Barlow has done is make it into a very partisan organization that I think is now little better than a front for the NDP. . . Maude has strong ties to the Canadian Labour Congress and it seems that at least some of her activities are being funded by the CLC. And of course, the CLC are strong supporters of the NDP. . . the rather tragic and duplici-tous action that Maude Barlow has taken will inevitably erode [the COC's] foundation. . . . My own suspicion is that Maude has taken this course of action because she wants to replace Audrey McLaughlin as the Leader of the NDP."

What was ironic about this is that I was still suspected by many in the labour movement and the NDP of being a secret Liberal. (At an NDP conference where I was asked to give a presentation a year later, Winnipeg MP Bill Blaikie gave me hell for not being a partisan New Democrat, and I shot back that "it's not my job to get you elected."

Soon after, Blaikie wrote a scathing essay that he circulated widely, castigating the Council and me for our non-partisanship.) Meanwhile, our right-wing opponents had a field day. Economist John Crispo claims he gave the National Party $2,000 because the stronger they were, the more they would split the opposition.

What was sad about all of this, of course, was the loss of a friendship that had meant a great deal to me. I had also turned to Mel for counsel many times over the years. I was missing this aspect of our relationship very much and wondered if jealousy had played a part in determining his actions and what I might have done to alleviate any such feelings on his part.

The National Party was a complete failure. It dissolved after the election in a pitched battle between Mel Hurtig and Bill Loewen, who had financed the campaign, and there are still ongoing court deliberations between the two camps to sort out the disputes about money. I wrote Mel to tell him how sad I was that it had ended for him like that and he sent me back a recent speech and a note that we should "talk sometime." It hasn't happened yet but I'm still hopeful. Mel Hurtig is an exceptional Canadian and still one of the most important influences of my life.

On New Year's Day 1994, the world woke up to what the media called "the first free trade war" — an uprising of Mayan peasants in Chiapas deliberately timed to coincide with the day NAFTA came into effect. Over the coming years, the Mexican government would institute a military crackdown on the local people with the eventual imposition of martial law and censorship of the press. Random killings began, including the horrific December 1997 massacre in the village of Acteal, where paramilitary gunmen shot and hacked forty-five men, women, and children to death.

I was very low and felt helpless to do anything about these new developments. In fact, I wasn't sure I could or should keep going. I was physically exhausted and Charles and Will urged me to quit or at least take some time off. The global nature of this agenda was beginning to surface, and I was frightened by the powerful forces aligned to drive it ahead and the energy it would take me to get the work to the next level.

The council was never intended to be a permanent organization, and I wondered if it weren't time to call it a day.

I wrote a very personal letter to our now 25,000 members and asked their advice. "We have lost twice now, and perhaps it is time to accept defeat and move on. I don't believe in keeping organizations going if there is no justifiable mandate." I asked for honest feedback and whether our members were prepared to continue to support us financially. (This wasn't a personal request for money. My work with the council has always been voluntary; I make my living on my writing and my non-council speaking engagements.)

The responses we received back were overwhelming. Our members said there was a more urgent need for the council than ever before exactly *because* we had lost the FTA and NAFTA fights. They committed themselves to helping us rebuild but made it clear we had to enlarge our scope of activity. Most important, they said, was the need to monitor the government closely for the economic, social, cultural, and environmental harmonization we anticipated and to be there to fight the cuts and privatizations we saw coming. I had a long talk with Andrew. I told him that this would be hard, slogging, often unrewarding work, and would probably limit my income. He replied that supporting my work was the most important thing he does and urged me not to give up now.

I also talked it over, as I do almost everything, with Helen. She has a career not unlike mine: neither of us has much security; every day is different; we are constantly taking chances; and we have to maintain a strong public face no matter how we are feeling. Helen had just set up the first story-telling theatre in Canada and was feeling excited and afraid at the same time. We went away for a weekend to a lodge near Toronto and walked and talked until we both got over our fears. (Sheila Purdy and Helen and I take regular trips together, and they often seem to come just when I need them most. In the early summer of 1989, after losing the first free trade fight, we spent two weeks walking the Pennine Way — the "spine of England" — from Manchester to the Scottish border. It was a magic time and all the years, husbands, children, and jobs melted away as we laughed all through the moors, covered in sheep droppings and mud.)

I found myself rejuvenated. Under the dynamic leadership of our new executive director, Peter Bleyer, and a terrific young team of activists, we set out to build a permanent citizens' movement in Canada. Our new mandate was to act as a citizen watchdog as governments abandoned our social programs and environmental regulations, and to promote alternatives to corporate-style free trade. We set up what we called our "Citizens' Agenda," a kind of manifesto of citizens' rights in a global economy and what people can do to claim them. Under the direction of a new board with key members like Susan Spratt of the Canadian Auto Workers and Jim MacFarlan of the British Columbia Teachers' Federation, we finally started to become the national grassroots citizens' movement we dreamed about being. (Jim has stayed on with the council and I have come to depend on his consistent good judgement, steadfast commitment, and unwavering friendship.) My role would be to publicly encourage Canadians to fight for their rights as governments across the country continued to vacate the public sphere, and to advocate for action by writing, speaking, and organizing. We would have our work cut out for us.

The Liberal Party under Jean Chrétien took up the Tory mantle and, goaded on by the surging Reform Party under Preston Manning, moved steadily to the right. After the infamous Martin budget of 1995, the cuts began. Over the next three years, the Liberals removed so much money from federal transfer payments to the provinces that social spending as a percentage of total government spending is now back to where it was in 1949 — a time *before* universal health care, public pensions, or family allowance. Cuts to health care were so deep that the federal government now accounts for just 20 per cent of all health care dollars spent in Canada, compared to 42 per cent in the mid-1970s. This has resulted in significant downsizing or closing of hospitals in all the provinces.

The Liberals killed the Canada Assistance Plan, an act which, as the National Anti-Poverty Organization explained, "transformed (Canada) from a country in which the right to adequate financial assistance for persons in need was a legal requirement, enforceable in court by individuals affected, to one in which there is no federal legislation recognizing this right or providing means of enforcing it." Protection for unemployment insurance dropped to below 40 per cent from a pre-FTA high of 87 per cent. Billions of dollars were cut from old age pensions. Together with huge cuts to welfare in the provinces, particularly Ontario, Alberta,

Manitoba, and New Brunswick, the Canadian government shifted from a 1960s-style war on poverty to a 1990s-style war on the poor.

When Ralph Klein first came to power in Alberta in 1993, he cut social welfare so deeply that, within two years, 45,000 welfare recipients, many of them single mothers, were cut off completely. Now in Alberta, a single person deemed employable receives assistance equal to just 36 percent of poverty-line income. Seniors with an annual income of over $10,400 had their benefits reduced; those with incomes over $18,000 lost them all, including health premium coverage, and dental, drug, and eye-care subsidies. Government House Leader Stockwell Day boasted, "In many ways, we're ahead of the Americans. We have deadlines here where there [will be] no more social assistance." As it turned out, Alberta was the petri dish for this social experiment, which was picked up by a number of other provinces. Ontario's Mike Harris took a page from Klein's book when he came to power a few years later. He justified cutting assistance for unemployed pregnant women saying they likely "spend it on beer."

The reality of getting cut off from society with the stroke of a pen hit home for me late one night when I returned a rental car to the underground garage of a downtown office building on Toronto's Bay Street. The attendant, a recent immigrant, had his whole family there — his parents, wife, young son, and brand new baby — set up for the night seven levels underground with sleeping cots, a kitchen table, and cooking equipment. The air reeked of car fumes. "What is your family doing here?" I asked, my heart in my mouth. He begged me not to tell the authorities, but said, "Where we live ma'am, is so much worse than this, I bring my family in for the night and take them home just before dawn. At least we're together here."

Whether we want to admit it or not (and many people do not) Canada is developing an entrenched underclass. While corporate profits and CEO salaries surge, a May 1998 report by Statistics Canada says that the incomes of most Canadians eroded in the 1990s to less than they were in 1980. John McCallum, the Royal Bank of Canada's chief economist, called it the "first protracted period of income decline since the 1930s." The majority of new jobs in the so-called "miracle boom" are part-time, insecure, and without benefits. Child poverty is at an all-time high in Canada — an increase of 58 per cent in the decade since parliament vowed unanimously to eradicate child poverty by the year 2000. Poverty among seniors is on the rise for the first time in three decades.

In culture, the story is the same — a 41 per cent reduction in indirect and direct federal spending since 1989. Transportation subsidies have been slashed 69 per cent by the Liberals, and funding to environmental and natural resource protection has been sheared to the point that, says the *Ottawa Citizen,* "the federal environment department has little influence on anything you eat, drink, or breathe."

Writer John Ralston Saul calls this retreat from governance a "*coup d'état* in slow motion." The COC fought it every step of the way, from town hall meetings to budget lockups to Parliamentary committees. For our pensions campaign, we brought together all the seniors groups across the country into a fighting force and collected over three-quarters of a million petitions to send to MPs. When Wal-Mart bought the 120 Woolco stores in Canada, we launched a national campaign to set standards on big box retailers so that they would fit into community life and wouldn't destroy the downtown heart of the small towns where they locate as they have done all over the United States. While we couldn't stop the Wal-Mart invasion, a number of communities did succeed in establishing local conditions on the size and location of the new stores. When we heard that the federal government was poised to grant the chemical giant Monsanto the right to market bovine growth hormone to Canadian farmers, one of our campaign officers, Alex Boston, put together such a strong national coalition that the government declared a moratorium on the decision and, to date, has not allowed the sale of BGH in the country.

The council is committed to working with other groups. We joined Kathleen Connors of the National Federation of Nurses' Union and the Canadian Health Coalition to stop the erosion of health care and to fight the growing influence of the big drug companies. We joined Keith Kelly of the Canadian Conference of the Arts and Gary Neil of ACTRA in their fight to stop the savage Liberal cuts to the CBC. We joined the Endangered Species Coalition to lobby the federal government to introduce protections for species and their habitats (only some provinces have species protection) — something they shamefully have not done to date. We worked closely with the gutsy Buzz Hargrove and Hassan Yussuff of the Canadian Auto Workers to forge alliances between organized labour and citizens. During the years since 1994, I have travelled across the country dozens of times, talking to groups, starting new council chapters, developing local strategies to cope with the cuts to services communities have been experiencing.

Everywhere I have gone, I have met Canadians at the grass-roots level who are committed to preserving their country, often at great personal cost to themselves. I work closely with Dorothy Inglis — my friend from the "porn wars" — an outspoken Newfoundland feminist and environmentalist with a great sense of humour. Dorothy warns that Atlantic Canada, and particularly Newfoundland because of its high unemployment, may become what she calls *Maquiladora North*, a place to dump toxic waste and open free trade zones. Mary Boyd (like Tony Clarke, fired from her job in the social affairs office of the P.E.I. Catholic Church for her outspoken views on poverty and the economy), and Leo Broderick, a high school principal, are leaders in the struggle to preserve social programs and public education in P.E.I.

Cynthia Patterson, an activist from the Gaspé, founded a very effective group on a shoestring called Rural Dignity that resisted, in some cases successfully, the closures of rural post offices. Don Kossick, social justice activist and outreach worker for CUSO in Saskatoon, keeps Roy Romanow's NDP government on notice all the time. Prolific writers and researchers Murray Dobbin and Ellen Gould of Vancouver turn out vital information on the Fraser Institute, the Reform Party, and the National Citizens' Coalition, which are, respectively, the research, citizen, and political arms of the radical right in Canada. Murray's best-selling books have been a great source of information for our work. Elizabeth May of the Sierra Club of Canada, den mother to the young activists of the world, is a strong ally. Her passionate campaign to protect Canada's forests and to set targets to reduce global warming has earned her respect across the country from friends and foes alike. David Suzuki is another environmental pioneer I am proud to call a friend and with whom the COC shares information and strategy.

Shirley Lord, Jim Silver, and John Loxley are part of a Winnipeg collective called CHO!CES. This innovative group developed a process to teach grass-roots activists to understand, critique, and write their own municipal, provincial, and federal budgets. With Bruce Campbell, economist Jim Stanford, and long-time firebrand researcher Ed Finn, they produce an "Alternative Federal Budget" every year, that, using the government's own fiscal targets, but armed with a very different set of priorities, presents the Canadian people with an alternative to the slash-and-burn budgets we have come to expect from the Liberals. This sense of choice is crucial to overcome the too-commonly held belief that there is no alternative to government downsizing.

An emerging role for the council is to be brought into a community to help the local citizens when the government cannot or will not fulfil its responsibility. I was invited to Swan River Valley in northern Manitoba where tireless forest environmentalists Don Sullivan and Ken Sigurdson were fighting the arrival of Louisiana Pacific, an American waferboard manufacturer convicted of serious environmental violations in the United States. Even though the pollution emission devices the company was planning to install were substandard according to both Manitoba and federal law, neither level of government would intervene. Lousiana Pacific had played to the crisis of unemployment in the town and the residents were deeply divided between those who needed jobs, and the farmers, Native peoples, small operation loggers, and environmentalists. We brought a national spotlight to bear on the dispute, and the company agreed to install state-of-the-art pollution control technology.

We were contacted by Dr. Shiv Chopra and other scientists at the Health Protection Branch where massive cuts have left them unable to do their job of protecting the country's drug and food supplies. The department has been ordered to operate on a "cost-recovery" basis whereby the big drug companies (still protected by twenty-year NAFTA patent rights the Liberals vowed to rescind) now account for 75 per cent of the funding to get their drugs approved. Needless to say, great pressure has been placed on these scientists (so great, that some, like Dr. Michelle Brill-Edwards, have left to sound the alarm from the outside) to approve drugs before tests are complete or even if they have disturbing evidence against a drug. The besieged staff, under pressure to shut up and make the drug companies happy, need the public support of a national citizens' group to disseminate information and give them protection if they are penalized for voicing their concerns.

Bill Farren and the New Brunswick Federation of Labour brought us in to help arbitrate a dispute with the local board of trade who were setting up the first "free trade zone" in Canada. Notorious for their human rights, labour, and environmental abuses (see Chapter Eleven), Export Processing Zones (EPZs) are usually established in the poorest areas of a country and displace domestic industry, rendering the economy dependent on their usually sub-standard jobs and leaving governments subservient to the demands of transnationals. Until recently, the federal government had responsibility to authorize the creation and location of EPZs but the Chrétien Liberals, ever anxious to help their business friends, removed this law from the books. Now any community can set up a zone, unregulated by the federal government.

The government of New Brunswick had chosen for its free trade zone a small community called Lorneville, where it had confiscated land years ago and built a toxic waste dump site. The goal was "Plastic Valley North" (after Silicon Valley in California) and the plastics companies of the world were being invited in, no questions asked. I had written a scathing op-ed piece on the history of free trade zones in other countries that was published in the local papers. The labour leaders and the residents of Lorneville had drawn up a "contract" they wanted the government and local business community to sign before the zone was established. The contract set out strict conditions that the zone bring good jobs and respect labour and environmental standards. All the players met around a table with the press outside the door, and the board of trade members agreed to work toward mutually acceptable conditions for the project. My presence ensured a public process and the Lorneville people know to contact the council if the agreement is broken.

In Alberta, we helped form a common front called "Defend the Rose" (the wild rose is Alberta's symbol) when the Klein government's first big cuts were unleashed. Trudy Richardson and Heather Smith of the feisty United Nurses of Alberta, and Julius Buski and Bauni Mackay of the Alberta Teachers' Federation gave strong leadership to this movement, which has partially succeeded in forcing the government to replace some of the lost funds. In this case, it was not my or the council's profile that was in demand, but rather our experience in organizing coalitions between diverse and sometimes competing groups.

We developed one clever tactic. Ralph Klein called all the "civil society" groups together for a "consultation." His agenda for the day might have read, "How you will help me cut your sector to ribbons and smile about it." The groups — assuming the right to their own power base — developed their own agenda items, and met Klein and his Cabinet as equals in a negotiation, laying on the table their competing itinerary and expectations. These groups, particularly the teachers and the nurses, have shown incredible leadership in this fight and they have been emulated across the country.

In 1994, I co-authored a book on education called *Class Warfare: The Assault on Canada's Schools.* I had been watching with growing concern the invasion of big-business interests into our increasingly cash-starved schools and the "reform" movement's push for charter schools and a tiered system that could lead to what one American writer calls, "survival of the children of the fittest." My co-author, Heather-jane Robertson, a teacher originally from Saskatchewan, is now a director at the Canadian Teachers' Federation. Heather-jane has also crossed Canada many times, working with teachers to develop what we call "political and economic literacy" and has gone on to do pioneering analysis on society's fixation on technology for the young.

We both spoke extensively against Charter schools — schools that are funded by public money but operate as private institutions and where parent boards set curriculum and hire teachers. I think we helped slow the enthusiasm for these schools in many parts of the country and helped arm educators with arguments against them, but we couldn't stop Alberta from setting up fifteen Charter schools. (Recently, one of the jewels in the Alberta Charter school crown has been closed in a swirl of controversy about its financing, but it hasn't stopped another proposal for a "Charter school of Commerce" that would require children as young as eight to wear shirts and ties and carry briefcases; study business reports in literature class; chart real estate and stock-market movements in math class; and receive lessons through headsets at computer-equipped individual work stations.)

The passions around this issue took me by surprise. In 1994, I was a speaker at the first national forum in Montreal of the Council of Ministers of Education, a body with no formal mandate that meets regularly to promote and streamline technology, testing, and private-sector partnerships in education. The conference room was filled with a mixture of politicians, academics, education bureaucrats, and (a few) real classroom educators. All the panellists spoke in what one observer called "Eduspeak" — a mixture of meaningless platitudes, slogans, and technical jargon used to force the square peg of public education into the round hole of the corporate economy. "Life-long cognitive skills" met up with "effective school-based initiatives" and promoted "practical resource-based programs" supported by "community-based partnerships."

I was very upset. "Here we are," I noted in my speech, "the supposed cream of the education community in Canada and no one wants to talk about child poverty, racism, or class. No one has mentioned the crippling cuts to education or the invasion of our schools by transnational corporations intent on reaching the last outpost of our society still off-limits to their propaganda. No one has acknowledged the assault on teachers and their unions or the undercurrent of privatization inherent in the language we are using here today." Half the audience stormed out in the middle of my talk. But the teachers loved it and the event turned into a real and open encounter over these issues. In the summary at the end of the conference, the chair said he had to break his remarks into two periods, BM and AM — "Before Maude and After Maude." Needless to say, I haven't been invited back to the education ministers' meetings.

When I attended a conference at a brand-new, state-of-the-art, high-tech school in Cole Harbour, Nova Scotia, on school-corporate partnerships, the audience was made up of equal numbers of teachers, students (all wearing T-shirts emblazoned with the partnership logo "NovaKnowledge"), and provincial and community business leaders. The principal, who called himself the "CEO" of the school, welcomed the business community and proceeded to apologize to them for the "disgraceful" job public schools had done and to give voice to every myth about school failure in the book. Drop-outs were at an all-time high, illiteracy rates were soaring, Canadians were falling behind other countries in testing. (Unfortunately for him, I was the keynote speaker right after him. In the first three chapters of *Class Warfare*, Heather-jane and I examined and refuted every one of those myths with precise and copious references and, referring to our research, I had great fun contradicting the "CEO" as he sat in the front row with all his corporate friends.)

At this event, the Nova Scotia education minister announced that he would never build another school in his province with public money. This one had been built by IBM, which received exclusive rights to supply the school with computers forever, and Maritime Telephone & Telegraph, whose CEO opened the day with the announcement that this school was the model. (That morning, I had debated the minister on CBC Radio and the host asked him what he thought of Charter schools. "I don't know anything about them," he admitted. "But if Maude Barlow is against them, then I'm for them.") One after another of the business leaders in the group rose to tell the students that there was no longer any such thing as a job and they should not expect security or pensions. "Think of yourselves as little entrepreneurs," said one, "Me Inc." Another told them schools had to produce "value-added students."

The Canadian manager of Pratt & Whitney, a transnational airplane-parts manufacturer with a large plant in the area, told the students that he didn't care if unemployment went up or down in Nova Scotia. He was from Great Britain on a two-year assignment in Canada and his next stop was Chile. "My only allegiance is to my shareholders. This may be hard for you students to accept, but if your schools turn out the kind of employees we want — competitive, flexible, and without a false sense of 'entitlements,' we'll keep our plant here. If not, we'll leave." The students were shocked. I was sitting at a table with a large group and encouraged them to speak up.

One young black woman from a nearby school (where race-based conflicts flared up a couple of years later) expressed her dismay at the money that was being poured into this school while her own was left to run down. "Why wasn't this fancy conference held in my school, where you get splinters in your backside from the chairs?" Another fifteen-year-old, her voice trembling and hardly audible, said, "We're not stupid, you know. We know that you are playing musical chairs with our futures and you don't intend to have enough seats for us all when the music stops." One businessman angrily accused the teachers of not liking change. A math teacher blurted out, "It's not change I don't like. It's you!"

Open-line talk shows were wild. People with a beef from their own childhood called in and Heather-jane and I were the subjects of pure hatred. "All" teachers were lazy, went home at 3 p.m., and took the summer off. One caller insisted anyone who worked for the public, including civil servants, nurses, and teachers, were "welfare bums," and should be fired. I slowly came to realize that much of this misplaced hate was, in fact, fear. Parents know the world is changing very fast. Globalization, however, is too abstract a concept to attack. The school their kid goes to is closer and more vulnerable.

In Calgary, I was a guest of the notorious Dave Rutherford, the Rush Limbaugh of Canada, who conducts his interviews with all the subtlety of a piranha. He was ruthless in his questions and frankly ignorant. Part of the show was televised, and, after the TV cameras were gone, and just before we were to go off the air, I said, "The audience can't see this, but Dave Rutherford is down on his knees begging me to forgive him for all the things he said to me over the last hour." "I am not!" Rutherford was protesting loudly when we went off air.

In Sydney, Cape Breton, I was invited to speak about education on the local radio show there, called *Talkback*. The host, another Dave, but very different in character, told me to drop any "big city" ways I had. "Everyone in Cape Breton listens to this show and they're all friendly." Sure enough, everyone who phoned in wanted to be kind. In their lovely Cape Breton lilt, one after another asked after my welfare. One wanted to know if I was "being fed properly." Then one man phoned in and gave the better part of his MasterCard number. Dave said, "Sir, why are you giving us your MasterCard? We don't need that." "Oh," replied the caller, "yes you do. It says right here. I'm looking for a lady companion and it says you need my credit card and my phone number." The host said, "Sir, I think you have the worst wrong number I have ever heard of. You're looking for an escort service. This is *Talkback*. Everyone in Cape Breton is listening to you right now." There was a deadly silence. Then the caller said, "Sweet Jesus, I hope the wife's not listening!"

Over the next few years, the teachers in Canada organized to defend themselves against these mostly false and mainly political assaults, and it has been my privilege to be part of this extraordinary development. The capable leadership of people like British Columbia teachers Jim

McFarlan, Ken Novakowski, and Elsie McMurchy, and Ontario teachers like Earl Manners and Eileen Lennon, is creating a new breed of political activists, people whose interests and work now range far beyond the classroom. I think my most rewarding work is with teachers; these are people, after all, who chose their profession because they love children and value learning. They are the defenders of democracy, equality, diversity, and inclusion — all anathema to the new economy and all under attack by school "reformers."

Meanwhile, my relationship with the Liberals wasn't improving. Mark Kennedy of the *Ottawa Citizen* wrote a story in October 1994 with the headline, "Nationalist Group Turns on Axworthy." It referred to our national campaign against the reforms to the social-policy review that Lloyd Axworthy, then human resources minister, had launched and that would end in the dramatic reduction of social security protection for Canadians. Kennedy quoted me saying that the reforms confirmed a prediction I had made that free trade would result in the harmonization of our social programs to the American level, and noted that Axworthy had been there, right at my side, saying the same things. "He was one of the most articulate people I ever met. He spoke right from the heart and the head. He wowed people, and he wowed me." I added that our campaign was "nothing personal" but Axworthy shot back not long after that "Maude has lost her role as legitimate social critic by going too far."

By now, Lloyd was striking out at critics everywhere. At a Vancouver conference on globalization that year, he rebuked a nurse in the audience who asked him how he could speak about globalization for a whole hour and not once mention free trade or his government's about-face on it. "Are you questioning my integrity?" he demanded with obvious anger. He shouted at university students at a Parliament Hill demonstration when they pelted him with Kraft Dinner (signifying that this would be all they would be able to eat after his funding reforms took effect). "If you don't want to hear the truth, that's your problem," he told them. He laid much of the blame for the failure of his review on his department's officials. "You won't believe the sort of barnacles I have," he told Ed Greenspon of the *Globe and Mail*. Jean Swanson of the National Anti-Poverty Organization had a dozen copies of a little pink button made up that says, "Axworthy screeched at me" and sent me one. I laughed, but at the same time, it made me a little sad for a lost friendship. I think Lloyd Axworthy is a genuinely progressive politician who would not have made these choices had he been prime minister. I think he took all this criticism so hard because, at some level, he knew he was betraying his principles.

(I told Ed Greenspon about the button for his book on the Liberals. When he couldn't trace it, he called and told me that, if I had made up a little fib, he wouldn't mind but he needed to know. Andrew drew up a notarized affidavit for me, confirming my story and giving Ed joint custody of "little screechie." The sheriff delivered the affidavit and the button to Ed. He hasn't returned it yet.)

Relations continued to deteriorate. In May 1995, I was asked to give the keynote address to the annual meeting of a national non-profit housing organization. Chaviva Hošek, former housing minister in the Peterson government and now a senior policy adviser to Jean Chrétien, was seated at my table. Just before I spoke, she was given the group's annual award for her housing advocacy on behalf of low-income people. Chaviva and I had been close colleagues in our days in the women's movement and I liked her very much. She is warm, personable, and very, very smart. So it was hard to watch her, like so many other fine, progressive people, get pulled into the Liberal Party where her talent has helped them deliver such a harsh agenda.

Chaviva was supposed to leave after her award but decided to stay to hear my speech. I was sorry, because my speech was a scathing indictment of the savage cuts to housing and everything else recently delivered in Martin's budget. I started by congratulating her for the award and thanking her for the good work she had done while in provincial politics. But I didn't change the speech; I said that the Liberals had abandoned the "Just Society" they had helped build and were betraying generations of Canadians who fought for a social heritage. Chaviva sat with her head down throughout and left immediately after my speech. Within half an hour, my office got an angry call from Terrie O'Leary, Martin's executive assistant, wanting a copy of the speech.

Not long after, my good friend and Martin confidante Richard Mahoney, called at Martin's request and asked me out for dinner. I told

Richard that I had to finish writing *Straight Through the Heart,* my book on the Liberals, first as I didn't want to be accused of using anything that was said at the meeting for my book. As soon as Bruce Campbell and I sent the manuscript off to the publisher, Richard, Paul, and I had dinner in a private room at a lovely old Ottawa private club called the Cercle Universitaire. Paul Martin is impossible not to like. Self-deprecating and genuinely funny, he embraces life with great passion. (When Cathy Mahoney cried during her wedding to Richard, Paul, who was sitting behind me, whispered, "I'd be crying too, if I was marrying Richard Mahoney.") He was a little miffed at me and started the evening with a lecture. But he couldn't stay angry. Soon, we were deep in conversation about politics, life, and choices.

Paul asked me to think of Canada as a shelter for homeless men that had run out of money. The choices were to close it down altogether or shut a wing down in order to save it. I asked him why it had run out of money and why government had money for Team Canada trade missions and corporate tax breaks but not for shelters. He seemed truly baffled at my position and we went round and round all evening. I said, "Paul, do you know what is happening to women's shelters and day care centres and programs for immigrants from your budget cuts?" "No," he answered. "I haven't had time for that, and those are provincial decisions now. I can't be responsible for it all. I just did what I had to."

I realized after that Paul Martin, who had been driven by limo to our meeting from a private golf course in Montreal, was a very decent man totally out of touch with the reality of most people's lives. I doubt if he had ever been inside a shelter for homeless men. I often say, "You are who you hang around with." Paul Martin hangs around with wealthy business friends, other politicians and, from time to time, the cream of the Canadian literary, media, and art world and sees life from a position of privilege. He is part of a new global royalty who have more in common with each other than they have with the majority of their own citizens. Such is politics in Canada as we approach the twenty-first century.

But this doesn't represent the real Canada — the thousands of dedicated ordinary Canadians who love their country and are proud of its history and fight every day to keep a "society" from becoming a mere "economy." Like many Canadians, I took my country for granted for many years, and only when I started to see it slip away did I realize I had to do something. The most important people in this country are not the power brokers. The most important people in Canada are those doing their bit to ease the burden of the "new economy" on the most vulnerable in our society: teachers, who are buying supplies, food, and even clothing for poor children in their care; front line nurses who double for the laid-off social workers in their hospital rounds and counsel needy patients; student activists fighting to stop the rise in tuition for future generations; seniors fighting to keep Medicare so that it will still be there for their grandchildren. These are the true heroes and heroines of Canada and they form the heart of this country.

The new royalty, on the other hand, has never had life sweeter. Corporate profits are up, corporate taxes are down, workers' wages are all but frozen, most politicians are obediently passing business-friendly laws (and undoing those that are not so friendly), and economic globalization is marching ahead. Perhaps most important, the mainstream press in Canada is now controlled by a small handful of older, white, wealthy, neo-conservative men who look and talk like the corporate elite, socialize with them, and use their editorial clout to promote their common interests.

10

CONFRONTING
CONRAD BLACK

"English Canada should prepare to submit, to its great profit
and comfort, and, ultimately, possibly even relief, to what
Mackenzie King described to General de Gaulle, in 1944, as
the gentle but 'overwhelming contiguity' of the United States."

Conrad Black

Over the years, I have had many opponents, some more worthy than
others. In spring 1996, I was to encounter one, the Right Honourable
John Crosbie, when I was honoured by Memorial University in
Newfoundland with a Doctorate of Laws. I was very moved by this
award. I get a lot of public criticism for my outspoken views and, while
I usually tolerate it pretty well, public recognition of my work goes a
long way to compensate. It is also a confirmation to council members
and other activists that this kind of work has meaning and is appreciated
by the community.

John Crosbie is a man I admire and like, although we have disagreed on just about everything, and, according to his 1997 autobiography, *No Holds Barred*, he doesn't reciprocate the feeling. Of our court challenge against Conrad Black, Crosbie wrote, "The perennially befuddled Council of Canadians, led by Maude Barlow, our version of Spain's La Pasionara, challenged the Southam acquisition in court on the grounds that our country and its institutions were somehow endangered by having too many newspapers controlled by one person. We can be sure of one thing: Maude and her motley crew would not have challenged the takeover if the purchaser had been a socialist or supporter of Liberal causes."

Born to an influential business family in Newfoundland, he was an accomplished scholar who hid his academic side under one of the most brilliant wits ever to grace Canadian politics. He served in the Newfoundland legislature under Liberal Joey Smallwood, but, disgusted with the corruption in Smallwood's government, switched to the Conservative Party, where he served in a number of key posts before leaving for federal politics. Crosbie was Joe Clark's finance minister and brought down the budget that toppled Clark's government. He ran for the Tory leadership against Joe Clark and Brian Mulroney in 1983, and carved out a clear position for himself on the hard right of the party. He was a fierce champion of free trade with the United States and he and Mulroney, who was opposed to free trade at this point, debated the issue many times on the campaign trail. He landed himself in hot water during the campaign when he defended his inability to speak French by joking that he didn't speak Chinese either.

Crosbie served on Mulroney's Cabinet in a number of important portfolios, including justice, and was the international trade minister during negotiations for the Canada–U.S. Free Trade Agreement. He admitted, some say boasted, that he had never read the deal and joked that critics' charges that it would lead to further Americanization of Canada was foolish, because Canada was already America's "love-slave." We had sparred many times through the media and Crosbie had more than once lost his (considerable) temper at the opposition the COC put up to this deal.

It turns out that John Crosbie is the chancellor of Memorial and, as such, his responsibilities include presiding over the sessions where the honorary doctorates are awarded. But he was furious that I was receiving this award and he refused to attend my ceremony. It was the talk of the campus. On the Saturday evening before my ceremony, my son Will and I attended a formal dinner put on for all those receiving honorary degrees, including the incomparable writer Timothy Findley and former Newfoundland Premier Clyde Wells. At the end of a wonderful meal, a professor sat down beside me and asked, "What have you done to John Crosbie that he hates you so much? He is sitting over there steaming, so angry he can't eat his meal." He'd had a little wine, as had we all, and he said, "I think you should go over and confront him." "I won't do that," I said, "but I will go over and say hello."

The whole room stopped talking as I approached him. Crosbie could clearly see me out of the corner of his eye but he sat rigid, his fists clenched, looking resolutely ahead. I knelt down in front of him, took both his hands in mine, turned him toward me and looked up into his face. "Well," he sputtered, "if it isn't little Maudie." I said, "Mr. Crosbie, I understand that you can't come to my convocation ceremony tomorrow. I know you must have something very important that keeps you from it and I want you to know that I understand. But the real reason I came over here is to thank you for honouring me with this wonderful degree. It means so much to me and I am so grateful you chose me for it." Clyde Wells, who was at Crosbie's table along with the president of the university, was laughing so hard tears were coming down his face and he rocked back and forth and pounded the table with his fists.

Crosbie mumbled something about my being "welcome, I guess" as I rose to walk back to my table. Half-way across the room, I stopped, turned, and called to him. "Oh John." As he turned to look at me, I smiled sweetly and blew him a kiss. To his credit, John Crosbie blew a kiss back. The whole room erupted in gales of laughter. Timothy Findley, sitting with Bill Whitehead, his partner of many years, said, "I must try kissing him too. I wonder how he'd take that!"

A much more personal and dangerous adversary is Conrad Black whose company, Hollinger, is the third largest newspaper corporation in the world. Black didn't get where he is by being nice. In 1984, he decided to "disassemble and liquidate" Dominion Stores, which he acquired as part of the acquisition holding company Argus Corporation in 1978.

"Preferably," he said at the time, "to foreigners." Black didn't like the "shiftless union" at the store (or anywhere else; he refers to unions variously as "scum" or "thugs" and "a mortal threat to any sense of community in an enterprise"), and he launched what he called a "war to the (commercial) death between the union and Dominion."

His tactics were ruthless. He brought in his right-hand man, David Radler, who "explicitly threatened shopping centre owners who wouldn't release us from our covenant . . . and, in a couple of cases had employees put rotting vegetables out in front of the stores to reduce the general ambience of the shopping centres." When the Retail, Wholesale, and Department Store Union fought back, Black boasted that he "recommended that a scythe be taken through the ranks of the low lives at the warehouse and it was."

In 1986, Hollinger withdrew the $38 million surplus from the pension fund for the unionized employees of the company, prompting Ontario NDP leader Bob Rae to describe him as "bloated capitalism at its worst." Black shot back that Rae represented "swinish socialist demagoguery at its worst" and said that Linda McQuaig, then a journalist with the *Globe and Mail* who had covered this case, should be "horse-whipped" but added, "I don't do those things myself and the statutes don't provide for it." The Ontario Supreme Court eventually ruled that the surplus be returned because the pension commission had failed to notify members of the plan of the withdrawal. The matter was eventually settled by splitting the funds between the company and the pension participants.

The only time I ever encountered Conrad Black socially was at a garden party at Kingsmere — Mackenzie King's estate, and the residence of the speaker of the House — during a visit from Charles and Diana in 1983. It was a beautiful early summer day. Women in big hats and flowing skirts and men in full evening dress rubber-necked to spot, or better yet, be spotted by, the young royals.

On a long table, almost impossible to get near for the crowds, were set large silver bowls of huge strawberries and warm chocolate for dipping. I came upon what I am sure was the last strawberry at the party at the same moment as Conrad Black. I smiled at him and said with a laugh, "Do you want to share or fight?" Before I could move, Black picked up a toothpick, speared the strawberry, dipped it in chocolate, popped it into his mouth, flicked the toothpick away, and walked off without a word. "That," I remember thinking, "is why you are rich and I am not."

I wrote about this years later in my column for the *Canadian Forum*. Someone must have given Black a copy for one day a lovely box of fat, ripe, New Zealand strawberries arrived at the office with a note from the man himself. "I cannot believe that I would have behaved in the discourteous manner you describe, but in the unlikely event that I was so overwhelmed by the ambience of Mr. King's ruins that I ate the last strawberry, I hope you will accept this penance." I sent him back a box containing several strawberry creams and his initials, CB, in dark chocolate, with a note that read, "Dear Conrad. Thank you for the lovely strawberries. You forgot the chocolates."

Unfortunately, those were probably to be the last kind words between us. In the spring of 1995, the Competition Bureau, which administers the Competition Act, gave Conrad Black's Hollinger Inc. the right to take over the entire Southam newspaper chain without even a public hearing. Our objection to his takeover was not personal; we were and are very concerned about the lack of diversity in the mainstream press. The Competition Act was written by a sub-committee of the Business Council on National Issues and enacted by the Mulroney government in 1986. It restricts access of the public to what are seen as purely commercial issues and it contains the weakest anti-combines provisions in the industrialized world.

No other country in the developed world has anywhere near the concentration of media as do we in Canada. In 1970 when the Davey Commission sounded the alarm about concentration in the media, 45 per cent of newspapers were controlled by just three corporations. By 1980, when the Kent Commission called for laws to deal with the problem, concentration had risen to 57 per cent. Today, it stands at 72 per cent, with one man, Conrad Black, controlling 60 per cent of the daily newspaper circulation. As well, private television, radio, and cable companies are increasingly owned by a small handful of companies who are sailing into the dangerous waters of cross-media ownership.

Communications Professor James Winter of the University of Windsor has done a study of Conrad Black's reach in the Canadian media. Through his control of newspapers that he directly owns and their holdings in Canadian Press and *Broadcast News,* Black reaches every newspaper in Canada but four, and 753 private and public broadcasting outlets across Canada. With his recent purchase of three more Thomson dailies on Vancouver Island, Black now controls 95 per cent of the circulation in British Columbia, 60 per cent in Nova Scotia, and has a virtual monopoly in Saskatchewan, Prince Edward Island, and Newfoundland. He also owns almost 70% of the dailies in Ontario and has recently taken control of the *Financial Post.* His wife, Barbara Amiel, editorial vice-president of Hollinger, is arguably the most widely read columnist in the country, with a piece in *Maclean's* magazine that reaches half a million families every month, and columns in 72 out of 105 Canadian newspapers. As well, the Blacks are launching their own national newspaper.

Aside from the issue of concentration, the COC is very concerned that Black uses his newspapers to promote his views, views already overly represented in the Canadian media. (Increasingly, the media are owned by those with fabulous wealth.) Hollinger President David Radler has said, "I am ultimately the publisher of all these papers, and if editors disagree with us, they should disagree when they're no longer in our employ." Asked by Peter C. Newman if the Southam papers had been forced to take Barbara Amiel's columns, Radler said, not exactly, but it wouldn't have been a very "career advancing" move to refuse them.

In England, Black openly used his powerful paper, the London *Daily Telegraph,* to campaign for Conservative prime ministers Margaret Thatcher (who claimed she was politically to Black's left) and John Major. In his autobiography, *A Life in Progress,* he describes how he gave a speech at the 1990 British Conservative Party annual conference written by a senior editor of his paper. He admits that, during a caucus revolt against Thatcher, "our editorial support of Mrs. Thatcher was unambiguous." One editorial in his paper declared, "As long as she seeks to retain that office, she may count on the support of this newspaper." In the 1992 British election, Black says the newspapers owned by him and other conservatives, "consistently warned of the consequences if Labour came in and raised income taxes and National Health Service payments."

He added that the Tory press "did a much better job of warning the people of the implications of a Labour victory than the government did," and added, "We own serious newspapers and reported fairly but went as far as we could in rational editorial arguments in favour of the government . . . our most powerful and elegant writers fired every cannon we had in promotion of the government's cause."

More recently, Black's *Daily Telegraph* played a central role in the attack on British Labour leader (now prime minister) Tony Blair and his wife, Cherie Booth, during the spring 1997 election. According to the *Globe and Mail*'s European Bureau, "If there is a silly picture to be had of Mrs. Blair, it can be found in the newspages of the *Telegraph* . . . . These are the awkward out-takes that newspapers usually reject as being needlessly demeaning of the subject or just plain juvenile." The reporter, Madelaine Drohan, speculated that this attack on Blair's wife was meant to unnerve him so that he would make a mistake in the weeks before the election.

Here in Canada, there are similar signs of editorial control. In October 1996, Black instructed his (then) fifty-nine Canadian daily newspapers to run a column he had written responding to "The Paper King," a CBC-TV documentary on Black's life which he called, "a smear job." As well, Hollinger President David Radler confirmed in an August 1996 interview with the *Toronto Star* that he and Black would impose their corporate will on the editorial content of their new newspapers in at least two areas: "One, the *Montreal Gazette* will stand up for the minorities who have been victimized by separatist governments. Two, any Hollinger paper that wants to support a Bob Rae-type socialist government better have pretty compelling reasons. We're not going to back a political party that seeks our destruction and the destruction of the capitalist system."

However, it is not necessary to intervene directly in a newspaper when you have hired the "right" kind of management. Both the *Vancouver Sun* and the *Ottawa Citizen* have swung hard to the right editorially and in their choice of columnists since Hollinger took them over in 1996 and replaced the senior staff. Now running the *Ottawa Citizen*, for example, are editor Neil Reynolds, former president of the Libertarian Party of Canada; editorial-page editor William Watson, former executive member of the right-wing Fraser Institute; and fellow editorial board members, Fraser Institute alumni John Robson and Dan Gardner (whose beat is education). These last two came directly to the paper, with no journalistic experience, from the office of then Ontario Education Minister John Snobelen (who once said if he couldn't find a crisis in education, he would create one). The *Citizen* carries the same chain-wide columnists that all the Southam papers now carry, right-wingers like Barbara Amiel, Andrew Coyne, George Jonas (Amiel's first husband), and former U.S. secretary of state (under Richard Nixon), Henry Kissinger.

One of my major concerns is the cross-fertilization of corporate, media, and political influence held by Conrad Black and his friends. Black's long-time newspaper partner, Peter White, was the principal secretary to Brian Mulroney when he was prime minister and is now chairman of the PC Canada fund and on the boards of both Hollinger and Southam. White was the chief fundraiser for Jean Charest when he was the federal Conservative leader and, in 1996 and again in 1997, he solicited funds for the party on Hollinger letterhead. Prior to the 1997 federal election, I put out a press release along with these shocking letters, condemning this flagrant abuse of White's position in the media to influence the outcome of the election directly; except for the *Toronto Star,* we were met with virtual silence from the media.

At the time of the Southam takeover, some of these incidents had already taken place and we were deeply concerned. I held a press conference with several other national groups to call on the federal Liberals to place a moratorium on the takeover and hold public hearings on what effect it would have on communities and diversity of views. When the government refused to intervene, we decided to launch a court challenge based on the argument that Canadians' Charter rights to freedom of expression were being violated by this level of media concentration. We had created a coalition called the Campaign for Press and Broadcasting Freedom with writers' groups and unions concerned about media concentration, but by the time we got the financial commitment to launch the case, a three-month deadline for challenges to the Competition Bureau's ruling had passed. Toronto lawyer Clayton Ruby, who has a formidable reputation in court and a strong sense of social justice, was hired to argue our case and ask the court to grant us the right to a trial even though we filed late, an option to which it could have easily agreed.

Black was asked by the *Globe and Mail* what he thought about me and the case before the court. He snorted, "I've never met her but to judge from her public efforts it's not hard to impute to her the motive of regret that the Southam papers may henceforth be less absolutely reliable and predictable mouthpieces of her feminist, socialist, envious, anti-American views than they have ever been."

The case as to whether we would go to trial was heard in Toronto on December 9, 1996, and we lost. The judge said that even if we hadn't missed the deadline, there really was no provision for groups like ours in the process. We appealed; we were heard again April 9, 1997, in Ottawa. I felt the judges didn't listen to one word of our argument; their minds were made up ahead of time. We lost here as well and were ordered to pay the other side's costs. My heart almost stopped beating. Peter Bleyer, our executive director, had been worried about just such a scenario. I took his hand for the four or five minutes the three justices took to determine the amount we owed and apologized for destroying the organization. Our penalty, however, was a slap on the wrist — $1,000. We were very relieved. But we were also very disturbed that there seems to exist no political will to stand up to Conrad Black in Canada.

On May 27, 1997, we decided to take our message to Hollinger's annual meeting at the Stock Exchange on Toronto's Bay Street. We had a cheque for Mr. Black — a twelve-foot long placard from the "Bank for Greedy Corporations," made out to "He Who Has So Much But Still Wants More" — and held a "street benefit" to raise the money. With music and handouts, Clay Ruby, Jim Winter, Gail Lem from the Communication, Energy, and Paperworkers Union, and many others in our coalition spoke to the Hollinger board members as they were entering the meeting. Most pushed by us, some with more than a little hint of violence. I asked board member Fredrik Eaton for a donation. "Conrad Black is so poor," I explained. Eaton roared with laughter. His company was in the midst of crisis. "We're a desperate company, Maude. Sorry. Can't help."

Conrad Black avoided us, entering by a back door. I did confront

David Radler as he was climbing out of his white stretch limo to attend the meeting. "Maude, you have to start your own newspaper," he said with a forced smile on his face for the cameras. "We don't have the money," I answered. "That's all it takes to be a businesswoman. Money is the key," he assured me.

Inside, the meeting was a wall of suits. Black looked tired and grumpy and ran the meeting like a drill sergeant. He introduced the board of directors, including Barbara Amiel, who stood on command and were recognized, then launched into a twenty-minute harangue, interrupted sporadically by applause and laughter from the mostly appreciative audience of shareholders, board members, employees, and various members of the Toronto establishment. He railed at the "politically primitive" country of Australia because it placed a ceiling on foreign ownership. He lashed out at the former staff of Southam, whom he had fired. Through the media present, he sent a warning to Southam minority shareholders that they should accept his buyout offer and not hold out for a better one, "as arithmetically-challenged fools and their money are soon parted."

The complaints continued. He ranted about the CBC, in particular the French-language network, which he described as a "house-organ of the separatist movement of Quebec." Endless concessions to separatists were wrong-headed: "There is no point throwing more raw meat to constitutional cannibals." He criticized the "lords of our national media," meaning the Toronto press, because a poll on Quebec separatism that Southam had commissioned was not picked up by the *Globe and Mail* and the *Toronto Star*. And he noted that the foolish court challenge by the Council of Canadians was over. Black was about to end the meeting, but first asked for questions from the floor. He was clearly enraged when Gail Lem, who had a proxy vote and could, therefore speak, and I took the microphone.

"We have listened to you today and are not reassured, especially hearing your views on Quebec. Mr. Black, newspapers are not just word factories and they are more than profit machines. The press has an integral role to play in democracy. Your increasing ownership of the media in this country is a dangerous development," she said to him. Gail warned the hushed shareholders that they were buying power and influence with their newspapers instead of running for election. "If you want that kind of power and influence, you should respect the democratic process and run for election and let the newspapers play the role they really need to play — the social role that is more than just making money."

Conrad Black was fuming. "These visitations from organized labour supplemented by the so-called Council of Canadians are getting a little tiresome," he said. "Miss Lem's perceptions are more deranged than I imagined. She is quite right not to be reassured by what we have done. If I were in her position, with her perspective and advocating what she advocates, I would not find the performance of this company reassuring either." He then proceeded to launch a vicious attack on unions which he said had "hobbled" the newspaper industry. Outside, he expressed contempt for our fears over his control of the news. "Owning [the newspaper in] Moose Jaw and the *Corner Brook Western Star* and the *Medicine Hat News*, in febrile Maude Barlow's little mind that may make me some kind of Goebbels of Canada but it doesn't."

I had been reading a fair bit about Black and Amiel's views and the more I read, the more concerned I became. Jim Winter and I decided it was important that Canadians know the views of the most powerful couple in Canadian media and so we wrote *The Big Black Book: The Essential Views of Conrad and Barbara Amiel Black*. What emerged from our analysis disturbed us. Black views his station in life as earned (his father was a millionaire) and defends the growing class system in Canada and elsewhere as the inevitable and natural consequence of liberty. As he explained to Peter C. Newman in his book, *The Establishment Man*, "It has always seemed to me that the real establishment in this country should be a handful of owners and a group of extremely capable managers so self-assured as to *behave* like owners, plus a battery of some lawyers and heads of large accounting firms and discreet stockbrokers who serve them well and with whom they are comfortable." He is so aggressive in his business dealings, we devoted a whole chapter to his views in this area.

Conrad Black approaches the world of business as a general approaches war. He views corporate acquisitions as a military manoeuvre and delights in outwitting his enemies. Like a professional military strategist, Black is a calculating adversary who lies in wait for the right moment to strike. Like a powerful general, he hones in on the weakness and moral flexibility of his opponents. "Most people are corruptible," he says. His writing is full of references to war; his military heroes are Napoleon, Admiral Nelson, General Douglas MacArthur, and Julius Caesar. Describing his business strategy in acquiring newspapers, he says that he keeps advancing "like a platoon of men through a forest, parallel lines moving in various directions. Wherever there is a breakthrough, I try to exploit it." Sometimes, he admits with more than a little relish, "to defeat the enemy, you have to inflict casualties as well as inconvenience."

Black was a great supporter of the Vietnam War and defended President Lyndon Johnson, who was a "great man." He wrote in one of his newspapers in the 1960s, that "a less patient and dedicated man, when taunted incessantly with the chant, 'Hey, hey, LBJ, how many kids have you killed today?' might have been tempted to reply: 'None, unfortunately.'" When the queen inspected the Governor General's Foot Guards during her trip to Canada in the summer of 1997, she was followed by a very sombre-looking Conrad Black in full military uniform and a huge beaver head-dress. For an "undisclosed sum of money" reported the *Ottawa Sun,* Black was allowed to dress up as an honorary colonel to attend the queen.

Black is openly contemptuous of "the locusts of feminism and multi-culturalism, the kleptocracy of organized labour" and says the Canadian concern for collective rights, "is, and always has been, recognized as a matrix for dictatorship, whether we are purporting to protect society from Communists, Jehovah's Witnesses, assorted bigots, wife beaters, gay bashers, office voyeurs, or discriminatory hirers." Bob Rae's Ontario government, about which he wrote relentlessly, was "a howling mob of single-issue fanatics: militant homosexuals, feminists, abortionists, eco-geeks, worker radicals, and social agitators, standing and shrieking on each other's shoulders."

Barbara Amiel has equally strong views, which she doesn't hesitate to promote. She is very clear about the women's movement. "The feminist reign of terror in Canada is such that it is better to proceed with charges of sexual assault that are patently false than risk feminist wrath if support is withdrawn from a so-called victim . . . . As evidentiary procedure changes to create kangaroo courts for accused males, our female judges, female Crown attorneys, and female elites remain mostly silent . . . . This reign of terror is their agenda . . . . 'What did you do, Mother,' Canadian children will ask in a decade or two, 'when men were imprisoned and reputations shredded in Canada's Feminist Salem?' . . . . For the past ten years at least, being a male has had aspects rather like being a Jew in Germany during the 1930s or a German in the postwar period."

Amiel has little patience for the culture or demands for justice of First Nations' people. "And what about the primitive work of Eskimos, Native peoples or Africans? It is of course of much anthropological or archaeological interest, if genuine. (If not, it is simply of no interest at all.) But it has the same relationship to art as an igloo to the Notre-Dame of Paris." In one article, she speaks forcefully about their claims for sovereignty. "Canada will . . . have to face the fact that, like every other nation on earth, it is founded on conquest . . . if the Indians are claiming sovereignty, then there is simply nothing to negotiate or renegotiate." Although she doesn't want to see men or women massacred, "it seems to me that a really strong show of force now is the only way to keep the casualties down to a minimum . . . . Perhaps at long last, we will bite the bullet and understand that the gun barrel created this country and that once more it will have to be used if Canada is to remain our home and native land."

Black and Amiel have both written extensively on Canada. Says Amiel, "Canada is still a better bet than a military junta, of course, but only for the politically unfree. Canadians themselves are becoming a sort of boat people, seeking friendlier environments." She is opposed to universal health care and education — "I prefer a society in which there is private medicine and private schools because their policies are decided by the people in charge of them" — and says the "nanny state" has gone entirely too far: "I would leave here as easily as I would have left Germany when its people elected Hitler to power." She adds, "There is no practical reason why any country in the world should bother learning about Canada when there are so many significant and pivotal international issues that require attention . . . . Canada is an immigrant's country and most often we have attracted people whose priorities are not very adventurous."

Black says Canada is "uncompetitive, slothful, self-righteous, spiteful, an envious nanny-state, hovering on the verge of dissolution and bankruptcy." He is opposed to regional equality programs. He has hardened his position on Quebec in recent years, saying that if it separates from Canada, it should be divided in two: an English-speaking part to remain in Canada and a smaller French-speaking portion to become independent. Canada would then be free to follow its real destiny. "Without Quebec, a majority of Canadians would be electors of Ralph Klein and Michael Harris."

Black talks openly about his love for the United States. "We could also draw officially closer to the United States, with whom, if we choose, we could make a much more rewarding arrangement than we have had with an unappreciative Quebec. Canada could negotiate arrangements with the United States that would preserve our regional distinctiveness as Texas and New England have preserved theirs . . . . Just 220 years after its founding, the most conceptually and materially powerful country in history would be virtually born again geopolitically by gaining access to Canadian resources and population . . . . Arguably, this could be at best achieved in one country rather than two."

Black writes of the great benefit that would accrue to the United States to have access to our resources, and says that in a new union Canada would have more influence on world affairs. Our few "folkloric" distinctions, such as Medicare and gun control, would "be accommodated in a fuller embrace with the United States anyway," and the only problem we would have to guard against would be an influx of "America's inner-city welfare cases, seeking to take advantage of Canada's extravagant social programs." This low view of Canada from a man who owns 60 per cent of the newspapers in this country!

When the book was published (by the very brave Jack Stoddart), we waited for the reaction to the material it contained. There was surprisingly little. I was concerned, not because of the book itself, but because the issues it raises were, for the most part, ignored by politicians and the media. I now believe that people are afraid of Conrad Black and Barbara Amiel.

This has been a disillusioning experience for me. I do not bash journalists as a group. On the whole, I think they do a good job under tight deadlines and some brave unions, like the one at the *Kingston Whig-Standard*, have gone on strike in recent months. But I can't help but wonder if the silence, or worse, the studied cynicism of so many journalists, especially those of the national press, comes from a fear of losing their jobs or a desire to get a place with Black's new national newspaper which is about to be launched. If that is the case, what future is there for independent journalism in Canada?

All that was left to us for now was to monitor the Hollinger-Southam merger. Under the capable hands of our then research director, David Robinson, the council undertook the most extensive content analysis of a media merger ever done in Canada by monitoring almost four thousand items in six Southam papers that had been acquired by Black's Hollinger. In the years covered by the study, 1991 to 1996, labour coverage plummeted, women's and aboriginal issues were almost totally ignored, and the odd bedfellows of business and lifestyle reporting grew.

While more money had been put into the bigger papers like the *Ottawa Citizen*, the *Vancouver Sun*, and the *Montreal Gazette*, we found the smaller papers were being starved, both for staff and money. Where there was no alternative, the local Hollinger paper had declined in every category. It was also clear that we were witnessing the recolonization of the Canadian press — the world seen clearly through the eyes of Conrad Black's London *Daily Telegraph*, *Jerusalem Post*, and *Chicago Sun-Times*.

The 1997 Southam Annual Report showed that, while labour costs had dropped dramatically, Southam's return on revenue was up by 63 per cent. Jim Winter confirms that Southam has laid off over two thousand employees since Black first bought into the company in 1992. In 1997, Hollinger had a profit of $171 million, up from $46 million the year before. While his employees were struggling, Black's pay packet rose 118 per cent to $5.8 million, not including a one-time special dividend he paid himself on his shares in Hollinger to the tune of $70 million. David Radler paid himself just under $5 million in the same year.

The Council of Canadians and the Communications, Energy, and Paperworkers Union have produced a blueprint for the kind of anti-trust legislation that could go a long way to dealing with the crisis of media concentration in Canada. Restrictions could be placed on the number of daily newspapers, radio, or television stations owned by any one company as well as the ownership of cross-media in total. The current

Competition Act could be amended to require that a proposed media merger is in the public interest. We also need measures to encourage diversity of ownership in Canada and ways to ensure industry accountability for the accurate presentation of news and diversity of content.

Such legislation is not extreme and would bring us into line with other industrialized nations. But under the present crop of Libertories, we don't have a ghost of a chance. Conrad Black has the field to himself.

11

THE FIGHT GOES GLOBAL

"There is no polite way to say that business is
destroying the world."

Paul Hawken
Businessman-turned-environmentalist

On October 3, 1997, the tenth anniversary of the Reagan-Mulroney
handshake that sealed the Canada–U.S. Free Trade Agreement, Bob
White, Tony Clarke, and I were invited to a small dinner gathering of the
victorious trade warriors at the stately Rideau Club in Ottawa to celebrate the publication of Gordon Ritchie's intriguing memoirs of that
fight, *Wrestling with the Elephant*. Bob was out of town but Tony and I
jumped at the opportunity to break bread with these powerful former
adversaries and find out what they were thinking about now. I was
escorted by security to the august Karsh Room past photo galleries of the
past and present politicians, civil service mandarins, corporate lawyers,
and business leaders (men all) who have run Ottawa for years and who
retreat after work to the quiet elegance of this most famous of the
Capital's private clubs.

192

They included: Gordon Ritchie, Canadian deputy chief negotiator of the Canada–U.S. FTA; Bill Merkin, U.S. deputy trade negotiator of the Canada–U.S. FTA; Bill Fox, senior Mulroney aide and chief public relations troubleshooter during the FTA years; Mike Apsey, head of the influential lobby, the Council of Forest Industries; Mitchell Sharp, former Liberal Cabinet minister and Chrétien adviser; Roger Tasse, former deputy minister of justice. Missing were Tom d'Aquino, head of the BCNI and passionate free-trade advocate who got tied up at a meeting, and lead FTA negotiator, Simon Reisman, who was too enraged by how he felt he was treated in Ritchie's book to attend. Publishers Jack Stoddart and Jan Walter were also present.

It was a remarkable evening. Besides being invited, which was remarkable enough, I was impressed with the civility and courtesy shown us. The dinner (spinach pasta roll, consommé, poached Atlantic salmon, lemon tart) was followed by port and cigars and talk, lots of talk. As often happens when adversaries come face to face in a social setting, I started to see the human side of my table companions. I realized that they had been a lot less sure of themselves than I thought at the time and that they wanted to be judged by history as having done right by their country. Bill Merkin recalled how little political weight the FTA talks had had in Washington (compared to the NAFTA talks with Mexico) and how hard he and Peter Murphy, senior U.S. trade negotiator for the talks (now dead of a brain tumour), had to work to convey the Canadian bottom line to busy American politicians who largely took Canada for granted.

They also seemed genuinely respectful of our position and the fight we had put up ten years earlier. Tony remarked that the free trade fight in Canada had not led to violence as it might have in other countries. Canada was special, he said, because we could have such deep and fundamental and public disagreements about the future and still sit down and have this kind of exchange.

Afterward, two observations stood out for me: their conviction that all was right with the world and the limited nature of the touchstones they use to make such judgements. Their assessment of the decade was one of pure success. Exports, the GDP, and corporate profits were up; productivity was down. The world was operating as it should. No mention was made of the cuts to social programs, the growth in poverty, or the deregulation of the environment. Sitting in that beautiful room, its walls covered with original Karsh photographs, I could see the allure of this life and how easy it would be to fall out of touch with the real world. These men, most of whom now advise or sit on the boards of global corporations, like Paul Martin, form the Canadian vanguard of globalization. Their views are becoming the norm in nations' capitals all around the world.

Economic globalization. This has become a term that means many things to many people. I have been working to understand and modify it since the day in late 1993 when I got a call from American writer and activist Jerry Mander to come to a meeting in San Francisco, where he lives, and join others from around the world engaged in work similar to mine. Jerry is an extraordinary man. He works for several American foundations established by Doug Tompkins, the controversial ecologist who founded the Esprit corporation and now lives on a ranch in Chile where he owns a huge swath of old growth forest that stretches across the entire country. Jerry is deeply concerned about the effect of technology on cultural and biological diversity and wrote a book, *In the Absence of the Sacred*, considered by many to be the most important case against television ever written. He has friends and allies all over the world.

In January 1994, about sixty-five of us, including myself and fellow Canadians Tony Clarke and Steven Shrybman (now of the West Coast Environmental Law Association) sat down together in the old Tompkins home on San Francisco's historic Russian Hill for the first time and started a global movement. I was overwhelmed by the people I met. Friends from the NAFTA fight were there. American environmental leaders such as Carl Pope of the Sierra Club; Brent Blackwelder of Friends of the Earth and Barbara Dudley of Greenpeace attended, as did David Korten (*When Corporations Rule the World)*, and Jeremy Rifkin (*The End of Work*). Leading community activists joined pioneers in the fight to control corporate power.

Celebrated international participants included Indian physicist, writer, and activist, Vandana Shiva; Third World Network director and veteran of years of global trade negotiations, Martin Khor; British conservationists and writers (*The New Protectionism*), Tim Lang and Colin Hines; Chilean environmental leader, Sara Larrain; Agnes Bertrand of EcoEuropa in France; aboriginal organizer Victoria Tauli-Corpuz from the Philippines; and *Ecologist* editor, Edward Goldsmith. These were some of the brightest minds in the world on the subject of economic globalization.

Although we came from different cultures, and had different histories with government (given their own history with brutal governments, some were surprised when we Canadians lamented the dramatic downsizing of our government), we started to forge an analysis of economic globalization that week that has opened the door for a kind of organized global activism none of us even dreamed of before. By the end of that first meeting, we had formed ourselves into the International Forum on Globalization, with a staff and a board of directors, on which I serve.

The notion of the inevitability of globalization is so widespread in academic, political, media, and corporate circles, that questioning it publicly brands one as a nostalgic, out-of-touch nationalist, protectionist, or Luddite. David Korten writes about this feeling of alienation from the dominant "paradigm" of our time. In his extensive travels, he found an almost universal sense among ordinary people that the institutions on which they used to depend are failing them and that the economic indicators that are touted by their leaders as proof that economic globalization is working have no meaning in their daily lives. Many are increasingly fearful of the future for themselves and their children, and are feeling estranged from their political rulers.

As Korten notes, "It is often the people who live ordinary lives far removed from the corridors of power who have the clearest perception of what is really happening. Yet they are often reluctant to speak openly of what they believe in their hearts to be true. It is too frightening and differs too dramatically from what those with more impressive credentials and access to the media are saying. Their suppressed insights may leave them feeling isolated and helpless. The questions nag: Are things really as bad as they seem to me? Why don't others seem to see it? Am I stupid? Am I being intentionally misinformed? Is there anything I can do? What can anyone do?"

We grappled with these questions at the IFG. The proponents of economic globalization say that a single global economy with universal rules for business is the most efficient system, allowing the creation of a global consumer market. For us, it is the spread of a single market ideology, a Western "monoculture of the mind," as Vandana Shiva describes it, that is exterminating cultural and biological diversity, creating an entrenched class system, and destroying the natural world. Our collective research tells us that there is a watershed global transformation taking place as great as any in history, and that it is not going well for the majority.

At the core of this transformation is an all-out assault on every public sphere of life. In 1997, US$157 billion worth of public government resources were transferred to private companies, up 70 per cent in one year. These include health care, education services, pensions, roads, prisons, hydro-electric facilities, transportation systems, and natural resources. The state of Texas has even decided to privatize welfare services, and is likely to give the contract to Lockheed Martin, one of the biggest weapons manufacturers in the world.

Increasingly, these services will be delivered by global corporations operating outside of any national or international law. The top two hundred corporations are so big, their combined sales now surpass the combined economies of 182 countries and they have almost twice the economic clout of the poorest four-fifths of humanity. These corporations, which have abandoned the nation-states of their birth, are creating new global law in the form of trade and investment treaties designed to knock down any remaining barriers to their free movement that governments have not already removed. A Japanese executive with the powerful *Keidanren*, Japan's largest business lobby group, explains kindly that "the nation-state is not really dead, but it is being quickly retired."

Transnational corporate profits have also escaped nation-state law and most countries are lowering corporate taxes to remain competitive. Citizens are left to shoulder the burden as stateless traders move on. An estimated $2 trillion in financial speculation moves around the globe every day in the global trading markets untouched and untouchable by governments. An entrenched underclass is being created in every country of the First World, and an elite class in the Third — a global south and north no longer related only to geography. The United Nations reports that the disparity in the level of income between the top 20 per cent and the bottom 20 per cent of the world's population is 150:1 and has doubled in the last thirty years. As countries line up one after another to privatize their social security, they are disenfranchising millions of their citizens who are left with no social programs, health care, or access to education.

Millions more are now working in Export Processing Zones — areas in which transnational corporations manufacture, process, store, and export goods duty-free. There are currently five hundred such zones world-wide, most of them located in the developing nations of Asia and Latin America (such as the ones I visited in Mexico), but they are spreading to the First World. (I discussed Canada's first planned experiment slated for Lorneville, New Brunswick, in Chapter Nine.) The designated area is sealed off behind high fences and often secured with private security forces. The zones form an enclave, separated from the rest of the country physically, economically, and socially.

Most of these free trade zones allow transnational corporations to operate outside the economic, labour, and environmental laws of the host country. Many countries abandon their workers in the zones, and local authorities openly ignore labour and environmental abuses forbidden in law. Labour organizing is strongly dissuaded, sometimes with violence. Conditions inside the EPZs are deplorable. For the corporations, it's a bonanza: they get a young, docile, usually female labour force; they are exempt from paying customs duties; they can export 100 per cent of their profits; they pay no income tax in the host country; and they are not required to transfer their technology to the host country or contribute to its industrial development.

The environment is very much at risk from economic globalization. Global treaties give transnational corporations the right to challenge national environmental laws if they appear to restrict trade. American laws to protect Asian sea turtles from shrimp nets and dolphins from drift nets used to catch tuna off the coast of Mexico have recently been successfully challenged at the World Trade Organization. The WTO says all "like" products have to be treated the same for the purposes of trade, regardless of the conditions under which they were caught or made.

An American corporation, Ethyl, sued the Canadian government for $350 million dollars because it banned the neurotoxin MMT from gasoline used in cars. The company claimed its rights under NAFTA to seek compensation for lost future profit caused by this ban, and the case was heard, in secret, by a panel of trade experts, not in a Canadian court. Outrageously, knowing it was going to lose the case, the Chrétien government capitulated to Ethyl before the panel ruled on it. In July 1998, it reversed its ban on MMT and agreed to pay the company's costs for the challenge. NAFTA was successfully sued to ensure the interests of a giant corporation over the health of Canadian citizens.

NAFTA also gives American and Mexican corporations the right to as much Canadian water as they want the minute we allow any Canadian company to export one drop of it for commercial purposes. The privatization of the world's forests and the deregulation of mining practices means essentially that transnational corporations are "self-regulating" in their environmental practices. Governments are fast losing the right to protect their natural resources and international trade agreements will see to it they don't get them back.

An international agency, the Codex Alimentarius, sets global food standards on allowable pesticide, additive, and contaminant levels, as well as the labelling of genetically altered foods. If any country establishes a higher standard for any food product than that set by the Codex, it can be challenged under the WTO for trade violations. Sitting on virtually every committee of the Codex are representatives of the largest food and chemical transnational corporations in the world. Coca-Cola and Nestlé sit on the committee that sets standards for child nutrition. These corporations are having a powerful impact on the standards now being set. At a Codex meeting on bovine growth hormone in the summer of 1997, Canada was prepared to impose no limit on the drug in meat or milk. Little wonder: our delegation included a senior executive with Monsanto, the company that manufactures BGH.

In a global economy, the role of agriculture is to produce profits for corporate interests instead of producing food for people. Food cultivation is being reduced to a mere industrial technique; farming is moving full speed towards becoming part of an integrated market-production system like other industrialized sectors, dominated by a handful of transnational corporations. Agriculture has been thrust suddenly and brutally into the international free trade arena with the creation of the WTO. Any marketing or regulatory system that impacts in any way on international trade can now be classed as a barrier to trade. Both the WTO and NAFTA ensure the privatization of the world's genetic inheritance by granting transnational corporations the right to challenge governments who continue to claim these properties as the common heritage of their people.

In the new system, plants are bred by corporate scientists — high-yielding, "improved" crops that are hybrids and cannot be replanted. Farmers cannot save the seed from their crops to plant again, but must purchase new stock each year from the seed companies. The farmers become dependent on international seed companies who are often part of larger corporations. Often, these corporations own the chemical manufacturing firms that produce the fertilizer and pesticides that the new "improved" seeds need to survive. If this trend continues, the world's farmers could become totally dependent on a small group of transnational agri-corporations whose sole goal is profit and whose activity will deplete the world of genetic diversity.

Tony Clarke has coined the term "corporate rule" to explain the new system of global governance. We at the IFG have come to believe that while politicians may govern, they no longer rule. In March 1997, I had a private breakfast meeting with British Columbia Premier Glen Clark — a decent man with not a touch of arrogance to his character — at a coffee shop near his house to talk about the Multilateral Agreement on Investment (MAI) and I put this to him. "You probably disagree," I said, "but some of us now think that transnational corporations have more power than governments." "Are you kidding?" he blurted. "I'm living with their power every day. Corporations tell all politicians what to do. They rule British Columbia. They rule Canada. They rule the world." (When I saw Glen Clark on television a year later wearing an IBM T-shirt because he was trying the lure the company to build a site in his province, I thought to myself that this must have been hard for a proud trade unionist to do.)

Certainly, business interests now rule the world of international relations. The Chrétien Liberals even merged Foreign Affairs and Trade into one department and the only group it invites on the Team Canada missions is the private sector. To Canada's shame, concern for human rights has been supplanted by the international trade agenda; we will do business with just about anybody. As a senior Foreign Affairs official explains, "We used to go in with lists of political prisoners we wanted released. Now we go in with lists of companies that want contracts."

To counter the commonly held notion that this is all inevitable and that there is no alternative to this form of economic globalization, we decided that massive public information and debate were needed and we resurrected the 1960s concept of teach-ins. Our first teach-in was held on a weekend in November 1995 at the historic Riverside Church in New York where Martin Luther King used to be a guest preacher. We didn't know what to expect. We were overwhelmed. The line-up started hours before the event and snaked around the church and down two blocks. Twenty-five hundred enthusiastic people stayed for an intense weekend of learning, sharing, and reflection. I was on the opening panel the Friday night and was moved to be standing in that pulpit in front of that audience. They were so clearly hungry for the information and point of view they were hearing.

We followed this with teach-ins in Washington and Berkeley, California, each time to sell-out crowds. Two years later, in November 1997, the IFG committee on corporations, chaired by Tony, brought ninety activists, scholars, economists, and writers who are leaders in the fight against corporate rule from around the world to the Canadian Auto Workers compound in Port Elgin, Ontario, where we held the First International Symposium on Global Corporate Rule. This was followed by the first International Teach-In on Global Corporate Rule in Convocation Hall at the University of Toronto.

It had the feel of a rock concert with thousands of young people, to whom this issue clearly speaks, trying to get in. We finally had to give up any attempt to sell tickets, as we would have been there all night, and opened the doors. At two thousand, the hall was full, and we had to close the doors. There was such energy in that hall that night. Our international speakers were greeted with such enthusiasm, some could hardly speak. I introduced Owens Wiwa, the brother of the Nigerian poet, Ken Saro-Wiwa, who was executed by the military dictatorship for fighting the environmental devastation perpetrated against the Ogoni people by Shell Oil. I no sooner said, "Tonight we honour a man who has been called on to sacrifice more than most of us can imagine," than the crowd roared to its feet and clapped and cheered for such a long time that Owens put his head down and wept. He told me afterwards that the evening gave him the courage to keep up the fight.

We took the fight to a political level, following the leaders of various countries to the meetings where they were to plan the next round of globalization. APEC — the Asia Pacific Economic Cooperation forum — is by far the boldest free-trade initiative in the world. Made up of eighteen member "economies" (they don't call themselves countries), APEC sets up a timetable for unrestricted foreign investment, unlimited export of profits, massive privatization of state assets, access to natural resources by transnational corporations, and the establishment of a superior class of visa for businessmen. Every year, a different "economy" hosts the forum. In 1996, it was the Philippines, and a small Canadian delegation went to participate in forums put on by our counterparts in Manila.

I knew that there were two types of visitors to Manila the moment I arrived. The prime minister and the Canadian delegation were whisked in air-conditioned limos on specially cleared roads, past "beautified" slums, to villas so fabulous that the Sultan of Brunei stayed an extra day to buy several. Those of us not in the official party were treated like criminal suspects and harassed at customs. A pipe bomb in a suitcase went off yards away from where we were standing at the airport, and the police, seemingly unconcerned for our safety, were a long time responding to calls for help.

The visiting VIPs were clearly more important than the citizens of the Philippines as well. President Ramos had vowed that there would be little or no protest and used military violence to suppress opposition. Protesters were beaten and arrested. "Friendship lanes" for foreign delegates were set aside, causing huge traffic jams, many accidents, and a dozen child deaths. Blue dye was poured into Manila Bay to beautify the water; thirty tons of dead fish floated to the surface, and many children became violently ill as a result of eating the contaminated fish.

Thousands of shanties were demolished in an attempt to create an "eye-sore-free" zone for visiting dignitaries. I was taken to visit several dozen brave fishing families who returned to their land on Manila Bay to protest this treatment. Young and old, they were living almost knee-deep in water from the dredging of the harbour and were regularly beaten up and had their protest signs burned in front of them. They had a "leader," a small, wiry man in his late seventies named Red, who escorted us through his community with great courtesy and formality as if we were visiting a palace, introducing his people to us, giving us a history of the oppression of his community. We stood on the now barren land, surrounded by a wall of concrete high-rises, and I felt that this man, who hadn't a hope of stopping the destruction of his village, was as dignified a leader as I had ever met anywhere.

(The land has since been confiscated and is now owned by a Hong Kong banker. It is slated to become the largest super-mall in the world, and will house the first Disneyworld of the region. The residents were not compensated, nor were they relocated. They just vanished into the slums of Manila.)

When I attended several alternative citizen forums to the APEC Summit, I was stunned by the raw nature of politics in the Philippines. These activists were the people who had brought down the Marcos regime, and the walls of the conference rooms were covered in gruesome photos of that struggle: clashes with police, torture victims, raped women, dead babies. At first, these images were too upsetting to bear, especially given the incongruity of sitting beside them through academic papers on liberalization in China, or the history of Japanese/Filipino relations. But I came to understand that these people had sacrificed a great deal for their (still fragile) political freedom and they wanted to stay close to that struggle and honour the memory of those who died for it. Out of the people's forums came statements of opposition to APEC that were handed on to the Canadians there, as the next APEC Summit was to be in Canada.

The Summit itself was held on the former United States naval base in Subic Bay where the leaders were flown in by helicopter. Our groups organized a massive and peaceful protest caravan from Manila, but the highways leading to Subic Bay were lined with thousands of non-military local citizens who had been armed with clubs and paid by local authorities to prevent the protesters from reaching Subic Bay and the march was stopped. I was among several Canadians and other foreigners who were secreted into Subic Bay where we saw the brutality up close. There, we stayed at a home for the abandoned children of American GIs and Filipino women called the Preda Foundation, run by Father Shay Cullen, a social activist for children, and a constant thorn in the side of local power brokers who plan to turn Subic Bay into a Hong Kong-like global free port for the rich. (Like the experiment run by the Catholic Church in Chiapas, the Philippine authorities don't dare shut him down for fear of an international outcry from his supporters all over the world.)

The compound sits high on a hill overlooking the naval base. We cut down sweet grass and sent "smoke signals of trouble" down the mountain, as we unfurled a gigantic banner that read, "APEC Hurts Children." For several days, we remained literally in an armed encampment, surrounded by armed military, fire trucks with hoses at the ready, and goons carrying clubs and bags of urine and feces with which to attack us. On the last day, a glorious sunny day with a high wind, Father Shay led us down to the end of the property to hold our protest.

We couldn't leave the grounds for fear of violence as we knew that local unarmed protesters walking to meet us had been assaulted with baseball bats and badly beaten. With all the children safely up on the balcony, cheering us on, we gave our speeches, with no crowd and no press (they were sequestered on the naval base and "discouraged" from leaving it). We called on our governments to deal with the crucial issues of human rights, child labour, and environmental crime in their negotiations down below us. I spoke on behalf of the Canadians there and urged Jean Chrétien to raise these issues because Canadians care about them and want their governments to stand for something beyond the bottom line. I have given many speeches in my life, but I don't think I have ever had a more important or appreciative audience than that little group of children on the balcony, clapping their hearts out.

That evening, we watched a play written and performed by a dozen of Manila's estimated 1.5 million street children, in which they told the story of their country. With amazing political sophistication, they told of the military invasion of the Japanese, the sexual exploitation at the hands of Americans stationed after World War Two at Subic Bay, and, dressed as McDonald's, Mitsubishi, Coca-Cola, and Shell, the economic occupation of their country by corporations. The leader of the troop, and by far the oldest, was a sixteen-year old street prostitute named Gerry who, without one day of schooling in his life, wrote and directed the play, designed the costumes, and composed the accompanying music. Then the children of the orphanage turned out all the lights and danced for us by candlelight.

Father Shay negotiated with the local authorities and late that night, we were escorted out of the compound, lying on the floor of the jeeps that would take us past the armed thugs and back to Manila. I was too emotional from the children's performances to be frightened for my safety, although I suppose I should have been. I had watched them in a trance, deeply moved, and was now lost in wonder that these extraordinary children could have gained such insight from their harsh lives. They had so very much to teach me. What would happen to them all. Would they just go back to the street? Was there anything I could do from home? I found myself thinking about my own country and how we take our freedoms so for granted. And how fragile democracy is, even, or perhaps especially, in a country like Canada, where we have come to think it is unassailable.

The next APEC Summit was held a year later in Vancouver, and the COC was part of a national coalition of women, church, human rights, labour, and environmental organizations that planned the alternative "Peoples' Summit." The Canadian government's outreach to "civil society" was not to work with the organized representatives of various communities but to hand-select individual youth, women, academics, and entrepreneurs who shared their vision. Under intense pressure, the APEC Secretariat of the Department of Foreign Affairs and International Trade finally agreed to meet with us, and the huge gulf between the sides became painfully obvious.

Officials kept talking about "the economy of Canada" and the prime minister as the "economic leader." Much to my dismay, Status of Women Canada had been brought in to organize a conference for women entrepreneurs of the "APEC economies" with the unbelievable title, "Stepping In, Stepping Out." It sounded to me like a debutante party. I knew several of the women there and felt sick at what the office was becoming. A senior official with the Environment Department kindly explained that environmentalists had not been invited to be a part of "consultations" on the impact of APEC on the environment "because the business community doesn't want you." People started shouting at each other. It got so bad, Elizabeth May left the room in tears at one point. I was the closing speaker for our side and with irony thanked the government representatives for doing in one afternoon what we in the citizens' groups hadn't been able to do in months of meetings — put aside our differences to approach and become one united team in opposition.

By the time of the November summit, the bloom was beginning to come off the rose of globalization. President Clinton had been denied his "fast-track" renewal which would have given Congress the power to pass trade deals intact. The financial crisis in Asia was just breaking, making it clear that the promised economic miracle for that region was still far away. Currencies were collapsing in countries like Indonesia and Thailand, whose hot economies until very recently had been considered invincible. The once-mighty Japan was going through a profound economic upheaval that would lead it into a full recession within the year, threatening the economy of not just the region but the whole world. For the last decade, Japanese investors had artificially driven up stock, real estate, and natural resource prices around the world. When the inflation bubble burst, the world's greatest lender took out the whole Asian economy with it. The *Globe and Mail* quoted a Toronto money manager, who said he now spends his time counting the country's debts, not its assets. He added that it might be all over for Japan. "They are probably the shortest-lived economic superpower in history."

At the time of the APEC Summit, the International Monetary Fund was giving dire warnings about the kinds of disciplines that would be needed to straighten up the economies of the "Asian Tigers," and the APEC leaders knew this would mean that millions of their citizens — the so-called emerging consumer class — were about to be thrust back into dire poverty. Hardest hit were people in the rural communities and inner cities. Already, reports were circulating about massive school drop-outs, widespread malnutrition, and increased death rates among children. For me, the fact that this suffering is being borne disproportionately by women is an added cause for anger at the politicians and economists who assured us that economic globalization was closing the great economic divide between men and women. Across most of Asia, it is still true that women are second-class citizens. If a child has to be pulled from school, it will be the girl. If an office worker has to be laid off, it will be the woman. Years of progress on the gender front are being wiped away as the false promise of the new economy ravages Asia.

As well, many Canadians were truly upset that our government was welcoming Chinese president Jiang Zemin, who in a visit to Washington just the month before had called the Tiananmen Square massacre "much ado about nothing," and President Suharto of Indonesia, a brutal dictator who has killed at least a million of his own people and about a third of the population of East Timor (and who has since been toppled in an extraordinary display of courage by the students of Indonesia). The Canadian media noted all of this, and the fact that the issues of interest to people were being discussed at our summit while the issues of interest to business were being discussed at the official summit.

When I gave the opening keynote at the Peoples' Summit, I took the gloves off and challenged Jean Chrétien. I deplored the massive corporate backing of the official summit and the fact that donations of a certain level bought the companies access to the political leaders. "It is with a great sense of shame that we Canadians are witnessing certain activities on the part of our governments here. While the brutal dictator Suharto is being welcomed with open arms, Canada has turned away several East Timorese activists for fear of embarrassing him. The Canadian government has declared the other APEC Summit site off limits to us dissenters. Well, Mr. Chrétien, I have news for you. We weren't put off by the bully boys in Manila and we won't be denied our fundamental rights for peaceful protest whenever and wherever we need to be this week."

These words seem prophetic considering the brutal pepper spraying and intimidation of protesters by the RCMP in the days that followed. Vancouver didn't feel all that different from Manila a year before. Security was so tight it shut down the core of the city. People were arrested for even holding peaceful signs of protest. But I did feel a change in the political wind. The triumph of the politicians was muted and it was clear our position was gaining respect. Even pro-APEC economists and academics were appalled at Canada's defence of Suharto and said so publicly. A BCTV reporter interviewed me in front of BC Place, the magnificent waterfront complex where the leaders were meeting. "You must feel vindicated," she said. "They look so out of touch and your side has captured everyone's imagination." I conceded that there were some signs of hope. But I knew that the big test was still to come.

12

SWEET VICTORY

"The MAI has probably rendered a service. The transparent
greed of the instrument; the overreaching for corporate power
and domination of every aspect of our lives went too far. The
pendulum is beginning to swing back."

Elizabeth May
The Sierra Club

In October 1997, I travelled to Paris as part of a Canadian delegation at
the invitation of the Organization for Economic Cooperation &
Development (OECD) to discuss the biggest global investment liberalization treaty ever negotiated. The OECD is made up of the twenty-nine
most powerful economies on Earth, home to 477 of the Global Fortune
500 companies. It is housed at a huge estate in the elegant sixteenth
arrondissement of Paris, once the stately palace of Baron Rothschild who
donated it to the governments of the industrialized countries to promote
joint economic liberalization policies. Its head is Donald Johnston, a
Canadian who held several Cabinet posts in the Trudeau government
and is such an avid free trader, he quit the Liberal caucus when John

Turner took his stand against the Canada–U.S. Free Trade Agreement. Though I didn't know it at the time, I was heading into a major confrontation with global stakes.

For years, the United States, prodded by its business community, has been trying to get a binding set of rules to protect its global investments. For years, other countries have held out, insisting on the right to attach conditions to foreign investment that would require it to create jobs and promote local economies. But recently, the heat has been turned up on this campaign. Corporations have become so large, and their lobby groups so powerful, that they are now demanding legal equality to nation-states in international law, including the right to challenge governments directly, and access to a judicial process to back them up.

Alarmed at this development, citizens' groups in the developing world have urged their governments, with some real success, to resist giving corporations such rights. They argue that most of their countries have very little domestic-owned industry, and that investment rules would dramatically favour the West. At the same time, citizens' groups in Europe and North America can see that these same corporations, even if they originate in their countries, are already using their clout to drive down environmental, labour, and social standards in their own societies, and they are worried that global investment rules will create a global "race to the bottom." Recently, recognizing their joint interests, citizens' groups in the Third World started to work with citizens' groups in the First World, including the Council of Canadians, to form an international movement to halt the common erosion of our rights posed by the demand for these new powers.

The United States has had some limited success. The last GATT talks led to the creation of the World Trade Organization (WTO) in 1995. But it wasn't until Canada and Mexico capitulated to the Americans in NAFTA, that the United States was able to gain real ground.

In the past, if an industry sector or a corporation had a dispute with its counterpart in another country, it had to convince its own government to launch a trade dispute with the government of the "offending" industry. Then the complaint would be heard before an independent panel of other governments. NAFTA, however, gave corporations (who were not signatories to the deal), the right to bypass their own government and sue directly for future lost profits if they could demonstrate that a law, regulation, or practice of another country had directly hurt them. This principle is now included in every bilateral deal Canada signs one-on-one with other countries.

Armed with this success, the United States (and subsequently Canada, a totally committed convert under Chrétien's Liberals) proposed a global investment treaty based on these corporate rights to the very first ministerial meeting of the newly formed World Trade Organization in December of 1996. The developing countries strongly objected to what they rightly saw as a form of neo-colonialism and said no. However, they did set up a working group to study the proposal. IFG member Martin Khor of the Third World Network was there and was not reassured. Martin had already sounded the alarm about this to an IFG gathering in San Francisco the year before and knew how determined the First World countries were to promote this process. In fact, he reported, a Multilateral Agreement on Investment (MAI) was by now also being quietly discussed at the OECD — the club of rich nations — where, once signed, it would be taken back to the WTO for global ratification.

As I had never heard of the MAI, I immediately called then Trade Minister Roy MacLaren's office about it. I was assured there was no such thing, that "discussions" were always going on to "improve" trade and investment rules, but that there was no MAI. Don't worry. Be happy. I was suspicious. Based on an OECD document Martin had given me that described the treaty, I wrote an op-ed piece that was carried in several newspapers expressing grave concern for what might be in this deal, the text of which we couldn't get our hands on. Resounding silence. We couldn't seem to get anyone, including other activists, interested. And we couldn't prove that it existed. Then one day in early March 1997, Tony Clarke obtained a draft copy of the proposed treaty, marked CONFIDENTIAL, and we had our proof.

I read this document on a plane from Vancouver and I was so upset at it that I phoned Tony three times from the air. (No wonder. We soon found out later that the first draft had been written by the International Chamber of Commerce.) Under the proposed treaty, governments would give up all rights to set conditions (called performance requirements) on foreign investment. Canadians would not be able to maintain domestic protection for our natural resources — our fisheries, forests, mines, and waters would be totally opened up to transnational corporations. Canadian culture would be totally exposed. Foreign investors would be able to sue the Canadian government if it or any province brought in any law or regulation, even for environmental, conservation, or health reasons, that could cost them future profits. They wouldn't even have to use our courts; they could challenge us under the "Rules of Arbitration of the International Chamber of Commerce" and the secret panel ruling would be binding. Canadian taxpayers would have to pay millions of dollars of compensation to corporations for the right to have their governments enact laws.

The only areas of life the negotiators thought important enough to exclude fully were law and order, and national security. Everything else that citizens might care about protecting — health care, labour standards, culture, education, pensions, natural resources — had to be put on a list of national "reservations," but then they would be subject to a clause called "roll-back" whereby governments would have to be prepared to give them up in future talks. To add insult to injury, this treaty would be binding for twenty years!

The possible threats to Canadians were legion. Under the MAI, if a province (like Alberta, which is already moving in this direction) decided to privatize hospitals, private hospital corporations like Columbia Health Care Corporation, an American-based transnational, could come into any province in Canada and set up shop. Under the MAI, Nova Scotia and British Columbia and other maritime provinces would not be able to preserve the fisheries for Canadians, but would have to allow foreign fishing fleets into our waters. Under the MAI, government subsidies to the CBC could be challenged by Disney Corporation as a form of illegal discrimination. Under the MAI, if a foreign mining company was leaking toxic tailings into a river system near its mine, and the province in which it was operating passed a law to stop the practice, the company could sue the government of Canada before an international panel for financial compensation.

I was stunned that our government would be any part of this. Tony quickly wrote an analysis of the text called *The Corporate Rule Treaty* (which was later published by the Canadian Centre for Policy Alternatives), and we wrote letters to five key Cabinet ministers expressing our concern about the MAI. Then we gave the text, analysis, and letters to Laura Eggertson, then of the *Globe and Mail,* where it was carried on April 3, on the front page, and put it on the Internet to all our IFG allies around the world. That very day the government put up its web site on the MAI and the war was on.

We knew it was essential to explain to ordinary Canadians that this dry, bureaucratic-sounding treaty being negotiated far away would have profound implications for their democracy. Decisions that they thought were being taken by their carefully elected governments, would, in fact, be made elsewhere by bureaucrats of the OECD and lobbyists for transnational corporations. If their governments passed or even, in some cases, enforced perfectly democratic laws and regulations, Canadian taxpayers might have to foot the bill. More likely, I felt, was the possibility of what we call the "chill effect" — corporations threatening governments with prohibitive compensation packages when laws are first being drafted. Would governments stand up to the tobacco and drug companies as some are trying to do? Would Canadians know how often and under what circumstances their governments decided it was too risky to even introduce certain legislation?

It was too early for the issue to take off during the spring federal election, although we did place several full-page ads in newspapers. Most Members of Parliament had never heard of the MAI. In June, Jack Stoddart, concerned about the implications of this treaty, approached Tony and me to write a book and we worked day and night to get it done on time. *MAI and the Threat to Canadian Sovereignty* was published in the fall.

By then a core group of activists was hard at work on the MAI: Keith Kelly and Gary Neil studied the negative effects on culture, including copyright, book publishing, and protections for Canadian magazines; Elizabeth May, Barbara Robson, Steve Shrybman, and Michelle Swenarchuk put out excellent material on the threat to the environment, including natural resources, endangered species, and existing laws; trade lawyer Barry Appleton wrote extensively on the legal ramifications of the deal, including the threat to the provinces and municipalities and to our social programs; Andrew Jackson of the Canadian Labour Congress published studies on the danger to working people and labour rights; Murray Dobbin published a paper on the impact on British Columbia, particularly in fisheries and forests, that sold thousands of copies; and Ovide Mercredi sounded the warning on the risk to aboriginal treaty rights and jobs programs and we distributed his paper to the six hundred Chiefs of the Assembly of First Nations. All across the country, local groups, teachers, health care workers, women's groups, seniors, and others were learning about the MAI and getting organized to fight it in their communities.

In October, the OECD MAI negotiators, concerned with the growing global opposition to the deal, invited a number of groups from the OECD countries to meet with them in Paris. Elizabeth, Michelle, and I went to represent Canada. On the first day, over seventy major citizen, environmental, and labour groups (many of them already coalitions of other groups) from thirty countries as far away as India, Hong Kong, Japan, and New Zealand, came together in the cramped offices of a Paris-based environmental group (entered through the back of a parking garage and up three flights of stairs) to forge a common position and a joint statement.

It was hard work. Some of the more conservative environmental groups like the World Wildlife Fund at first wanted to modify rather than totally oppose the MAI. In the end, we agreed to put a list of demands to the negotiators the next day, including a suspension of the talks and the abandonment of the spring 1998 deadline for closure of the deal in order that full public hearings could take place in all of our countries. If our government delegations approved our demands, we would be willing to sit down and talk with them. If not, we agreed, we would stand together in our resistance and take our statement back to all our countries.

The meeting took place in an enormous high-ceilinged boardroom of the former Rothschild estate with red velvet chairs, crystal chandeliers, and gold leaf panelling around a very large board table — the government negotiators at one end, us at the other. A CBC *National Magazine* crew was doing a story on the MAI and following me around Paris. We asked that they be allowed to stay in the room, at least for our opening statements, but the answer was no. They were unceremoniously escorted out: as they left, they filmed the heavy wooden doors closing behind them, thereby catching for their documentary the perfect visual image they needed to expose the exclusive nature of this club.

OECD Secretary General Donald Johnston (who earns $365,000 tax-free a year and has a home, car, and driver supplied to him free as well) was clearly annoyed at having to deal with this outbreak of democracy. He welcomed and then scolded us for the "disinformation you — especially the Canadians! — have been putting out on the MAI." He said he hoped the day would clear things up for us as if we were all delusional and just in need of a good talking to. The chairman of the MAI negotiating group, Franz Engering, explained that the meeting was operating under "Chatham House rules" — no comments could be attributed to any speaker or delegation. Our side was ably chaired by the WWF's Charles Arden Clarke.

Each side, starting with the government negotiators, put forward its case. We had done our homework and it showed. (I had chaired an early-morning meeting of our coalition in a room off to the side of the grand ballroom, where we decided who would present from our side and what tactics we would use.) The government delegates, on the other hand, spoke in generalities, refusing to deal with the substantive issues of the treaty itself. (This approach to the MAI has become so commonplace now, I am amazed if I find anyone from the other side who has even read it.)

The one issue they seemed to pick up on was our description of the Ethyl case under NAFTA, whereby Canada was then being sued for banning a toxic substance manufactured by the company. (Canada recently reversed its ban on MMT under this threat, proof that our concerns are real.) This is exactly the kind of legal challenge that can be expected to proliferate under a global deal, and the delegates seemed genuinely puzzled by it. They had never heard of the case and expressed shock that a clause on expropriation compensation in the MAI similar to one in NAFTA might lead to such challenges. We were perplexed, as the right of corporations to sue for such damages is so clearly written in the draft text of the MAI.

At the break, Elizabeth, Michelle, and I met with chief Canadian negotiator, Bill Dymond, and the rest of the Canadian delegation. When I asked Dymond point blank about the morality of negotiating a deal with such serious implications for Canadian social programs, culture, and natural resources, he said that they were trying to put forward "reservations" in these areas. We reminded him these reservations would be subject to the "roll-back" clause and, therefore, only temporary. Would he sign if we didn't get real and lasting protections in these areas? Dymond told us these questions could only be decided at the political level. He had been given a mandate to close a global investment treaty and that was what he was doing.

Back in the larger meeting, the debate was heated, and, at the end of the day, we had reached an impasse. We explained that we were not opposed to a global treaty on investment. In fact, we said, it would soon be imperative to have one. But this one was completely one-sided, with all the rights granted to corporations and all the obligations placed on governments and citizens and we demanded time to work with our governments and other groups back home to create something very different. The delegations said it was beyond their power to remove the spring 1998 deadline; only our own governments could do that. I told them we would be waging an all-out campaign against the MAI back in our home countries and we left the meeting.

All the next day, we worked to form a global citizens' movement to fight the treaty. We agreed to exchange strategy, research, and information and to coordinate our campaigns and then held a press conference to announce the birth of our coalition. Since that day we have circulated our joint statement of opposition to the MAI around the world and several thousand groups (five hundred from Canada alone) have now signed on.

Now we had to take the fight back home. The day I returned from Paris, we held a press conference announcing the formation of both this global citizens' coalition and a national Canadian coalition co-chaired by the Council of Canadians and the Canadian Labour Congress, of over forty national groups from every sector affected by the deal. The government finally knew it had to respond, and so it directed the House of Commons Standing Committee on Foreign Affairs and International Trade to hold hearings on the MAI. The committee didn't travel outside Ottawa, and only sat for several weeks, but it did give groups a chance to appear before their elected representatives and tell them how they felt. The majority of groups and individuals who testified were opposed.

The Council of Canadians had asked Barry Appleton to give us a legal opinion on the reservations to the MAI that the Canadian government had filed in Paris. When Barry presented it to the committee, he pointed out that the Canadian position failed to protect Canadian social programs. The definition was too general and could be interpreted by an international court not in Canada's favour. As well, in "reserving" social programs, the government forgot to name the provinces explicitly, who are, of course, responsible for delivery of the very programs in question. This oversight meant that only those social programs delivered by the federal government to armed forces personnel were protected. We were wondering who was in charge of this process and how they could so consistently botch it. In the end, the committee members did, in fact, seem to consider our concerns legitimate, and advised the government to accept the MAI only if it "fully protects Canadian culture, the environment, labour standards, health, education, and social services." Finally, we were getting somewhere.

But I felt I had to take our message to ordinary Canadians. In the first six months of 1998, I undertook the most gruelling national speaking tour I have ever had, visiting sixty communities right across the country. I spoke in churches, libraries, union halls, and high school auditoriums. Almost every event was packed — seven hundred in Guelph, more than five hundred in St. John's, twelve hundred people in Victoria — and filled with young people, a very important development. The Raging Grannies, wearing gingham, bonnets, and protest buttons, opened many an event with songs of political resistance, and the audiences, hungry for information, would pummel me with questions until my voice gave out. When I spoke to the annual convention of the Canadian Auto Workers in a huge downtown Toronto hotel ballroom, a thousand workers rose to their feet in unison to loudly affirm their solidarity with the council's campaign.

Dozens of anti-MAI coalitions sprang up across the country and, with the help of the Council of Canadians, put out an astonishing quantity of fact sheets, buttons, petitions, and bumper stickers. Research on every aspect of the MAI was undertaken, and, in the spring, the Canadian Centre for Policy Alternatives published an excellent collection of essays called *Dismantling Democracy* on the effects of the deal on every sector of Canadian society.

It was clear we had to encourage the press to start covering this issue. I put together teams to meet with the editorial boards of a number of newspapers and magazines, and we saw the direct effect of that in the reporting that followed. In a meeting with a room full of journalists and editors at the *Globe and Mail*, I pointed out that the MAI wasn't necessarily a left-right issue, and, as proof, I offered the fact of widespread concern over the MAI on the part of the governors of the western United States — "Not leftists by anybody's standards, except perhaps yours, Terence" — I said smilingly to Terence Corcoran. He grunted by way of reply.

One particularly effective publicity tactic was the creation of "MAI-Free Zones" which were set up at people's offices and homes and on university campuses and even adopted by some municipalities. Many groups took their case to their municipal politicians, and dozens of city councils, including Toronto, Montreal, Victoria, Kamloops, Saskatoon, Red Deer, Hamilton, and Sydney, adopted resolutions of concern about or downright opposition to the MAI. Seniors became involved in the fight. On Vancouver Island, seniors set up MAI-Information sites at libraries all over the island. Students were rallied by tireless youth workers across the country, and they organized the extraordinary student demonstration of May 25 in Montreal, when peaceful protesters sealed off the entrances to a conference on the globalization of the world's economy and over one hundred were arrested by an army of riot police, in full gear.

One thing is certain: the opposition to the MAI was a grass-roots movement and came right out of communities, campuses, and churches. The team at the council worked overtime for months keeping up with the volume of requests for information, from all over Canada and the world. The fight had reached right into provincial capitals as well. British Columbia, the Yukon, and Prince Edward Island came out completely against the MAI; Saskatchewan and Alberta both registered strong concerns. British Columbia Premier Glen Clark even commissioned a study on the impact of the MAI on the province and made it clear he would not feel bound by the deal if the federal government went ahead and negotiated it without his government's involvement. As well, the NDP's Alexa McDonough took a strong stand against the MAI and was raising it whenever she could in the House of Commons. Over these months, I met with dozens of provincial politicians, both in the house and opposition parties.

Sergio Marchi, the minister for international trade, called this phenomenon (which he was hearing about everywhere) a "shopping cart" crossing the country into which Canadians were putting all their anxieties about other things. He was partly right. The MAI had come to represent something larger than itself — it was now a kind of catchment issue for the decades of cuts, downsizing, lost jobs, lower living conditions, and assaults on the environment. But he was wrong to characterize this concern as rootless "anxiety." The debate became a metaphor for the value system that underpins economic globalization and has given Canadians the occasion to debate the very meaning of democracy and citizenship and to define the kind of world we want as we approach the millennium.

On one open-line show, a nurse called in, clearly close to tears. She said to me, "I couldn't stop the cuts to health care. I couldn't do anything about it when they granted the big drug companies twenty-year patent rights. I see the tragic results of child poverty every day in my emergency room, and I can't seem to do anything about it." Here her voice cracked. "But I will *not* put up with the MAI!" she shouted. When the clearly surprised host asked her why a dry investment agreement being negotiated halfway around the world would evoke such passion, she answered, "Because they wrote it down! They are so cocky, they couldn't even be bothered to be subtle in their langauge, and now I know what they're up to. And, by God, I'm going to stop them!"

It was evident that the government had been caught completely off-guard and had not anticipated this reaction to their MAI initiative. Few in government or the business community would come forward to defend the treaty in public. Economists like Owen Lippert from the Fraser Institute, and trade experts like Michael Hart of Carleton University, would venture into the fray occasionally and drive me crazy with their insistence on not debating the actual MAI, but the "notion" of a global set of rules for investment. I "debated" one trade academic from the University of British Columbia, who, like the rest, had clearly not read the transcript of the deal. When I raised one particular concern, he chided me for "fear mongering" until I whipped out my text and read it to him. On air, he said, "I could never support signing that!"

We knew a similar grass-roots campaign was needed in other countries as well. Because Canada had created a campaign first, we had an important role to play in getting the word out to our colleagues in other OECD countries where the MAI was almost unknown. Tony took charge of this process. He drafted and circulated a document called "Operation Monkey Wrench," essentially outlining a strategy to enable citizens' groups to inform each other of politically sensitive issues concerning their government's negotiating positions and then use the information to establish friction between the different government delegations. He travelled several times to Europe with fellow IFG member Lori Wallach from Public Citizen's Global Trade Watch to help jump-start citizen campaigns against the MAI.

Tony knew that, in Canada, only politicians and bureaucrats from the trade area knew anything about the deal, and that as soon as others from MAI-sensitive areas such as culture and environment had got wind of it, trouble would follow. He correctly guessed that it would be the same in Europe and worked with groups to expose these ministries in their governments to the threats posed to their portfolios by the MAI. As a result of this strategy, pressure grew from within governments to exempt many new areas from the treaty, and the second wave of national reservations followed, more than doubling the number of contentious issues to thirteen hundred. This in turn slowed the negotiating process dramatically.

Grass-roots organizers used the Internet brilliantly (an advantage we didn't have in either of the other free-trade fights). All the groups that had originally met in Paris were hooked up on a daily basis; we shared our campaign strategies and materials regularly. This work included groups in the developing world; all they needed was one modem and a good communication system of their own to be immediately plugged in to whatever was going on worldwide. The cultural community in Canada was particularly successful in reaching out to its counterparts in the other OECD countries. In France, the emcee of that country's version of the Academy Awards — the "Cesars" — read a prepared statement condemning the MAI (or *l'AMI*, as it is in French), and got a prolonged standing ovation from the audience, all caught on national television. The story led the news for days.

Piece by piece, we moved forward. By February, we had active citizen campaigns forming in twelve countries. That month, the

International Forum on Globalization put full-page ads in several international papers, including the *New York Times*, and received thousands of requests for information as a result.

A confidential report from a member of the Canadian delegation to that month's OECD MAI negotiating meeting shows just how successful our campaigns were becoming. The chairman of the OECD MAI negotiating group, Franz Engering, had called for the meeting as a way of "breaking the log-jam on major issues," and the memo noted that Engering "relapsed into evangelism" to try to save the process. "There is ample blame to go around for this melancholy state of affairs," said the report: the United States for admitting the MAI didn't fit into its 1998 calendar; the Europeans for protectionism, and "the Chair and the Secretariat [of the OECD] for repeated fundamental errors in the management of the negotiation." The role of citizen opposition was recognized, and the resulting disagreement over culture, environment, and labour standards were of "profound concern." The memo made it clear the negotiators were looking for some compromise for the public, as "any postponement of conclusion beyond April without 'some' agreement on key issues would result in a loss of momentum and in conceding victory to MAI opponents."

In March, the European Parliament passed a resolution, 437:8, urging its members to reject the MAI in its present form. In the Netherlands, Franz Engering was followed by activists everywhere, and students occupied his office. The campaign there, in the capable hands of youth activist, Olivier Heodeman, succeeded in getting the government of the Netherlands to limit what its own trade minister could commit to at the upcoming crucial talks in April. This put him in direct conflict with his fellow countryman, Franz Engering, who expressed his frustrations publicly on the eve of the meeting, and let the world know there were serious internal problems with the MAI process if he couldn't even deliver his own government.

Meanwhile, Tony and I launched an American version of our MAI book. In Washington, Public Citizen and a number of other groups put on a special event, and Ralph Nader warmly praised the work of the Canadians on this issue: "another Canadian first," he said, a reference to his book of that name. Dealing with the American media is like entering another planet. What is good for General Motors is surely good for all. I appeared on the business show of CNN and once we had established that the MAI would be good for big American business, the host couldn't think what to ask me. Who else mattered? A journalist with the *Washington Post* read in our book that once a natural resource is privatized, ownership must be opened to global competition. He asked me to give him an example that would bother me. I said, "Our government in Ontario is planning to privatize Ontario Hydro. We worry that Disney or Mitsubishi will be able to buy Niagara Falls." He said, "What's wrong with that? Do you think they will move it?"

The Canadian government was getting edgy and nasty. Andrew Jackson, Kathleen Connors of the National Federation of Nurses' Unions, Tony, and I asked for a meeting with House Leader Herb Gray on the MAI. We felt that his history of fighting for Canadian sovereignty would make him sympathetic to our concerns and wanted to find a way to open a dialogue. It was a mistake for me to go. Herb had been a friend and mentor when I was involved with the Liberal Party. In his quiet way, he had fought against foreign domination of Canadian industry, natural resources, and culture all his life and I went into the meeting with expectations of a sympathetic hearing and even personal goodwill. Within minutes, however, it was clear that we were meeting with a fierce Liberal partisan.

Gray had not read the MAI and knew very little about either its contents or our concerns. He asked aggressive questions and argued our every point, which I wouldn't have minded, had he even read the document. But because he had not, he was arguing for the sake of argument and we couldn't "prove" anything to his satisfaction because his own lack of knowledge prevented him from corroborating or countering our statements. At one point, he said that the trade department assured him there would still be some controls on foreign investment over $150 million. Was this true? I said "no" just as Andrew said "yes." We were both right. I was referring to the MAI text itself, which has no mention of such an exemption; Andrew was acknowledging the fact that Canada had filed a reservation (not yet accepted) to protect this right. Gray seized on what he saw as a disagreement between us and kept asking, "Well, which is it?"

I felt my heart pound with fury. For once, I was too close to losing my temper and saying things that couldn't be unsaid. I picked up my papers, declared the meeting was a waste of my time and left. Later, I apologized to my colleagues; I explained that my anger had been unexpectedly personal. I had truly admired Herb Gray and felt myself close to tears with disappointment at his transformation. After all, this was the man who had carried the banner of Canadian nationalism in the Liberal Party for over thirty years and authored the famous Gray Report in 1972, which called for a screening agency to monitor and place conditions on foreign investment in Canada. The Foreign Investment Review Agency (FIRA) was set up in 1973 largely as a result of his work.

I had a run-in with Sergio Marchi as well. He was already angry with me, and told a friend, "Please tell Maude Barlow I don't go to bed every night wondering how I can hurt the children of the world the next day." I actually like Marchi. He comes from the progressive side of the party and has twice had to deliver on policy he wouldn't have dreamed up himself. As immigration minister in the Liberals' first term, he had to sell the infamous "head tax," which he openly admitted would have kept his Italian family out of the country when they had emigrated from Argentina where he was born.

In opposition, Sergio Marchi was a vocal critic of free trade, which he said would jeopardize the future of workers as transnational corporations moved jobs offshore. In 1991, he advocated reopening the FTA to renegotiate the energy provisions, and said in the House of Commons, "Who in their right mind would treat Americans as Canadians in times of energy crisis?" Two years later, he called the FTA, NAFTA, and the Goods and Services Tax (all of which the Liberals would embrace once they formed the government), "a crown of thorns for the country." When he became the minister of international trade after the 1997 election, he sent out signals that he would concern himself with more than the bottom line, commenting publicly that he would also put forward concerns about human rights and labour standards.

This set off alarm bells in the business community. Tom d'Aquino of the BCNI warned that these concerns should never be part of any trade deals but said he was confident that bureaucrats and the federal Cabinet as a whole would bring the new minister into line. "The portfolio and the issues drive the minister, not the other way around." Soon after, Marchi was sent out to sell the biggest economic globalization treaty the world has ever seen. He inherited the project from two gung-ho free traders, former trade ministers MacLaren and Art Eggleton, and it is my opinion that, although he was going to do his best to be a good team player, he could never muster their enthusiasm for the deal.

In March, the coalition asked Marchi for a meeting and the only day he had available was one on which Tony and I were to be in Washington for our book launch. My office tried to find other leaders of the national anti-MAI coalition to attend, but had to cancel the meeting when, for one reason or another, they couldn't muster a proper delegation. Marchi heard from his American counterparts that I was debating an MAI negotiator from the U.S. State Department on National Public Radio that day, and put out a press release on Department of Foreign Affairs and International Trade letterhead, castigating me for not making the meeting, as I was "too busy" selling my book! In an open letter to the council, he added, "It appears regrettably, that you and your organization do not want your fear-mongering to be impeded by knowledge of the facts." I knew that Marchi was under the gun to shut me up; the insider report of that confidential February meeting made it clear that governments were to go back and deal with the opposition "in order to ensure that a potential MAI can be accepted by the civil society in OECD countries." But I was surprised that he would put out such a childish release on government letterhead.

On March 20, to coincide with the annual policy convention of the federal Liberal Party in Ottawa, we held a national protest against the MAI with events taking place in dozens of communities across the country. Outside the Ottawa Convention Centre, we held up a hugh anti-MAI banner and handed out hundreds of "Liberals Against the MAI" buttons, many to convention delegates who sported them on their jackets. On the final day of the convention, the prime minister and the entire Cabinet sat on the stage in a "bear-pit" session where the two thousand delegates got to raise any issues they wanted. The MAI came up again and again, and seemed to be the only issue causing real dissent. After one particularly hostile question on the MAI, all the lights on stage suddenly went out, and the prime minister, in complete darkness, said, "That Maude Barlow. She's everywhere!"

The April OECD MAI meeting was a "ministerial meeting," meaning that the political leaders had been summoned to see if they could rescue the clearly faltering deal. Our groups knew we had to be present for this event, and Tony and I went to represent Canada. Once again, we met with our counterparts from the other countries and held a widely reported press conference to issue our manifesto of opposition not only to the OECD process, but to the plan to send the MAI on to the WTO, which several countries, including Canada, were pushing for.

Before he left Canada, Sergio Marchi, under growing pressure, adopted the Parliamentary Committee's report and promised he would hold out for "ironclad" reservations to protect Canadian health, education, social programs, culture, aboriginal hiring practices, and natural resources. I actually think Marchi had come to see the merit in some of our arguments and was determined not to be seen as the man who exposed Canada's heritage to the forces of unchecked globalization. The U.S. government, meanwhile, had hardened its position that such exemptions would never be allowed. By the time the BMWs and Mercedes Benzes rolled up to the gates of the OECD early on the eve of April 27, the negotiations were already stalled.

Hours later, a grim-faced OECD President Donald Johnston emerged. He told a packed press conference that they had failed to meet their deadline, that talks were "on hold," and blamed the failure on a campaign of "disinformation" propagated by the treaty's opponents. We weren't allowed in to hear any of this, of course, and had to stand for hours outside waiting for the news. We knew, however, that Marchi would be holding a press conference at the Canadian compound down the street and we walked right in, flashed the guards our passports, and sat down at the back of the room before anyone knew we were there. By the time Marchi and Secretary of State for Financial Institutions Jim Peterson arrived, we were well ensconced among the press, and all they could do was limit the questions to "legitimate" journalists.

Marchi was disarmingly open about the failure. He admitted his government had not handled the whole process well and even admitted that some of our concerns were "substantial" (although he still insisted the fear of the "minestrone soup" of globalization anxiety was the biggest problem). But he showed flashes of real anger when asked about the role of the OECD and Donald Johnston. "They have a staff of fifteen hundred," he said. "What have they been doing all this time?" Each country was calling the six-month delay something different — for the French, it was a "suspension"; for the Americans, a "pause." "What did you call it?" a journalist asked Marchi. The minister looked right at us and said, "a period of redemption." Then he left for Canada to be in the House of Commons for the Hepatitis C vote. The negotiators, meanwhile, stayed up until 4:00 a.m. the next morning, hammering out the wording for their joint communique to put the best face on a bad situation.

The next day Tony, writer and philosopher Susan George, and I were hooked up to over one hundred Canadian activists on a coast-to-coast conference call to report the up-to-the-minute happenings in Paris. Susan, in elegant French and English, told them about the incredible movement that had grown up over the last year and the rally, complete with speakers, musicians, and performers, that was being held at that very moment in a beautiful old park right across from the OECD. When I told them the news of the moratorium and the way it was being reported in the European press (a "rout"), a huge cheer came blasting over the phone, a message of solidarity from Canada we took to the rally that evening where we formed a human chain around the compound, watched by bewildered OECD bureaucrats inside the gates.

Donald Johnston was not happy. The European press was widely interpreting his failure to negotiate an MAI as a personal loss and the possible end for the "anachronistic" OECD. Johnston was the OECD's first non-European head ever and had got the post only after extensive lobbying by the Chrétien government. European critics said at the time that Johnston didn't have the international experience needed for this job; now they would have the ammunition to dump the Canadian when the post comes open again in 2001.

A furious Johnston went on CBC's *National Magazine* that evening and said that the Canadian government should have done a better job of "handling" the opposition back home and vowed he would resuscitate the deal. In an interview that immediately followed him, I said that the days of exclusive meetings like this were over and the "no ordinary people allowed" sign that had been hung outside this particular club had come down forever.

225

(Johnston and I had debated several months before on *Lateline*, Australia's leading current affairs show. He was so rude to me that night — I didn't know anything; I was making things up; I was lying — I actually said on air that I was glad there was a continent between us. The next morning, at about 5:00 a.m., a man from the Australian outback called me. He had seen the program and driven to the nearest town, found a library with a computer, looked up the Ottawa phone book and called two other Barlows before he got me. "I'm a Vietnam vet, working with victims of Agent Orange, and I can smell bullshit a mile away," he said. "That Donald Johnston fellow was talking the highest grade — uncut. How can I help you, mate?" My office put him in touch with the groups in his country fighting the MAI and sent him a package of material. I smiled all day.)

Back in Canada, it was roundly seen as a "win" for us. I was worried about this, as it was clear to me that the *notion* of an MAI was not going to go away. The thing was like a hydra — we might have cut one head off, but it was already growing others, at the WTO, the International Monetary Fund, in the expanded free trade of the Americas. Nevertheless, a *Globe and Mail* front page headline declared "How the Internet Killed the MAI." Journalist Madelaine Drohan said the "high-powered politicians" were no match for a "global band of grass-roots organizations" and that international negotiations had been "transformed" by this development. One senior diplomat admitted, "This is the first successful Internet campaign by non-governmental organizations. It's been very effective."

The *Financial Times* compared the fear and bewilderment that seized the governments of the industrialized countries in the wake of the MAI's collapse to a scene from the movie *Butch Cassidy and the Sundance Kid*, where politicians and diplomats looked behind them at the "horde of vigilantes whose motives and methods are only dimly understood in most national capitals" in close pursuit, and asked despairingly, "Who *are* these guys?" The paper said the hordes — "an international movement of grass-roots pressure groups" — claimed their first success in this fight and "drew blood." It quoted a veteran trade diplomat who said, "This episode is a turning point. It means we have to rethink our approach to international economic and trade negotiations."

Ed Greenspon wrote an article called "That Sinking Feeling," for the *Report on Business* magazine in which he called the MAI "globalization without representation . . . offering up nothing or little for the things that concern anxious ordinary people, like workers' rights or environmental protection. These agreements are meant to assist corporate interests, plain and simple." He basically said that the government blew it on the MAI. It broke the cardinal rule of politics: don't let your adversaries define your position. While the negotiators were busy tending Brussels, Geneva, and Paris, Greenspon said, I was tending to Kamloops, Saskatoon, and Fredericton. The lesson, according to Greenspon: our trade gurus have to stop thinking Paris and start thinking Kamloops.

I knew that there would be a backlash and I knew it would be highly personal. Our opponents had to make the whole thing appear like the work of a very small band of extremists, and not the wide-spread movement it had really become. Terence Corcoran of the *Globe and Mail* predictably derided my "tiresome crusade" and dismissed the opposition as an "international gaggle of leftists, unionists, greenists, and Naderites, who spent much of the past year attacking the project as a corporate plot to turn control of the world over to McDonald's and Mitsubishi." A lead editorial in the same paper said anxiety about globalization "was cleverly fanned by narrow special-interest groups with more time and Internet access than common sense and scruples."

"Maude and the MAI" was the headline of one of Andrew Coyne's columns for the Southam newspaper chain. He accused me in one paragraph of launching a "worldwide campaign of hysteria and misrepresentation" against the MAI and in another, said the retreat on the MAI "had very little to do with Maude Barlow." Owen Lippert of the Fraser Institute despaired of these "trivial skirmishes" and said it was "irritating" to see victory bestowed upon me and others like Tony Clarke and Barry Appleton. Attacking me eight times in the one article, he warned darkly that his side wouldn't let this happen again. "Work lies ahead in stiffening Liberal spines to defend their own policies . . . . The MAI will come back. Next time, we need to be better prepared."

In the House of Commons, Reform MP Paul Forseth savaged Marchi for being so inadequate. "He lets Maude Barlow and others lie

bald-faced to the nation and deceive communities right across this country with their socialist, small-minded inferiority complex." Donald
Johnston accused us of spreading "misinformation" and "nonsense,"
and added that the MAI would be signed within the year. "It's a question of 'when,' not 'if.'" He had come to Canada in early May to defend
the MAI and the continued relevance of the OECD. My concerns were
sheer "demagoguery, totally unfounded, utter nonsense."

"How can you withstand such a relentless barrage of belittling criticism?" asked a friend. I replied that it depended on where it was
coming from. I was reminded of my mother's wise words, "Serious
people have serious enemies." While I don't compare myself to her in
any way, I am very moved and motivated by the words of Burmese
dissident and Nobel Prize winner Aung San Suu Kyi who says, "If you
want to indulge in honest politics, you've got to be prepared to be
reviled and attacked." If we hadn't hit a raw nerve, they wouldn't be
attacking in this way. What I couldn't (and can't) get over is that, while
my critics all accuse me of misrepresenting the facts, claiming that I
cannot grasp the meaning of the MAI, they refuse to debate me on the
substance of the deal or even answer specific concerns. I know the
PMO regularly examines our material for mistakes, for we have copies
of their lengthy briefing notes to MPs giving them "responses" to use
when confronted with questions about pensions or their annual
budgets based on our material.

(When I was on a 1995 book tour for *Straight Through the Heart*, I
debated then Member of Parliament, Mary Clancy, on a CBC Radio call-
in show in Halifax. Mary pulled from her briefcase an extensive analysis of
my book, prepared by the Privy Council Office, and marked CONFI-
DENTIAL. Mary seemed to think I was being unfair when I announced
this fact to the audience.)

I don't play the gender card often or easily, but I cannot help but
wonder if the refusal to debate me on ideological grounds is related to
the fact that I'm a woman. These people are not used to losing and
certainly not to a woman. Ah, you may say, but there are now women
among them, like Charlene Barshevsky, the U.S. trade representative.
This is true. But in my experience, a certain number of women will be
welcomed into the club as long as they behave. They give it legitimacy

and convince the men in charge that they are really an open bunch after all. The global club, it seems, is yet another old boys' network.

In any case, I am able to take this criticism because I believe I am right. Not on every detail. I am fallible. But I am engaged in an ideological fight over the direction in which the world is headed. I have made the choice to act upon my beliefs. I am not naïve; I know that challenging the power structure is risky. There will be retaliations. In fact, the more successful we are, the greater the retaliations.

The reactions to my work that matter to me more, and what keeps me going, are the letters and cards from ordinary Canadians from across the country who write to tell me I have given them hope and reason to keep fighting for justice. This is the victory here, not the temporary setback of the MAI. The simple fact is that as we approach the end of the twentieth century, governments no longer listen to the people in the way they listen to business, and other avenues to express our democratic rights have to be found.

I have great faith in the generation now in high school. Helen Porter says every generation seeks what it was raised without, and I think young people, so steeped in materialism, are seeking meaning in their lives. Recently, I spoke to a high school conference on globalization in Oakville where the students were a multicultural microcosm of the whole world. I told them about the joys of global interdependence that could come to us if we could build a world that respects cultural and biological diversity and strives for international standards to protect humanity and the Earth. But I warned them about the global monoculture of rootless capital we were building instead.

I said, "This I know. It is better to stand for something, to *be* about something, to make a difference, than to just take your place in the global shopping mall. Your life will be infinitely richer if you make the choice to make a difference." For over an hour after I spoke, about forty students surrounded me in a circle and we just talked — about life and values and parents and history and the deep and abiding knowledge we humans have of the infinite possibilities of true political and spiritual emancipation. "How can I be you?" asked one young woman. "I've got a better idea," I said. "You're going to be you and the world had better watch out!"

229

AFTERWORD

"No problem can be solved from the same consciousness that
created it."

Albert Einstein

As I look back, I can honestly say that the first part of my life has been
an extraordinary journey, with all the highs and lows that come from
creating one's own way. It has also been one of constant growth as my
own life experience has continually challenged me to deepen my analysis
and move beyond previous assumptions.

For instance, I am still very much a feminist although my understanding of what that means has changed. Where I once wanted to see
women in every sphere of life, from the boardroom to the shop floor,
now I want us to use our talent and organizing skills to challenge the
fundamental precepts of the new economy. It pains me to see women
ascend to the highest level of government and business, only to pick up
the most deplorable traits of powerful men. When she was natural
resources minister, Anne McLellan basically turned the environmental
monitoring of oil and gas production over to the industry and presided

over cuts of almost two-thirds to the budget for natural resource protection in Canada. *Financial Post* editor Diane Francis uses her important public forum to slam social programs and foment divisions between French and English in Quebec. Maureen Kempston Darkes, head of General Motors in Canada, provoked one of the most bitter plant occupations in the history of the Canadian car industry when, in 1996, she tried to remove the dies — the moulds from which automobile parts are made — from the Oshawa plant, which would have destroyed the union.

Not long ago, I gave a speech to a senior group of women in education — principals and vice-principals, university deans, and some provincial deputy-ministers. I listed a series of acronyms and asked them to put their hands up when they recognized any one of them: CHST (Canada Health and Social Transfer, the 1995 legislation that replaced the former and superior system of federal transfer payments for social programs to the provinces); C-91 (the 1993 law giving transnational drug companies twenty-year patent rights that came up for renewal in 1997); APEC; NAFTA; MAI, and a few others. Not one hand went up for any but the NAFTA reference. I then explained what every one of those references stood for and how they were eroding the hard-earned gains of women. "Twenty years ago, you were on the leading edge of social change," I said. "But now, you are on the verge of becoming part of the problem." They all had good salaries, tenure, and pensions. They could afford, like many influential men around them, to mentor a few young women coming up after them to make them feel they were still making a difference to women's lives, tune the rest of the world out, and reap the material rewards of their work.

A few women in the room were clearly annoyed with me, but many took the challenge I laid out before them: if feminists do not address the issues of economic globalization and government restructuring, we will not only lose many of the rights we have so recently won, but will risk becoming irrelevant to the most important issues of our time.

I have also undergone a similar transformation in my understanding of the word "sovereignty." I am still a passionate Canadian nationalist and believe we must continue to fight for our economic and cultural sovereignty in order to maintain even the most basic democratic control as a people in a world run by transnational capital. But it is harder and harder to defend my country as being a moderate voice for progressive change, given our abandonment of the poor, our blatant disrespect of our natural heritage, and our aggressive role in creating international trade agreements with no minimum standards. I now work for what I call "popular sovereignty," the fundamental right of people in Canada and all over the world to food, housing, jobs, education, health, democratic choice, and dignity, and the obligation of nation-states to secure and protect these rights.

This second shift has mirrored a third — my journey from partisan politics to citizen politics, or what American writer Lillian Hellman loosely defined as the "politics of decency." While I understand that we still need committed and principled politicians like New Democrats Alexa McDonough and Svend Robinson and former Liberal Warren Allmand, I now believe there is very little they can accomplish in the absence of an independent, well-organized on-the-ground movement free to organize resistance to the growing tyranny of corporate rule all over the world. David Suzuki recounts a rueful little story American Vice-President Al Gore told him. Gore is an ardent environmentalist who went into high-level politics in large part to create tougher laws to curb pollution and protect America's threatened natural resources. He now says he had greater influence as an activist than he's had as vice-president, caught as he is in Washington's power politics.

To me, it comes down to making the conscious choice to exert influence over the values of society rather than seek personal power. I am increasingly convinced that power cuts most people off from their roots and gives them a false sense of entitlement with all the privileges that attend this status. I would be grateful to be remembered as someone who helped to build the global citizens' movement that finally brought the rule of law to stateless and lawless transnational corporations. Martin Luther King said, "Legislation may not change the heart, but it will restrain the heartless."

I am not, contrary to constant accusations from the business press, anti-business. There are many fine local business leaders who care deeply about their communities but who are hurt, I believe, by being cast in the public eye as one with global corporations whose very size and mandate have separated them from the needs and rights of human beings. Nor am

232

I against rules for trade and investment. In fact, the Council of Canadians is using the temporary set-back of the MAI to launch public hearings on a "Citizens' MAI," rules for global capital that would be based on the fundamental principles of citizens' rights, nation-state obligations, and corporate accountability. (Our membership now stands at 100,000 and has over fifty active chapters right across the country, making us the biggest public advocacy group by far in Canada.)

I have learned two things on my journey. The first is to be content with my life and grateful every day for what I have — a roof over my head, clean water to drink (more and more of a rarity in the world), friends, family, and meaningful work. I have come to believe that our late twentieth century obsession with gaining ever more material possessions is an addiction that threatens our spiritual well-being and the natural world.

The second is that, to find oneself, it is necessary to lose oneself in a greater cause. Material comfort and the individualization of our society has created a generation of people in North America obsessed with finding out who they are; after great amounts of time spent with therapists and new-age spiritual guides, they discover the often disappointing reality that they, like most of us, are just ordinary people. Extraordinary lives are lived by people who have an extraordinary passion for something greater than themselves.

I have also become deeply disturbed about two emerging trends and will be spending more time and energy in confronting them in the future. One is the wanton destruction of other animal species by humans. We seem unable to see other living creatures as having value, and, therefore, rights. Only if they can be useful to us — to eat, shoot, photograph, or enjoy in zoos — do we recognize them at all. In referring to concerns that the MAI could lead to harm of the natural habitat of endangered species, Jim Sheehan, an economist with the Competitive Enterprise Institute in Washington, said, "If an animal goes extinct that is not economically useful, no human is going to care too much." This appalling attitude toward animals makes me think that maybe the wrong species evolved.

I read recently that psychiatrists are seeing more and more people, particularly women, who are having troubling dreams about the end of the Earth. I think it no coincidence that women are having these dreams. As the givers of life, we are perhaps more aware of the imminent danger we humans pose to the very survival of the planet. I too have terrible dreams. In one, I emerge from a plane onto a world that is exquisitely, pristinely white. Only when I look closely can I see that every living thing is dead, replaced by fine white plastic dust, covering the horizon as far as I can see.

This I know: if we do not hear the cries of the Earth and soon learn to respect the rights of other species, we are doomed. This requires addressing the long-standing grievances of the First Nations of this land, the one group among us capable of showing us what we must do. Phil Fontaine, Grand Chief of the Assembly of First Nations suggests a bumper sticker that reads, "My Canada includes the First Nations."

The other trend that worries me is the rise of Fascism everywhere in the world. It can be as apparently innocuous as the sudden appearance of swastikas on mailboxes all over Ottawa or as horrifying as the ethnic cleansing and racist violence that attends the rise of the right in many parts of the world. I look at our overheated economy in North America and I feel that the conditions that spawned the economic crash and the Depression of the 1930s, as well as the rise of Nazism, are all here again today: an overheated stock market, a huge and growing gap between rich and poor, merger mania based on falsely inflated market values, and a shredded social safety net. Those who really rule the world — transnational corporations — have no capacity or will to deal with the social fall-out of their system. As Tommy Douglas warned: "Fascism need not wear a brown shirt or a green shirt. It may even wear a dress shirt."

In the liberation movements of Latin America and elsewhere, they use a term to explain how hope and freedom are kept alive no matter how many people are killed or how much of their work is removed from the public record. It is called "dangerous memory" and refers to the fact that the search for social justice inevitably brings people into confrontation with the power elites of society and that their work can expose them to great personal danger. I am fortunate, I know, to live in a time and place where my political work does not pose this kind of personal risk, but I am fully aware that it has not always been so for others in Canada, who were beaten up, sent to prison and even, in some cases, killed, for their beliefs, nor is it now for many contemporaries around the world. A Mexican friend told me that she gets regular anonymous telephone calls asking if she knows where her school-age children are. I cannot imagine the courage it takes for her to continue her work.

I am constantly amazed at the determination of ordinary citizens to fight for their rights in the face of overwhelming odds. In the last year alone, there have been a number of important success stories. Recently, the Lubicon, a small First Nations band in northern Alberta, won a crucial three-year court battle against the corporate paper giant Daishowa, who had to give the band back a large tract of land in order to end a successful European boycott the Lubicon had led against the company's products. Chief Bernard Ominayak worked tirelessly with Kevin Thomas and other environmentalists from a grass-roots group called Friends of the Lubicon to stop this $14-million assault on their democratic rights and to bring the big company to its knees.

A small group of community activists, concerned about the fate of their small-business sector, kept Wal-Mart from setting up shop in Guelph after a three-year fight. A math teacher on an Ontario Catholic board picketed in front of his school until it reversed a decision to allow a daily commercial half-hour of "edutainment" to be shown, corporate ads and all, to the students in his school district.

My favourite story is one from India. My friend Vandana Shiva tried to stop her country from signing the GATT in 1995 because it would, among many other things, allow transnational corporations to take out private patents on the genetic heritage of rural India. She was unsuccessful, and since the signing of the GATT, many patents, including ones for basmati rice, and the neem tree — a sacred tree of great spiritual and healing properties referred to in India as "the tree of life " — have been filed by First World companies who will try to force anyone using these "products" to pay them royalties. Unable to get her government to stop this practice, Vandana trained a group of young lawyers to go out into the Indian countryside and have the peasant and rural farmers, most of whom have no formal schooling, go into their fields and farms, woodlands, mountains, and wild spaces, and gather every living plant species they can find. The seeds are then catalogued in a "community seed register" where they are forever held for the community and are, therefore, forever off-limits to be patented by private corporations. Transnationals are scrambling as they cannot keep up with this grass-roots movement now sweeping not only India, but Africa and Latin America as well.

One of my most precious possessions is a hand-made book Vandana sent me relating this story and which contains photos of the farmers — men and women, in local dress, grinning from ear to ear — holding "their" seed, or leaf, or touching "their" tree, bursting with pride at the miracle they have wrought. The book is called *The Seed Keepers,* and Vandana signed it with the words, "From one seed keeper to another." I have never received a greater gift.

This is my vision now: that ordinary Canadians and citizens from all over the world will see ourselves as seed keepers and organize accordingly to do the work that bears our name. Leadership is no longer coming from the places it used to. With rare exceptions, leadership to help us deal with the fall-out from economic globalization is not coming from our political parties, mainstream media, or our universities. It is coming from ordinary people: teachers, the keepers of the seed of public education; front-line health care workers, the keepers of the seed of public health; environmental and anti-poverty activists, young people, seniors, new Canadians, aboriginal peoples, the poor. It is coming from you and me, the seed keepers of democracy.

For me, to be alive at this time in our history and to be part of this extraordinary movement — this is enough.

ACKNOWLEDGEMENTS

I am deeply indebted to Phyllis Bruce not only for suggesting this book, but for her patience in guiding me through its writing. I am also very grateful to the whole team at HarperCollins, particularly copy editors Beverly Endersby and Michael Redhill, who have supported this project with such enthusiasm and energy.

I know, as well, that I have been enormously fortunate in my private life. As a result, I am devoted to my parents in their old age. Sunday dinner is my favourite time; baking bread and cooking a good meal for them grounds me, especially if I have been away or involved in some highly stressful issue, and it gives me great peace. Time with them is a priority, and I treasure every moment with them.

My husband, Andrew, is an extraordinary partner with a great sense of humour. He has supported my work in every way. Every summer, we retreat to the sea with our twelve-year-old otterhound, Pasha (who has kept me company for every one of my books), for a few weeks to recover from the year and to ride our bikes, swim, and hike, and spend time with our family. We have a circle of friends, closest among them Janice Hopkins and Glen Wolfson, social workers with the Region of Ottawa-Carleton who are also raising two great little boys. My women friends — Bonnie Diamond, Sheila Purdy, and Helen Porter in particular — have become more important to me as I get older and I am so grateful to have them, as well as my sisters, Pat and Christie, in my life.

My sons are still my pride and joy. Charles, a captain with the Black Watch, served a year in Bosnia and has started his own small business. A strong athlete, he swims, skis, bikes off-road, and teaches wilderness survival with his unit. Will is an editor with Hansard. He is also a gifted musician and is soon to earn his black belt in karate. Both are married to fine, independent women; Charles to Lynn Smith, Will to Pam Dakers. They have been a gift in my life as have been Michael, Scott, Lynn, and Jennifer, my sisters' children.

I am also blessed with superb colleagues in the staff, board, and members of the Council of Canadians. The council has grown so much that I cannot list every one of our employees by name, but I give great credit to our brilliant executive director, Peter Bleyer, who has assembled an excellent staff. My day-to-day life is run by my pitbull assistant, Patricia Armstrong, a sixty-seven-year old dynamo who rollerblades in her spare time and to whom I am deeply indebted. My travel load has been lightened this past year by my energetic travelling companion, Victoria-Gibb Carsley, whom we hired to build our organization on the ground.

My colleagues and co-authors, Bruce Campbell, Jim Winter, and Heather-jane Robertson, have also become close friends and essential to my sanity, and I know without question that I could not do my work without my political partner, Tony Clarke. I think he is a Canadian hero.

To all of my other international colleagues — too numerous to mention — I say thanks for your tireless and inspiring work.

Finally, I wish to acknowledge the members of the Council of Canadians who have been my bedrock. No matter where I go in this country, no matter how weary I am, my friends and colleagues are there to care for me, give me energy, and inspire me with their tireless work and commitment.

INDEX

Y